REFERENCE GUIDES IN LITERATURE
NUMBER 9
Ronald Gottesman, *Editor*
Joseph Katz, *Consulting Editor*

Katherine Anne Porter and Carson McCullers: *A Reference Guide*

Robert F. Kiernan

G. K. HALL & CO., 70 LINCOLN STREET, BOSTON, MASS.

Library of Congress Cataloging in Publication Data

Kiernan, Robert F
   Katherine Anne Porter and Carson McCullers : a
reference guide.

   (Reference guides in literature ; no. 9)
   Includes indexes.
   1. Porter, Katherine Anne, 1894-   --Bibliography.
2. McCullers, Carson Smith, 1917-1967--Bibliography.
Z8705.7.K53 [PS3531.O752]   016.813'5'208   76-2357
ISBN 0-8161-7806-2

This publication is printed on permanent/durable acid-free paper.
MANUFACTURED IN THE UNITED STATES OF AMERICA

Contents

Introduction

Katherine Anne Porter has enjoyed the attention of important and influential commentators from almost the beginning of her career. In 1924, for instance, the promise of her first story was noted by Edward J. O'Brien, the renowned editor of The Best Short Stories anthologies, and with the publication of Flowering Judas in 1930 she found champions in Allen Tate, Yvor Winters, and Ford Madox Ford. Nurtured by the praise of such critics, her reputation spread quickly, and it was not long before her stories became touchstones of literary taste. Indeed, Porter's enthusiasts established her reputation so quickly that by 1933 The New York Times could chide Sylvia Chatfield Bates, the prominent editor and teacher, for failing to include Porter's work in an anthology of twentieth-century stories. The keynote of this attention was clear from the beginning: Porter was a distinguished, serious writer, one who had produced mature work in Flowering Judas, and from whom great things were expected.

A tone of guileful astonishment runs through much of the early commentary. Where had she come from, this dedicated, meticulous craftsman, and what was her apprenticeship? Allen Tate praised her style as the richest and most efficient in American fiction; Yvor Winters thought some of her work superior to the work of almost every other contemporary writer; Llewelyn Jones predicted that Porter would be for the thirties what Willa Cather had been for the twenties. On the basis of a single book of stories, such enthusiasm now seems excessive and part of a cult rhetoric, but Porter has always enjoyed the benefits of intelligent criticism as well as influential criticism, and the enthusiasm was perceptive. Again and again her reviewers noted the delicacy of her phrasing, the firmness of her technique, and the economy of her means--the substantial qualities upon which her permanent reputation was to be based.

When critics have acclaimed a first book their tendency to retrench with the second book is a physical law according to Tennessee Williams, but no such reaction greeted the 1935 publication of an expanded Flowering Judas. Charles Angoff described Porter in American Spectator as a writer "of obvious maturity and unimpeachable honesty," and William Troy insisted in The Nation that she was among the most distinguished writers of fiction in America. For Eda Lou Walton,

INTRODUCTION

writing in the New York <u>Herald Tribune</u>, Porter was simply the finest short story writer in the country. Doubts were expressed about the success of "Hacienda," but a tone of respectful adulation continued to dominate Porter criticism, and Glenway Wescott, Kay Boyle, and Malcolm Cowley added their names to the growing list of Porter enthusiasts.

The publication of <u>Pale Horse, Pale Rider</u> in 1939 was greeted by the reaction that failed to materialize in 1935. For a number of reviewers Porter's work was still above reproach, and one reviewer compared her solemnly with Hawthorne, Flaubert, and James. A significant number of reviewers, however, expressed dissatisfaction with one or another of the stories, and a few reviewers were openly hostile. As a whole, the criticism is curiously inconsistent. "Noon Wine," for instance, was censured by Clifton Fadiman for its obviousness, yet praised by Christopher Isherwood for its subtlety; "Pale Horse, Pale Rider" was censured in <u>The Nation</u> for its slick quality, yet praised in the Manchester <u>Guardian</u> for its poignancy, wit, and charm. Such inconsistencies suggest that a quarrelsome spirit was in the air and that the time had come to qualify Porter's reputation.

Specifically it was time for serious critics, armed with leisure and perspective, to enter the field, and they entered it almost immediately under the aegis of the Southern and Southwestern literary journals, Glenway Wescott publishing in <u>The Southern Review</u>, Paul Crume in <u>The Southwest Review</u>, and Lodwick Hartley in <u>The Sewanee Review</u>. Again, Porter was fortunate in her early commentators. The celebration of Porter's achievement was to become a motif of Wescott's own career, and Hartley was to become a lifelong apologist of Porter's work, publishing over the years some of the most distinguished essays in the field.

Porter was especially fortunate, however, in attracting the pen of Robert Penn Warren. Warren's 1942 essay "Katherine Anne Porter (Irony with a Center)" illumined Porter's concern with "the delicacy of phrase, the close structure, the counterpoint of incident and implication," and focussed on the ironic stance which gave point to this concern. Effectively, Warren fixed the terms in which Porter was to be discussed and the values against which she was to be measured, for so inevitable were his terms and so apt his values that they form the unchallenged basis of all subsequent discussion. The academic interest in Porter during the 50s and 60s is traceable almost entirely to the Warren essay, and it remains today the single most important statement about Porter's work. Indeed, like <u>The Well-Wrought Urn</u> and the textbook <u>Understanding Fiction</u>, "Irony with a Center" has become a classic within the Brooks-Warren canon, an example of the New Criticism at its most persuasive and in its most genial mood.

Unlike the reviews of <u>Pale Horse, Pale Rider</u> and influenced, perhaps, by the academic criticism which had intervened, the reviews of

The Leaning Tower were overwhelmingly favorable. Too frequently, however, the reviews are unconvincing: the praise of Porter's style seems more dutiful than inspired by actual analysis; the praise of the title story seems to have its source in contemporary Germanophobia rather than in any literary criteria; and the general lack of enthusiasm for the Miranda sketches suggests a subtle prejudice against their scale and form. The problem which haunts the reviews is the unevenness of the collection--its new and unexpected range of style, genre, idiom, and technique. The critical need was no longer for a qualified statement of Porter's achievement, but for a comprehensive vision of her work.

Major essays on Porter's work began to appear at this time and until 1960 at the rate of about one a year, and their primary effort was to fulfill this need for a synthetic overview of Porter's work. Ray B. West's "Katherine Anne Porter and 'Historic Memory'" and Charles Kaplan's "True Witness" attempted to get at the work genetically by attending to Porter's use of her personal memories, a method Porter encouraged with her 1956 essay "'Noon Wine': The Sources." F. O. Matthiessen, Charles Allen, and S. A. Poss attempted to get at the work thematically and through the techniques of characterization, as did Harry J. Mooney in the first book-length study of Porter's work. The most ambitious and most influential synthesis of Porter's work, however, is James William Johnson's 1960 essay "Another Look at Katherine Anne Porter." With considerable ingenuity, Johnson synthesized the separate statements of the individual stories into an embracing "fictional philosophy" which incorporates virtually the entire life of man and which remains true to the stories despite its rather startling contrivedness.

If The Leaning Tower created the need for an overview of Porter's work, the publication of Ship of Fools in 1962 unsettled the attempts at synthesis by the simple expedient of doubling her published output. The book was widely reviewed, and the majority of reviewers found it admirable for its intelligence, its characterizations, and its style. For Mark Schorer, writing in America, the book was a second Middlemarch, and for Sybille Bedford, writing in England, the Great American Novel had appeared at last. A vocal and sizeable minority of critics, however, were disappointed by Ship of Fools: they found its tone misanthropic, its allegory clumsy, and its style pedestrian. This minority were careful to qualify their judgment and to suggest that inflated rumors about the novel had invited disappointment, but their judgment has generally prevailed. Indeed, for all of its anger, Theodore Solotaroff's attack both on the novel and on those who had liked it is the most significant essay inspired by Ship of Fools. Subsequent writers of book-length studies try invariably to make a case for Ship of Fools (M. M. Liberman most notable among them), but the general feeling today is that Porter should have heeded her own advice to Eudora Welty and avoided the novel that every writer of short stories is expected to publish.

Introduction

The attempt since the publication of <u>Ship of Fools</u> to synthesize
Porter's work has been carried on most notably in a series of
pamphlet- and book-length studies. Harry J. Mooney's revision of his
<u>The Fiction and Criticism of Katherine Anne Porter</u> (1962) was the
first of these, and it was followed in short order by Ray B. West's
pamphlet <u>Katherine Anne Porter</u> (1963), William L. Nance's <u>Katherine
Anne Porter & the Art of Rejection</u> (1964), George Hendrick's <u>Kather-
ine Anne Porter</u> (1965), Winfred S. Emmons' pamphlet <u>Katherine Anne
Porter: the Regional Stories</u> (1967), M. M. Liberman's <u>Katherine Anne
Porter</u> (1971), and John Edward Hardy's <u>Katherine Anne Porter</u> (1973).
While these works have their individual excellences, none has been
particularly successful in establishing an inescapably persuasive
overview. West and Emmons are barely interested in doing so, while
Nance is too eager, forcing his thesis unconvincingly. Mooney, Hendrick, and Hardy argue loosely for thematic patterns in the work, but
they do so primarily to establish a framework for discussion of the
individual stories, and Liberman's book is more a collection of dis-
crete essays than a sustained reading of the <u>oeuvre</u>. The attempt to
synthesize Porter's work has been carried on also in a number of essays which survey isolated themes of the work. Porter's attitude
toward the South is the most frequent of these, but her attitudes
toward childhood, toward Blacks, and toward Mexico and Mexicans have
increasingly absorbed the critics, and Porter's use of her own memories and experiences is an abiding concern.

The publication of Porter's <u>Collected Stories</u> in 1965 occasioned
another summing-up, less premature than earlier efforts, but less
ambitious too. There were no major attempts this time to illumine
the pattern of her work or to bring her themes into new focus. Indeed, there is a sense in the reviews that all possible positions
have been taken, and Granville Hicks probably sounded the truest note
when he observed simply that Porter's reputation would rest with her
stories rather than with <u>Ship of Fools</u>. Again and again the reviewers observe that Porter's stories have earned a permanent place in
American literature despite their grimness and despite their misan-
thropy and that they are successful by any standard of measurement.
"It is indeed difficult to define the exact quality of Miss Porter's
stories and short novels," wrote Hicks, agreeing with an earlier
statement by Edmund Wilson, ". . . and yet one has the feeling, with
almost every story, that it is absolutely right." The publication of
<u>The Collected Essays and Occasional Writings</u> in 1970 occasioned much
the same sort of response, although many reviewers noted predictably
that the collection was uneven.

Studies of individual works have usually been more provocative
than the synthesizing studies, but relatively few stories have been
given major treatment. The elaborate symbolism of "Flowering Judas"
and "The Grave" have made them particular favorites of the explicators, and Ray B. West, Leon Gottfried, and Daniel Curley have written importantly about them. Symbolistic interest seems also to have
inspired the several treatments of "Theft" and "The Jilting of Granny

INTRODUCTION

Weatherall," with particularly significant essays by Joseph Wiesenfarth and Peter Wolfe. "Noon Wine" has attracted commentary on a
number of levels. The frequent and elaborate analysis of these stories has resulted in some interesting disagreements and exchanges,
and, predictably, in some redundancy as well. Redundancy in the
critical literature is minimal, however, and it does not seriously
mar the generally high quality of Porter commentary.

*   *   *

In preparing this research guide, I have listed all books and
pamphlets about Porter's writing, and all periodical reviews and essays, interviews, unpublished dissertations, and chapters, headnotes,
or significant passages in books which bear upon her reputation, as
well as reviews from the major newspapers. I have cited single references to prizes and awards where they seemed to reflect Porter's
reputation. In my abstracts of reviews and essays, I emphasize
critical judgments, and in my abstracts of interviews, bibliographies,
and biographical notes, I emphasize scope except in the case of very
brief items. Where it has been impossible to lay hands on an item, I
have marked it with an asterisk and noted a source for the citation,
and in order to distinguish between collections and their title stories, I have standardized the use of italics for the titles of the
collections and quotation marks for the titles of the stories even
when the sources do not follow this usage. My index lists all treatments of Porter's work by title and by author and all significant
treatments of a work under the name of that work as well. Subject
headings have been used in the index where appropriate. Reprints are
not indexed under the titles of Porter's works but are cross-indexed
within the bibliography itself.

No bibliography of this kind is ever complete, but within the
limits I have set this guide is as comprehensive as I can make it
through 1973. I have included items for 1974 of which I am aware,
but the entries for that year are undoubtedly incomplete.

I would like to express my appreciation to Professor Mary Ann
O'Donnell of Manhattan College for technical advice in the preparation of this book, and to Ms. Maíre Duchon, Acquisitions Librarian of
the Cardinal Hayes Library, Manhattan College, for her assistance in
obtaining some obscure materials.

Abbreviations

AL   American Literature
ArQ   Arizona Quarterly
BA   Books Abroad
BB   Bulletin of Bibliography
BNYPL   Bulletin of the New York Public Library
BuR   Bucknell Review
CathW   Catholic World
CE   College English
CEA   CEA Critic
CLAJ   College Language Association Journal
ColQ   Colorado Quarterly
Crit   Critique
EJ   English Journal
ESA   English Studies in Africa
Expl   Explicator
GaR   Georgia Review
HudR   Hudson Review
LaS   Louisiana Studies
MFS   Modern Fiction Studies
MHRA   Modern Humanities Research Association
MinnR   Minnesota Review
MQ   Midwest Quarterly
MQR   Michigan Quarterly Review
MR   Massachusetts Review
NY   New Yorker
PMLA   Publications of the Modern Language Association of America
PR   Partisan Review
SatR   Saturday Review
SCR   South Carolina Review
SDR   South Dakota Review
SHR   Southern Humanities Review
SLJ   Southern Literary Journal
SoQ   Southern Quarterly
SoR   Southern Review
SR   Sewanee Review
SSF   Studies in Short Fiction
SWR   Southwest Review
SWS   Southwest Writers Series

ABBREVIATIONS

TamR   Tamarack Review
TCL   Twentieth Century Literature
TLS   Times Literary Supplement
TUSAS   Twayne's United States Authors Series
UMPAW   University of Minnesota Pamphlets on American Writers
UMSE   University of Mississippi Studies in English
VQR   Virginia Quarterly Review
WHR   Western Humanities Review
WR   Western Review
WSCL   Wisconsin Studies in Contemporary Literature
WVUPP   West Virginia University Philological Papers
XUS   Xavier University Studies
YR   Yale Review

Writings About Katherine Anne Porter, 1924 - 1974

1924 A BOOKS - NONE

1924 B SHORTER WRITINGS

   1   O'BRIEN, EDWARD J., ed. The Best Short Stories of 1923 and
       The Yearbook of the American Short Story. Boston: Small,
       Maynard, p. 454.
          Biographical note.

1930 A BOOKS - NONE

1930 B SHORTER WRITINGS

   1   ANON. Review of Flowering Judas, New York Times Book Review
       (28 September), sec. iv, p. 6.
          The controlled language of "María Concepción," "Rope,"
       "He," and "The Jilting of Granny Weatherall" has an in-
       ·tensity missing from more superficial fiction. "Magic" is
       the only inferior story in the collection.

   2   BOGAN, LOUISE. Review of Flowering Judas, New Republic, LXIV
       (22 October), 277-78.
          The stories of Flowering Judas are straightforward on
       the whole. "Flowering Judas" is remarkable for its firm-
       ness and delicacy, and "Rope" is very nearly as good.
       Only "Magic" and "María Concepción" seem mannered, the
       first in its monologic structure, and the second in its
       unnecessary details and unconvincing characterizations.
       Reprinted in Selected Criticism (1955.B1) and partially
       reprinted in A Library of Literary Criticism (1969.B2).

   3   DAWSON, MARGARET CHENEY. "A Perfect Flowering," New York
       Herald Tribune Books (14 September), pp. 3-4.
          Porter uses her imagination to get at our subcutaneous
       sensations in all of the Flowering Judas stories. "María
       Concepción" shows a remarkable sensitivity on Porter's
       part to the Indian mentality, and a considerable emotion

1930

(DAWSON, MARGARET CHENEY)
is conveyed through its precise diction. "Magic" is ter-
rifying, hilarious, and bawdy, all at once. "Rope" is
both painful and sophisticated, and its use of indirect
discourse imparts a wonderful sense of reality. "The
Jilting of Granny Weatherall" and "Flowering Judas" are
superb revelations of the human mind.

4   RICHARDSON, EUDORA RAMSAY. Review of Flowering Judas, Book-
man, LXXII (October), 172-73.
Porter's career is worth watching, for the Flowering
Judas collection is "exquisitely done, with feeling for
dramatic values, with clarity, with delicate delineation
of characters, and in language transcendentally beautiful." Porter is a versatile artist, and the stories range
widely in setting and theme.

5   TATE, ALLEN. "A New Star," Nation, CXXXI (1 October), 352-53.
Unlike the majority of American writers, Porter has an
instinctive feel for her background material; she falls
into the traps neither of overworking her style nor of
developing her background sensationally. Indeed, Flowering Judas is a mature work of art, and Porter's style is
both the most economical and the richest in American
fiction.
Partially reprinted in A Library of Literary Criticism
(1969.B2).

1931 A   BOOKS - NONE

1931 B   SHORTER WRITINGS

1   JONES, LLEWELYN. "Contemporary Fiction," in American Writers
on American Literature, edited by John Macy. New York:
Horace Liveright, pp. 488-502.
Porter will be for the next decade what Willa Cather
has been for the present decade.

2   WINTERS, YVOR. "Major Fiction," Hound and Horn, IV (January-
March), 303-05.
The stories in Flowering Judas are unevenly successful.
The themes of "Magic," "Rope," and "He" are narrow, unable
to bear the weight of Porter's ironic method, while "María
Concepción" suffers from an excess of ornament. "The
Jilting of Granny Weatherall" and "Flowering Judas" are
"major fictions," however, and, together with "Theft,"

(WINTERS, YVOR)
    they surpass the writings of all living Americans except
for one story by W. C. Williams.

1933 A BOOKS - NONE

1933 B SHORTER WRITINGS

  1   ANON. Review of Twentieth Century Short Stories, edited by
        Sylvia Chatfield Bates, New York Times Book Review
        (21 May), p. 7.
          In her otherwise excellent anthology, Bates has omitted
        "some of the very newest and most promising of our Ameri-
        can writers"--Porter among them.

  2   ANON. "Mr. O'Brien's Short Story Selections for 1933," New
        York Times Book Review (2 July), p. 6.
          In a collection not conspicuous for its brilliance,
        Porter's "The Cracked Looking-Glass" has a "racy vigor and
        a rich authenticity."

  3   ANON. "French Song Book," New York Herald Tribune (Paris),
        (25 December), p. 5.
          Porter's translations in her French Song Book are both
        remarkable and admirable, losing none of the charm or
        meaning of the originals.

  4   CHAMBERLAIN, JOHN. "Books of the Times," New York Times
        (20 October), p. 17.
          Ford Madox Ford is currently championing Porter's work.
        Her Flowering Judas is among the best books of short sto-
        ries written by an American.

1934 A BOOKS - NONE

1934 B SHORTER WRITINGS

  1   ANON. Review of Katherine Anne Porter's French Song Book,
        New York Herald Tribune Books (28 January), sec. vii,
        p. 18.
          Porter's translations of favorite French songs convey
        more of the songs' original spirit than translations are
        usually able to do. Each song is prefaced by an appropri-
        ate, informative note.

1934

2   ANON. Review of <u>Katherine Anne Porter's French Song Book</u>,
        <u>Poetry</u>, XLIII (February), 290.
            Porter's skill in this book is as apparent as it is in
        her books of fiction. The volume includes her transla-
        tions of her favorite old French songs, brief notes on the
        songs, and copies of the authentic tunes.

3   ANON. "Books: Some Christmas Suggestions," <u>NY</u>, X
        (15 December), 141.
            "Hacienda" is by Porter, "which means it's distinguished
        work."

4   CHAMBERLAIN, JOHN. "Books of the Times," <u>New York Times</u>
        (10 December), p. 19.
            Porter's "Hacienda" is first-rate writing, and it is
        full of precise description. It deals with how slowly
        Mexican life changes.

5   GANNETT, LEWIS. "Books and Things," New York <u>Herald Tribune</u>
        (8 December), p. 13
            If Porter had not said that the characters and situa-
        tions in "Hacienda" were imaginary, one would be reminded
        of Eisenstein's adventures with Upton Sinclair.

6   HART, ELIZABETH. "Slight and Short Stories," <u>New York Herald
        Tribune Books</u> (16 December), sec. vii, p. 15.
            Although Porter is one of our best short story writers,
        "Hacienda" is a disappointment. There is rich material
        in the story, but it seems to be little more than notes
        for a novel. Despite the author's disclaimer, the story
        is clearly based on Eisenstein's filming of ¡Que Viva
        <u>Mexico</u>!

7   POORE, CHARLES G. "A New Story by Katherine Anne Porter,"
        <u>New York Times Book Review</u> (23 December), sec. v, p. 4.
            "Hacienda" is a "quietly diabolic" story about Eisen-
        stein's filming of <u>Thunder Over Mexico</u>. It is unfortunate
        that the game of identification dominates the story and
        that Mexico has served so often in fiction as a back-
        ground for a conflict among artists. Still, Porter's
        wonderfully-developed style makes the book superior to the
        books of lesser writers. Hers is a style which comes
        close to expressing the unutterable.

1935 B   SHORTER WRITINGS

1   ANGOFF, CHARLES. "An Honest Story Teller," American Specta-
        tor, III (November), 11.
            Porter is a writer of "obvious maturity and unimpeachable
        honesty," and her chief topic is the confusions of the
        heart. "Rope," "Magic," "He," "Theft," "Flowering Judas,"
        and "Hacienda" are the less successful stories of the col-
        lection, for their insights are commonplace, while the
        best stories are "María Concepción," "The Jilting of
        Granny Weatherall," and "The Cracked Looking-Glass." The
        latter story is one of the most powerful in contemporary
        American literature.

2   ANON. "Notes on Fiction," Nation, CXL (27 March), 369.
            "Hacienda" is a painful and disturbing story about the
        crumbling of a feudal Mexican estate, and many readers
        will think they recognize the source of the story. One
        wants the book to be longer than it is, for the material,
        the implications, and the manner of the story are not
        slight.

3   ANON. Review of Flowering Judas, Christian Century, LII
        (6 November), 1426.
            The stories in Flowering Judas are "remarkably good
        stuff."

4   ANON. Review of Flowering Judas, Booklist, XXXII (December),
        110.
            The stories of Flowering Judas are distinguished by a
        "delicate precision of style" and by a "clarity and econo-
        my of words."

5   ANON. Review of Flowering Judas, New York Times Book Review
        (1 December), sec. vi, p. 37.
            Porter displays humor, vitality, and a wide range of
        subject matter in Flowering Judas. She is an eminent
        stylist.

6   ANON. "Complexity and Depth," SatR, XIII (14 December), 16.
            Porter's stories are simple on the surface, but they
        combine complexity, depth, and beauty in their concern
        with brutal facts. "María Concepción" is the best story
        in Flowering Judas; indeed, it is the only story which is
        fully resolved and fully comprehensible. "The Cracked
        Looking-Glass," "Theft," "That Tree," and "Hacienda" have

1935

(ANON.)
>less form than Porter's earlier stories, and "Hacienda" is
>the least successful of all her stories.

7   BAKER, HOWARD. "Some Notes on New Fiction," SoR, I (July),
>188-89.
>>The novelette "Hacienda" does not deal directly with the
>>climate and feudal society of Mexico so much as it conveys
>>them through the timbre of its prose. Both the theme and
>>the fable of the story lack strength, but Porter's style
>>is marvelously adapted to conveying the nuances of people,
>>things, and situations.

8   CHAMBERLAIN, JOHN. "Books of the Times," New York Times
>(11 October), p. L-23.
>>One can always count on Porter for good prose. The sto-
>>ries published in the first edition of Flowering Judas are
>>still fresh in the second edition, and, among the new sto-
>>ries, "That Tree" is "a very understanding bit of work."

9   CLARK, ELEANOR. "Cameos," New Republic, LXXXV (25 December),
>207.
>>Porter's style compels one to pay more attention to word
>>patterns than to substance in her miniature-like stories.
>>"Flowering Judas," "María Concepción," and "The Cracked
>>Looking-Glass" are perfect stories by any standard, but
>>the understatement, rigid selection, and sympathetic music
>>that characterize all of the stories in Flowering Judas
>>are less successful in a story like "Hacienda."

10 COWLEY, MALCOLM. "Books in Review," New Republic, LXXXIII
>(29 May), 79.
>>While "Hacienda" has not the "desperate emotion" of a
>>story like "Flowering Judas," it is "rich in gossip," the
>>burden of its interest springing from its relationship to
>>Eisenstein's Thunder Over Mexico. Porter treats all as-
>>pects of the Eisenstein quarrel with equal malice.

11 DICKSON, THOMAS. "Absorbing Characters," New York Daily News
>(13 October), p. 84.
>>Flowering Judas is a series of absorbing vignettes with
>>particularly good characterizations. Porter has learned
>>much from Maugham, but she stands on her own two feet.

12 HIGGINS, CECILE. "Short Stories," New York Sun (26 October),
    p. 10.
        The stories of Flowering Judas are the work of a mature
    artist. Each is a compact unit of cause and effect, yet
    each abounds in depth, naturalness, and skillful
    characterization.

13 NASH, ANNE. "A Vivid Awareness," Carmel, California Pacific
    Weekly (11 November), p. 228.
        The stories of Flowering Judas are richly impression-
    istic: we identify with Porter's characters and experi-
    ence the atmosphere of Mexico vividly.

14 TROY, WILLIAM. "A Matter of Quality," Nation, CXLI
    (30 October), 517-18.
        Porter's output is essentially qualitative. Her stories
    are founded on an honesty which avoids both artificiality
    and self-conscious sincerity. She adheres strictly to
    facts for what facts can produce and thus makes the over-
    tones of fact clear to us. One can fault her for an oc-
    casional failure to crystallize her theme adequately, as
    in "Hacienda" and "That Tree," but "María Concepción" and
    "The Cracked Looking-Glass" alone would place her among
    the most distinguished writers of fiction in America.

15 WALTON, EDA LOU. "An Exquisite Story-Teller," New York Herald
    Tribune Books (3 November), sec. vii, p. 7.
        Porter is probably the finest short story writer in
    America. Her especial ability is to create the effect she
    wants with absolute precision and without apparent strain.
    "The Cracked Looking-Glass" is the best of the new stories
    in Flowering Judas, while "Hacienda" and "That Tree" lack
    the perfect focus of the other stories.

16 WALTON, EDITH H. "Katherine Anne Porter's Stories and Other
    Recent Works of Fiction," New York Times Book Review
    (20 October), p. 6.
        The new stories in the second edition of Flowering Judas
    make clear Porter's development and progress. Although
    "Hacienda" is a little too chaotic, "Theft" and "The
    Cracked Looking-Glass" are richly developed and justify
    Porter's reputation.

17 _____. Review of Flowering Judas, Forum and Century, XCIV
    (December), ix.
        Flowering Judas establishes Porter as one of our best
    short story writers. Her style is as subtle and lovely as

1935

(WALTON, EDITH H.)
Kay Boyle's, while she has greater vitality and less
rarefied mannerisms.

18   WOLFE, BERTRAM D.   "Books of the Age," Workers' Age
(19 January), p. 2.
"Hacienda" is a "rather long, slightly novelized and
insubstantial essay in exquisitely polished prose." Porter knows her Mexico and includes every type of Mexican in
her story except the new Mexican worker.

1936 A   BOOKS - NONE

1936 B   SHORTER WRITINGS

1   ANON. "Mexican Contrasts," TLS (18 April), p. 333.
Except for "María Concepción," the stories in Flowering
Judas are simply psychological studies; they need more
patterning if they are to make sense.

2   ANON. "Book Notes," New York Herald Tribune (22 December),
p. 21.
"Noon Wine" will be published in February, and Glenway
Wescott, Josephine Herbst, and Kay Boyle say it is Porter's best work to date.

1937 A   BOOKS - NONE

1937 B   SHORTER WRITINGS

1   ANON. "Four Forgotten Books Win $2,500 Prizes," New York
Times (30 January), p. 15.
Porter has been awarded a prize of $2,500 by the Book of
the Month Club for Flowering Judas. The award is given to
books of outstanding merit that have not sold well.

2   BELITT, BEN. "South Texas Primitive," Nation, CXLIV (15 May),
571.
"Noon Wine" deals with its theme in terms of "the vil-
lage 'primitive'" rather than in the psychopathic terms
that are more appropriate to the material of the story.
The effect is one of "gangling artlessness," and it rings
false inasmuch as all of the simplicities are clearly
stratagems.

3 GANNETT, LEWIS. "Books and Things," New York Herald Tribune
        (30 January), p. 11.
          Porter has had more praise than most short story writ-
        ers, but the public does not buy books of short stories in
        numbers.

4 MORSE, SAMUEL FRENCH. "Style--Plus," Reading and Collecting,
        I (April), 14.
          "Noon Wine" is a solid, finished work. If the strong
        themes of some of Porter's stories have lacked strong
        treatment, this story does not.

5 THOMPSON, RALPH. "Books of the Times," New York Times
        (30 January), p. 15.
          Porter is "indubitably among the most brilliant of our
        writers of short stories." She equals Katherine Mansfield
        in perception and surpasses her in forthrightness.

6 WALTON, EDITH H. "An Ironic Tragedy," New York Times Book Re-
        view (11 April), sec. vii, p. 7.
          "Noon Wine" has the incidental charm that characterizes
        all of Porter's work, but the climax of the story is in-
        explicable and the point of the story is elusive. The
        reader is left dissatisfied, convinced that the story is
        too ironic for ordinary mortals.

7 WINSTEN, ARCHER. "Presenting the Portrait of an Artist," New
        York Post (6 May), p. 17.
          Biographical sketch based on an interview dealing with
        Porter's childhood, juvenilia, decision to leave home,
        movie career, newspaper career, Mexican adventures, writ-
        ing habits, interests, and future publications.

1938 A BOOKS - NONE

1938 B SHORTER WRITINGS

1 BAKER, HOWARD. "The Contemporary Short Story," SoR, III
        (Winter), 595-96.
          Porter's greatness is linked to her social conscious-
        ness. In "He" she illumines the predicament of the par-
        ents of an idiot child; in "Old Mortality" she illumines
        what we are like insofar as the past lives on in us; and
        in "Noon Wine" she illumines the human tangle within a
        violent and ruinous tragedy.

1939

1939 A BOOKS - NONE

1939 B SHORTER WRITINGS

1   ANON. Review of Pale Horse, Pale Rider, Time, XXXIII
        (10 April), 75.
            Pale Horse, Pale Rider belongs with the best American
        writing in the form of the short novel, and it is subtle
        without falling into the preciousness that mars Porter's
        earlier work. Porter is a newcomer to the Southern lit-
        erary center that has been established at Louisiana State
        University. She does not worry about how slowly she
        writes, and she is working on a novel to be called
        "Promised Lands."

2   ANON. Review of Pale Horse, Pale Rider, Booklist, XXXV
        (15 April), 271.
            The delicate and humorous stories of Pale Horse, Pale
        Rider contain much beautiful writing that is particularly
        interesting for its technical skill.

3   ANON. "Away from Near-War Consciousness," TLS (27 May),
        p. 311.
            A poetic quality gives distinction to Pale Horse, Pale
        Rider at a time when few novels have any distinction at
        all. The poetic effect is too assiduously cultivated,
        however, and real beauty is not achieved.
        Reprinted in American Writing Today: Its Independence and
        Vigor (1957.B1).

4   ANON. Review of Pale Horse, Pale Rider, North American Re-
        view, CCXLVII (Summer), 399.
            "Pale Horse, Pale Rider" is verbose and unimpressive,
        but "Old Mortality" and "Noon Wine" are among Porter's
        best stories. "Noon Wine" achieves an effect rare in
        American literature.

5   ANON. Review of Pale Horse, Pale Rider, Wisconsin Library
        Bulletin, XXXV (October), 168.
            The three short novels of Pale Horse, Pale Rider are
        distinctive for their admirable prose style and for their
        degree of emotional awareness.

6   FADIMAN, CLIFTON. "Katherine Anne Porter," NY, XV (1 April),
        77-78.
            The three stories of Pale Horse, Pale Rider are "mar-
        moreal" in quality, for Porter writes carefully, wasting
        nothing and giving us genuine works of art. The title

10

(FADIMAN, CLIFTON)

story is the best of the three; it is "a bitter story that does not shout aloud its bitterness; an anti-war story that on the surface has no social point of view whatso-ever; a story about Liberty Loan drives, four-minute ora-tors, the influenza epidemic, but which is dateless." It contains agonizing insights into love, death, war, and sickness. "Noon Wine" is a more studied tale, slightly tainted by obvious technique, but with characters perfect-ly comprehended and developed. "Old Mortality" is a beautiful story, but it is the weakest of the three.

7   GANNETT, LEWIS. "Books and Things," New York Herald Tribune (30 March), p. 23.
    Porter is possibly one of the great contemporary Ameri-can writers. "Old Mortality" has genuine insight with acute characterizations and subtle awareness of the con-flicts between generations.

8   HARTUNG, PHILIP T. Review of Pale Horse, Pale Rider, Common-weal, XXX (19 May), 109-10.
    Pale Horse, Pale Rider establishes Porter as a prose stylist of the first rank. "Old Mortality" is the best of the three stories.

9   ISHERWOOD, CHRISTOPHER. Review of Pale Horse, Pale Rider, New Republic, XCVIII (19 April), 312-13.
    Porter should be better known in England than she is. ·She has a great deal of talent, if she is no genius, and, unlike Katherine Mansfield, she is fundamentally serious and close to the earth. "Noon Wine" is a subtle, psycho-logical story that evokes Maupassant, and it is the best of the three stories in Pale Horse, Pale Rider. Porter fails her reader only by providing no "vulgar appeal," for one does wish that she would condescend to make her reader cry or laugh aloud. Partially reprinted in A Library of Literary Criticism (1969.B2).

10 MOULT, THOMAS. Review of Pale Horse, Pale Rider, Manchester Guardian (30 June), p. 7.
    Pale Horse, Pale Rider is a fine collection. The first two stories depend heavily on atmosphere and are slightly marred by vagueness and turgidity, but the title story is perfect in every way--clear, poignant, witty, and charming.

1939

11   REID, FORREST.   "Fiction," The Spectator, CLXII (9 June),
         p. 1010.
           The British publisher of Pale Horse, Pale Rider does
         not seem to expect it to sell well in England, but "Old
         Mortality" and "Noon Wine" are brilliantly accomplished
         stories, and the title story transcends the class of
         ordinary war stories. Porter has surely discovered the
         perfect form for her talent.

12   RICE, PHILIP BLAIR.   "The Art of Katherine Anne Porter,"
         Nation, CXLVIII (15 April), 442.
           Porter is justly praised as a stylist, but one should
         not fail to note that she has all the other skills of a
         good fiction writer. She is sensitive to both pace and
         construction, she handles colloquial dialogue well, she is
         observant, and she is intelligent. Porter is at her best
         in her short stories and not in her novelettes, however.
         "Pale Horse, Pale Rider," in particular, descends to slick
         magazine writing. Partially reprinted in A Library of
         Literary Criticism (1969.B2).

13   ROSENFELD, PAUL.   "An Artist in Fiction," SatR, XIX (1 April),
         7.
           Porter's fiction belongs with that of Hawthorne, Flau-
         bert, and James. It is accomplished, beautifully formed,
         and unobtrusive in its workings. Porter's usual subject
         is the "eternal discord and harshness of things." "Noon
         Wine" is the most perfect of the three stories in Pale
         Horse, Pale Rider. Partially reprinted in A Library of
         Literary Criticism (1969.B2).

14   S., M. W.   "More Flowering," Christian Science Monitor Weekly
         Magazine Section (13 May), p. 10.
           In Pale Horse, Pale Rider Porter is still writing for
         the more sensitive reader.

15   SOSKIN, WILLIAM.   "Rare Beauty of Good Writing," New York
         Herald Tribune Books (9 April), sec. ix, p. 5.
           Both "Old Mortality" and "Pale Horse, Pale Rider" sug-
         gest that long periods of thought went into their making,
         and one could wish that writers who aspire to Porter's
         emotional suggestiveness and essential story values would
         also allow their materials to gestate properly. The in-
         teriority of "Old Mortality" and "Pale Horse, Pale Rider"
         contrasts with the strange and melodramatic "Noon Wine,"
         a tale that reminds us of Caldwell's comedies and which
         demonstrates Porter's versatility as an artist.

16   STEGNER, WALLACE. "Conductivity in Fiction," VQR, XV (Sum-
        mer), 443-47.
            The three novelettes of Pale Horse, Pale Rider are mas-
        terfully crafted by one of our most subtle writers. "Noon
        Wine" is the best of the three, however, because it has
        "conductivity"--it sets up a rapport with its reader that
        makes it more convincing and exciting than reality. The
        other two stories are more carefully structured than "Noon
        Wine," but they do not "conduct" so well.

17   THOMPSON, RALPH. "Books of the Times," New York Times
        (30 March), p. L-21.
            Pale Horse, Pale Rider confirms Porter's high reputa-
        tion. Its stories are substantial and honestly moving,
        and few of Porter's contemporaries could match them. The
        title story is the best of the three, and "Noon Wine" is
        the most artificial.

18   WALTON, EDITH H. "The Delicate Art of Katherine Anne Porter,"
        New York Times Book Review (2 April), p. 5.
            "Old Mortality" is flawless and completely charming.
        "Pale Horse, Pale Rider" is not so good a story as "Old
        Mortality," but it has an appealingly haunting quality.
        "Noon Wine" is a good, clever story, but it is essentially
        a tour de force. Indeed, the three stories justify all
        that has been claimed for Porter as a writer. They show,
        too, that she has a sense of humor unusual in a stylist
        which brings a large audience within her reach.

19   WESCOTT, GLENWAY. "Praise," SoR, V (Summer), 161-73.
            An unabashed morality permeates "Noon Wine" and the sto-
        ry has an epic quality reminiscent of Milton. Hatch is
        Porter's Lucifer, "not to blame for anything except his
        being, and his happening to be just there, in juxtaposi-
        tion with [the] others." Porter might fittingly be
        linked to the early Joyce or to Forster, but it is wrong
        to classify her as a stylist for hers is a "bare art" and
        it is the story which is laid bare. She has never "com-
        promised with inability," making a method of it or playing
        tricks with it, nor has she affected false humility. She
        is the sort of writer that we now need: one who maintains
        standards against which literary excesses and fads may be
        evaluated.

20   WEST, ANTHONY. "New Novels," New Statesman and Nation, XVII
        (27 May), 832, 834.
            Pale Horse, Pale Rider is fundamentally shallow, explor-
        ing certain emotions under the influence of certain

1939

(WEST, ANTHONY)
circumstances rather than exploring important ideas. It
is completely satisfying in its power to please and charm,
however.

1940 A   BOOKS - NONE

1940 B   SHORTER WRITINGS

1   ANON. Publisher's Weekly, CXXXVII (13 April), 1490.
       Porter has received the first gold medal awarded by the
    Society for the Libraries at New York University. The
    medal was awarded for Pale Horse, Pale Rider.

2   BLOCK, MAXINE, ed. "Porter, Katherine Anne," in Current Bi-
       ography. New York: Wilson, pp. 657-58.
       Biographical essay dealing with Porter's ancestry, early
    interest in writing, newspaper experience, work in Mexico,
    Guggenheim Fellowship, work in Germany, lecturing in Amer-
    ica, divorce, writings, ideals of writing, and interests.

3   CRUME, PAUL. "Pale Horse, Pale Rider," SoR, XXV (January),
       213-18.
       Porter seems more an essayist writing about a story than
    a teller of tales, but she writes for the connoisseur and
    uses her language with fine exactness. "Old Mortality" is
    the strongest tale in the Pale Horse, Pale Rider collec-
    tion, although all of the stories are very fine. (Bio-
    graphical details are included relevant to Porter's youth,
    her working in Denver, her living in Greenwich Village,
    her writing of My Chinese Marriage, her living in Mexico,
    and her interests.)

4   HARTLEY, LODWICK. "Katherine Anne Porter," SR, XLVIII (April-
       June), 206-16.
       Porter's narratives are difficult to classify and one
    senses that she mistrusts the short story form. "Magic"
    and "He" are starkly economical, while "María Concepción,"
    "The Jilting of Granny Weatherall," and "Hacienda" encom-
    pass more than the usual range of short stories, and "The
    Cracked Looking-Glass" is as much a novel as Madame Bo-
    vary. Porter's achievement is variable, too. "Rope" and
    "Noon Wine" are structurally very fine, whereas "Theft"
    and "Flowering Judas" have too obvious a moral, and "Old
    Mortality" and "Pale Horse, Pale Rider" are defective in
    plan. Porter is at her best when she is most objective,
    as in "Magic," "He," "The Cracked Looking-Glass," and

(HARTLEY, LODWICK)
"Noon Wine," and when she is evoking detail, as in the fetal rabbits passage of "The Grave" and the Mexican life passages of "María Concepción"; judged by any part of her work, however, she is one of our most talented writers. Partially reprinted in A Library of Literary Criticism (1969.B2).

5   MARSHALL, MARGARET. "Writers in the Wilderness: Katherine Anne Porter," Nation, CL (13 April), 473, 475.
Throughout her life Porter has absorbed her narrative material intuitively, and this explains the lack of apparent strain in her writing. She will never write a "novel of American life," however, because generalizations are alien to her. She is content to work with the "thumbprint in the wilderness." Partially reprinted in A Library of Literary Criticism (1969.B2).

6   MILLETT, FRED B. "Porter, Katherine Anne," in Contemporary American Authors. New York: Harcourt, Brace, pp. 96, 528.
Porter is sometimes too subtle a writer, but her prose has an incomparable poetic power.

7   van GELDER, ROBERT. "Katherine Anne Porter at Work," New York Times Book Review (14 April), sec. vi, p. 20.
[Interview.] Porter writes infrequently, partly because she requires absolute privacy for her work and finds privacy difficult to arrange. Robert Penn Warren's ability to write easily amazes her. She does not write specifically for connoisseurs, but her quickly-written stories go through a long incubation. She works directly on a typewriter and never shows her work to anyone until it is finished. She has held a number of jobs, and "Pale Horse, Pale Rider" (which she considers her best story) is based on her newspaper experience. Reprinted in Writers and Writing (1946.B4).

1941 A BOOKS - NONE

1941 B SHORTER WRITINGS

1   BATES, H. E. The Modern Short Story: A Critical Survey. Boston: Writers, Inc., pp. 185-87.
Porter is the most accomplished of American short story writers in that she is the most versatile. She has not

1941

(BATES, H. E.)
confined herself to working with a single technique, a
single region, or a single psychology.

2   BOYLE, KAY. "Full Length Portrait," New Republic, CV (November), 707.
Porter says a number of profoundly true and sensitive
things about Eudora Welty in her preface to A Curtain of
Green.

1942 A   BOOKS - NONE

1942 B   SHORTER WRITINGS

1   ANON. Review of The Itching Parrot, NY, XVIII (21 March), 70.
Porter's introduction to The Itching Parrot is more in-
formative than strictly necessary and fails to defend
adequately the book's dullness.

*2   ANON. "Writing a Short Story," New York Herald Tribune
(6 April), p. 8.
Unlocatable; cited in A Bibliography of the Works of
Katherine Anne Porter and A Bibliography of the Criticism
of the Works of Katherine Anne Porter (1969.A2), p. 163.

3   CHAMBERLAIN, JOHN. "Books of the Times," New York Times
(20 March), p. L-23.
Porter's introduction to The Itching Parrot is alone
worth the price of the book, and her translation and edit-
ing are narrative delights.

4   GANNETT, LEWIS. "Books and Things," New York Herald Tribune
(28 July), p. 15.
Porter's introduction to Fiesta in November is elusive:
she should have shared with the reader her basis for the
catalogue description of contributors to the volume.

5   GARNETT, EMILY. Review of The Itching Parrot, LJ, LXVII
(1 March), 225.
Lacking the picturesque language and the concision of
Lazarillo des Tormes, The Itching Parrot will not interest
the general reader.

6   JONES, HOWARD MUMFORD. "Lizardi . . .," SatR, XXV (4 April),
14.
Porter's translation of El Periquillo Sarniento ("The
Itching Parrot") is both adequate and idiomatic, but her

(JONES, HOWARD MUMFORD)
    biographical essay on the author is wholly fascinating.
Porter should write a series of essays on Mexican literary
figures.

7   RUGOFF, MILTON. Review of The Itching Parrot, New York Herald
        Tribune Books (22 March), sec. ix, p. 9.
           Porter has given us an edition of El Periquillo Sarni-
        ento stripped of its moral and political disquisitions and
        turned into pure picaresque.

8   RYAN, EDWIN. Review of The Itching Parrot, Commonweal, XXXVI
        (24 July), 331-32.
           Porter's translation of El Periquillo Sarniento is well
        done; she has wisely omitted passages which retard the
        action.

9   SMITH, REBECCA W. "The Southwest in Fiction," SatR, XXV
        (16 May), 12-13, 37.
           Porter is said not to think of herself as a Southwestern
        writer, but she is Southwestern in her roots and she deals
        knowledgeably with the Southwest in many of her stories.
        Indeed, the Mexican stories of Flowering Judas are the
        best in that volume, and "Old Mortality" is the best of
        the stories in Pale Horse, Pale Rider.

10   TRILLING, LIONEL. "Mexican Classic," Nation, CLIV (24 March),
        373-74.
           Porter's introduction to The Itching Parrot is more in-
        teresting than the book itself, and her translation is a
        model of firm, simple prose.

11   WALTON, EDITH H. "Bygone World," New York Times Book Review
        (10 May), p.22.
           Porter's introduction to The Itching Parrot is
        excellent.

12   WARREN, R. P. "Katherine Anne Porter (Irony with a Center),"
        Kenyon Review, IV (Winter), 29-42.
           Porter is justly praised as a stylist, but we should
        note that the various devices of her prose always take us
        to the core meaning of a scene and from there to the
        theme of the story, which is usually ironical. Passages
        from "Flowering Judas," "Noon Wine," "The Cracked Looking-
        Glass," and "Old Mortality" all make clear that Porter's
        ironical structures imply "a refusal to accept the formu-
        la, the ready-made solution"-- that they affirm "the need
        for a dialectical approach to matters of definition, the

1942

(WARREN, R. P.)
  need for exercising as much of the human faculty as possible." This is "irony with a center" rather than irony
  for its own sake.
  Reprinted in Contrasts (1951.B3), in Selected Essays
  (1958.B2), and, in slightly revised form, in Katherine
  Anne Porter: A Critical Symposium (1969.A1).

13 WOLFE, BERTRAM D. "Picaresque," New Republic, CVI (22 June),
    868-70.
      Porter's editing of The Itching Parrot has made the re-
    lationship of its rogue to his sixteenth-century anteced-
    ents wonderfully clear, but Porter is mistaken in her ex-
    cellent introduction when she observes that this work is
    almost the last of its kind.

1944 A BOOKS - NONE

1944 B SHORTER WRITINGS

1 ANON. Review of The Leaning Tower, LJ, LXIX (1 September),
    699.
      The Leaning Tower collection is recommended. "A Day's
    Work" is a wonderful depiction of a James Farrell world,
    and "The Leaning Tower" is an excellent study of Berlin
    and its inhabitants.

2 ANON. Review of The Leaning Tower, Chicago Sun Book Week
    (24 September), p. 8.
      The collection of episodes in The Leaning Tower is the
    sort of thing that Porter does well. The title story and
    "The Downward Path" deserve special mention.

3 ANON. Review of The Leaning Tower, Time, XLIV (25 September),
    103-04.
      Six of the stories in The Leaning Tower seem parts of a
    continuous, nostalgic memory, rather than discrete sto-
    ries. They are "gentle, affectionate epitaphs for a dead
    world." Some readers may prefer the title story--a horri-
    fying tale of a country on the edge of tragedy.

4 ANON. Review of The Leaning Tower, Christian Century, LXI
    (11 October), 1170.
      The stories of The Leaning Tower are skillful in tech-
    nique; they will appeal not only to general readers but to
    writers as well.

5 ANON. Review of The Leaning Tower, Booklist, XLI (15 October), 59.
    The stories of The Leaning Tower are skillfully and beautifully written, but they will probably appeal only to discriminating readers.

6 ANON. Review of The Leaning Tower, Commonweal, XLI (20 October), 20.
    Porter's "poetic sensibility" has given us a distinguished collection of short stories in The Leaning Tower.

7 ANON. Review of The Leaning Tower, CathW, CLX (November), 189.
    Porter displays complete mastery of her medium in The Leaning Tower as well as considerable feeling for life and insightfulness into character.

8 ANON. Review of The Leaning Tower, American Mercury, LIX (December), 766.
    The title story of The Leaning Tower is wordy, oversymbolical, and unclear, but stories such as "A Day's Work," "The Downward Path," and "The Old Order" are enormously better, respectively heart-breaking, insightful, and charming.

9 BOUTELL, CLIP. "Authors Are Like People," New York Post (21 September), p. 23.
    [Interview.] Porter is quoted as having to develop her talent slowly and being ready to publish "No Safe Harbor" in the Spring.

10 DOWNING, FRANCIS. Review of The Leaning Tower, Commonweal, XL (29 September), 572.
    The sculptured vignettes of The Leaning Tower would satisfy the aesthetic demands of both James and Poe, and the sensitivity and subtlety of such stories as "The Old Order" and "The Grave" are a tribute to the human spirit.

11 HANSEN, HARRY. "The First Reader," New York World Telegram (14 September), p. 22.
    Porter is particularly interested in character in The Leaning Tower. The title story is neither unjust nor obvious in its distaste for Germany. "A Day's Work" is evidence of Porter's versatility.

12 JONES, HOWARD MUMFORD. "A Smooth Literary Texture," SatR, XXVII (30 September), 15.
    The stories of The Leaning Tower may appear casual, but they are the product of fundamental brainwork and are exqui-

1944

(JONES, HOWARD MUMFORD)
sitely right. The stories might gain in dramatic power
while losing nothing of their delicacy, however, if Porter
were not quite so carefully casual in developing them. It
is ironic that American short story writers have gone full
circle, eschewing the neatly plotted short story in favor
of the older, slice-of-life mode.
Partially reprinted in A Library of Literary Criticism
(1969.B2).

13   KELLEY, GILBERT H. Review of The Leaning Tower, LJ, LXIX
(1 September), 699.
The Leaning Tower is recommended to readers. "A Day's
Work" recalls the work of James T. Farrell, and the title
story is an excellent portrait of Berlin.

14   MOLLOY, ROBERT. "The Book of the Day," New York Sun (15 September), p. 20.
The Leaning Tower establishes Porter as without rivals
in the area of the short story. The stories have ease,
grace, and technical finish, and they present more than
meets the eye.

15   PRESCOTT, ORVILLE. "Books of the Times," New York Times
(18 September), p. 17.
The Leaning Tower is not so appealing as Porter's earlier
work. The six stories that begin the collection are in-
conclusive and unsubstantial: they seem almost to be
fragments from an unwritten novel. "The Downward Path to
Wisdom" is very nearly a masterpiece, a "truly terrible and
a profoundly pitiful story," and "A Day's Work" is excel-
lently conceived. The title story, however, is only hind-
sightfully critical of German psychology and the German
civilization.

16   _____. "Outstanding Novels," YR, XXXIV n.s. (Autumn), 190.
The Leaning Tower is written by one of the best stylists
of our time. Some of the stories deal nostalgically with
childhood, and they have the haunting inconclusiveness of
Katherine Mansfield's stories. "The Downward Path to Wisdom" is the best of the stories.

17   SAPIEHA, VIRGILIA. "By Katherine Anne Porter," New York Herald Tribune Book Review (17 September), sec. vi, p. 2.
Most of the stories in the Leaning Tower collection are
"sharp little genre paintings," but the title story, by
far the best, deals with the gulf between hopeful America
and embittered Europe, the "chief problem of our time."

(SAPIEHA, VIRGILIA)
The story makes clear that the gulf cannot be bridged before Americans learn a great deal more than they now know.
"The Downward Path to Wisdom" is the most incisive of the
other stories, and the general level of craftsmanship in
the collection is high.

18   TRILLING, DIANA. "Fiction in Review," Nation, CLIX
(23 September), 359-60.
"The Leaning Tower" is a literary-political document
about the culture which spawned Hitler, and almost everything in it portends catastrophe. It is the best tale
Porter has ever written; only the handling of Charles Up-
ton is inadequate. The rest of the stories in The Leaning
Tower collection are "fugitive sketches," marred by "a
faint perfume of sensibility" that may spring either from
their abbreviated length or from their autobiographical
basis.

19   WEEKS, EDWARD. "The Atlantic Bookshelf," Atlantic Monthly,
CLXXIV (November), 131, 133.
The Leaning Tower is a disappointment after Porter's
earlier work, for her usual fastidiousness of phrasing and
precision of observation have no vitality in this book and
the characters arouse neither curiosity nor sympathy.
Style is tedious when not accompanied by warmth.

20   WESCOTT, GLENWAY. "Stories by a Writer's Writer," New York
Times Book Review (17 September), sec. vii, p. 1.
Most of the stories of The Leaning Tower are wholly unself-
conscious in method and wonderfully transparent in style.
Only the title story is self-conscious in its method, and
it is the only story of the collection that is not quite
satisfactory. "The Leaning Tower" seems to signify that
Porter has novelistic ambitions, however, and one might
look forward to a womanly War and Peace from her.

21   WHICHER, GEORGE F. "Books and Things," New York Herald Tribune (14 September), p. 19.
Porter's style in The Leaning Tower is better than flawless, and the stories are very fine in every way. The at-
mospheric effects of the title story are memorable; "A
Day's Work" suggests Porter's skill in capturing an alien
idiom; "The Downward Path" has ghastly depths; and "The
Grave" is the most striking tale in the collection.

1944

22 WILSON, EDMUND. Review of The Leaning Tower, NY, XX
         (30 September), 72-74.
         Porter's stories are so lucid and unpretentious that it
      is difficult for the critic to suggest their quality. Her
      stories are usually about the shifting phases of human
      relationships, and they fall into three distinct groups:
      stories of working- and middle-class households, more suc-
      cessful stories of foreign countries with a sense of de-
      stroyed human values, and stories about women. The last
      stories are Porter's best: their meanings may be elusive,
      but they make clear a natural human spirit upon which all
      of the forces of society bear and against which they are
      appraised.
         Reprinted in Classics and Commercials: A Literary Chroni-
      cle of the Forties (1950.B3).

1945 A BOOKS - NONE

1945 B SHORTER WRITINGS

1 ANON. Review of The Leaning Tower, TLS (10 November), p. 533.
         Since the death of Katherine Mansfield, American writers
      seem more able than British to tell a story simply, with
      the lightest, implicit emotion. Porter's "The Source" is
      such a story. The other stories in The Leaning Tower are
      lively, intelligent, humorous, and touching, but not so
      perfect as "The Source."

2 BEACH, JOSEPH WARREN. "Self-Consciousness and Its Antidote,"
         VQR, XXI (Spring), 292-93.
         Porter is neither a humorist, a moralist, nor a philos-
      opher, and her writing is in no way self-conscious. Her
      whole interest is in the spiritual state of her charac-
      ters. Her method is to draw her characters clearly and to
      place them in established cultures in which they work out
      a relationship between self-respect and the circumstances
      of their lives. The result has the ring of truth.

3 BUCKMAN, GERTRUDE. "Miss Porter's New Stories," PR, XII
         (Winter), 134.
         Porter's The Leaning Tower collection proves her much more
      than a stylist: she gives us "authoritative and substan-
      tial" images of entire societies. She sees the horrors
      perpetrated by human beings, but love lifts her above mere
      sensationalism. These stories are not so good as her pre-
      vious ones, but they have her essential purity and
      delicacy.

4   MATTHIESSEN, F. O. Review of The Leaning Tower, Accent, V
         (Winter), 121-23.
         Porter's stories frequently rest on a discovery of "the
     living intricacy in any relationship," and the fragmentary
     sketches that begin The Leaning Tower chart such discov-
     eries very well. Violence is often compounded with the
     discovery, as in "The Circus" (the best story in the col-
     lection) and "The Downward Path to Wisdom." Porter is
     more a virtuoso than a regionalist, as the different en-
     vironments of "A Day's Work" and "The Leaning Tower" make
     clear, and in the title story her virtuosity is combined
     beautifully with moral penetration.
         Reprinted as "That True and Human World" in Accent An-
     thology (1946.B3) and in The Responsibilities of the
     Critic: Essays and Reviews by F. O. Matthiessen
     (1952.B10).

5   READ, MARTHA. "The Mind's Delineation," Quarterly Review of
         Literature, II (no. 2), 150-52.
         The stories of The Leaning Tower dwell on inner lives
     and fragile emotions, but Porter in no way sacrifices
     depth or comprehensiveness, and she maintains a "light
     touch" throughout. "The Grave" is the best story in the
     collection.

6   SPENCER, THEODORE. "Recent Fiction," SR, LIII (Spring),
         300-01.
         The title story of The Leaning Tower is a microcosmic
     picture of post-war Germany without false emphasis or ex-
     aggeration, and it reminds us of Porter's ability to see a
     situation organically. None of the stories in the Leaning
     Tower collection are as good as "Pale Horse, Pale Rider"
     and many of the stories are very slight, but Porter's work
     is still among the best in contemporary American fiction.

7   YOUNG, MARGUERITE. "Fictions Mystical and Epical," Kenyon Re-
         view, VII (Winter), 152-54.
         The stories of The Leaning Tower have as a theme "the
     continuity of the individual's experience, his sense of
     the past in the present, and his sense of the indestructi-
     bility of that brave human spirit which rejects the arti-
     ficiality of chaos, even as an abstraction." Porter im-
     parts new stature and significance to the short story, in-
     asmuch as the forms of her stories are absorbed wholly
     into the matter, imparting the effect of an "immense mu-
     sical spaciousness" and an "epic state of mind."

1945

8   YOUNG, VERNON A.   "The Art of Katherine Anne Porter," New
        Mexico Quarterly Review, XV (August), 326-41.
           Porter is "the most flawless realist of her generation."
        She is careful to retain the color and background of her
        characters and she has a real genius for stylistic veri-
        similitude.   Her governing themes are incomprehension and
        incompatibility, and she traces these themes realistically
        and with psychological insight.   Her sense of irony is
        crucial to the realism of almost all her stories, and a
        story such as "The Leaning Tower" is inferior to her
        others primarily because it is insufficiently ironic.   In-
        deed, Porter's realism should be the gauge for testing
        literary realism among American authors.
        Reprinted in American Thought (1947.B5).

1946 A   BOOKS - NONE

1946 B   SHORTER WRITINGS

1   ALLEN, CHARLES.   "Southwestern Chronicle: Katherine Anne Por-
        ter," ArQ, II (Summer), 90-95.
           Porter's themes derive their power from a rich and com-
        plex characterization.   The depth of characterization is
        made possible by her conviction that man's irrational im-
        pulses emerge when he is under pressure, by her explana-
        tion of people in terms of cultural conditioning, and by
        her sensitive use of tone.   A large part of Porter's work
        is superior to anything written in English in the twenti-
        eth century.
        Partially reprinted in A Library of Literary Criticism
        (1969.B2).

2   BROWN, JOHN L.   "Readers and Writers in Paris," New York Times
        Book Review (3 March), p. 14.
           Marcelle Sibon's translation of Flowering Judas is re-
        ceiving appreciative reviews in France.

3   MATTHIESSEN, F. O.   "That True and Human World," in Accent An-
        thology, edited by Kerker Quinn and Charles Shattuck.   New
        York: Harcourt, Brace, pp. 619-23.
        Reprinted from Accent (1945.B4).

4   van GELDER, ROBERT.   Writers and Writing.   New York: Scrib-
        ners, pp. 42-44.
        Reprinted from New York Times Book Review (1940.B7).

1947 A   BOOKS - NONE

1947 B   SHORTER WRITINGS

1   SNELL, GEORGE. The Shapers of American Fiction: 1798-1947.
    New York: Dutton, p. 301.
      One finds some of Hawthorne's love of shadows and alle-
    gory in Porter's stories, as well as James' love of invo-
    lution, but Porter has still to find her own voice as a
    writer. The short story does not seem to give adequate
    range to her talent.

2   SYLVESTER, WILLIAM A. "Selected and Critical Bibliography
    of the Uncollected Works of Katherine Anne Porter," BB,
    XIX (January), 36.
      A listing of eighteen uncollected items, both fictional
    and non-fictional, "arranged in order of interest from the
    'belletristic' point of view." The first appearances of
    collected stories are not included.

3   WANNING, ANDREWS. "The Literary Situation in America," in The
    Novelist as Thinker, ed. B. Rajan. London: Dennis Dob-
    son, pp. 156-57.
      Porter continues to be a model for younger writers.
    Both Eudora Welty and Carson McCullers show her influence.

4   WEST, RAY B., JR. "Katherine Anne Porter: Symbol and Theme
    in 'Flowering Judas,'" Accent, VII (Spring), 182-88.
      "Flowering Judas" contains three "fields" of symbolism.
    Religious symbols invoke Christian ideology; secular,
    machine-linked symbols invoke Marxist ideology; and love
    symbols evoke erotic, secular, and divine love. In the
    interaction between these fields of symbolism, it becomes
    clear that both orthodox religion and Marxist socialism
    are sterile unless joined to love, and that love is im-
    possible without the objects provided by either religion
    or socialism. The symbolic interaction makes clear that,
    unlike Braggioni, Laura is not redeemed, and that Laura is
    the Christ-like Eugenio's Judas.
      Reprinted in Katherine Anne Porter: A Critical Symposium
    (1969.A1), in Critiques and Essays on Modern Fiction:
    1920-1951 (1952.B20), in American Literature: Readings
    and Critiques (1961.B13), and in slightly revised form in
    The Art of Modern Fiction (1949.B2).

5   YOUNG, VERNON A. "The Art of Katherine Anne Porter," in
    American Thought. New York: Gresham, pp. 223-38.
      Reprinted from New Mexico Quarterly Review (1945.B8).

1948

1948 A   BOOKS - NONE

1948 B   SHORTER WRITINGS

   1   HERBST, JOSEPHINE.   "Miss Porter and Miss Stein," PR, XV
          (May), 568-72.
             In attacking Gertrude Stein, Porter fails to understand
          her, as Picasso did, in relation to her period and in
          relation to human nature. The frailties that Porter in-
          dicts are not Stein's alone, and Porter's distaste for
          Stein's "frivolity" fails to perceive that Stein was re-
          sponsible within her chosen orbit.

   2   ORVIS, MARY BURCHARD.   The Art of Writing Fiction. New York:
          Prentice Hall, pp. 27-28, 54, 66, 97, 105-07, 123-25,
          167-68.
             Porter's stories have much to teach the aspiring writer:
          "The Downward Path" depicts the making of a neurotic; "He"
          depicts a conflict that cannot be resolved; "Rope" uses
          conversation in an extraordinarily skillful way; "Theft"
          is distinctive for its manipulation of tenses; and "He"
          delineates Mrs. Whipple perfectly without using physical
          detail.

   3   SUMMERS, RICHARD.   Craft of the Short Story. New York: Rine-
          hart, pp. 283-85.
             Biographical note and listing of Porter's work. Porter
          writes slowly and has never asked others to criticize her
          work.

1949 A   BOOKS - NONE

1949 B   SHORTER WRITINGS

   1   MATTHIESSEN, F. O.   "The Pattern of Literature," in Changing
          Patterns in American Civilization, edited by Dixon Wecter,
          et al. Philadelphia: University of Pennsylvania Press,
          pp. 52-53.
             The Grapes of Wrath has a more important subject than
          Porter's "Pale Horse, Pale Rider," but Porter's more ex-
          acting craft results in a more persuasive "moral meaning"
          than Steinbeck's less careful craft.

   2   WEST, RAY B., JR.   "Katherine Anne Porter: Symbol and Theme
          in 'Flowering Judas,'" in The Art of Modern Fiction, edit-
          ed by Ray B. West, Jr. and Robert Wooster Stallman. New
          York: Rinehart, pp. 287-91.

(WEST, RAY B., JR.)
　　Reprinted in slightly revised form from Accent (1947.B4)
　　and reprinted in Katherine Anne Porter:　A Critical
　　Symposium (1969.A1).

1950 A　BOOKS - NONE

1950 B　SHORTER WRITINGS

　　1　ANON.　"Authors Honored by National Institute," New York Times
　　　　(18 January), p. 23.
　　　　　Porter has been elected a vice-president of the National
　　　　Institute of Arts and Letters.　She is the second woman to
　　　　be named an officer of the Institute.

　　2　HEILMAN, R. B., ed.　Modern Short Stories.　New York:　Har-
　　　　court, Brace, pp. 192-94.
　　　　　Porter emphasizes in " Flowering Judas" the entanglement
　　　　of the political with the whole of life.　She opposes an
　　　　idealistic, political novice to a ruthless, professional
　　　　politician, and focuses the ironies of this contrast by
　　　　making the novice suffer inner conflicts while the pro-
　　　　fessional is at peace with himself.　By making the ideal
　　　　tangible, religious diction gives especial point to the
　　　　conflict between the real and the ideal in the story.

　　3　WILSON, EDMUND.　"Katherine Anne Porter," in Classics and
　　　　Commercials:　A Literary Chronicle of the Forties.　New
　　　　York:　Farrar, Straus, pp. 219-23.
　　　　　Reprinted from NY (1944.B22).

1951 A　BOOKS - NONE

1951 B　SHORTER WRITINGS

　　1　COWLEY, MALCOLM.　"Twenty-Five Years After," SatR, XXXIV
　　　　(2 June), 7.
　　　　　Mexico City was Porter's Paris and Taxco was her South
　　　　of France.

　　2　STRAUMANN, HEINRICH.　American Literature in the Twentieth
　　　　Century.　London:　Hutchinson House, pp. 91-93.
　　　　　Porter is like Carson McCullers in her taste for subtle,
　　　　psychological detail and in her distaste for overt ex-
　　　　planations of her fictional events.　Her "genteel irony"
　　　　is entirely her own, however, and she is particularly

1951

> (STRAUMANN, HEINRICH)
> skilled in counterpointing ordinary events with symbols
> which point to a catastophic climax. This is especially
> true of "Flowering Judas," "The Leaning Tower," and
> "Hacienda."

3 WARREN, ROBERT PENN. "Irony with a Center: Katherine Anne
>   Porter," in Contrasts, edited by Robert E. Knoll. New York
>   Harcourt, Brace, pp. 492-502.
>   Reprinted from Kenyon Review (1942.B12).

4 WHICHER, GEORGE. The Literature of the American People, ed-
>   ited by Arthur H. Quinn. New York: Appleton-Century-
>   Crofts, p. 925.
>   Porter is a master of "stylistic resonance" and exotic
>   atmosphere, and her prose is "an instrument of marvelous
>   precision."

1952 A BOOKS - NONE

1952 B SHORTER WRITINGS

1 ANON. Review of The Days Before, Bookmark, XII (November),
>   33.
>   The Days Before is distinguished by clarity, wit, and
>   precision.

2 ANON. Review of The Days Before, Booklist, XLIX (1 November),
>   86.
>   The essays of The Days Before are varied in subject, but
>   "all bear the imprint of their author's conviction of the
>   high mission of the artist."

3 ANON. Review of The Days Before, NY, XXVIII (1 November),
>   134.
>   The title essay of The Days Before is finely drawn; the
>   essay on Willa Cather is "a model of tough-minded sensi-
>   tivity," and the essay on Gertrude Stein must change our
>   understanding of its subject. The more personal writings
>   in the collection are nearly a self-portrait.

4 BAKER, CARLOS. "A Happy Harvest," New York Times Book Review
>   (2 November), sec. vii, p. 4.
>   The collected writings in The Days Before have the fas-
>   cination of a great novel. Despite their grouping, all
>   are critical and all are personal and particular, and

(BAKER, CARLOS)
together they tell of "artistic growth and its enemies, the perennial pests, the recurrent blights."

5   BROOKS, CLEANTH, ROBERT PENN WARREN, and JOHN T. PURSER. An Approach to Literature. 3rd ed. New York: Appleton-Century-Crofts, pp. 218-19.
"Noon Wine" is about "the difficult definition of good and evil." The world of the Thompsons is established in ample and vivid detail, justifying the scale of the work and involving us in the emotional lives of the characters.

6   FREMANTLE, ANNE. "Yesterdays of Katherine Anne Porter," Commonweal, LVII (7 November), 122.
Porter deals unkindly with Gertrude Stein in The Days Before, but she is perceptive about Katherine Mansfield, appreciative of Eudora Welty and Willa Cather, and intelligent about Edith Sitwell and Virginia Woolf. Her essays on the problems of women are a bit naive, but pleasantly old-fashioned and Christian.

7   HEILMAN, ROBERT B. "The Southern Temper," Hopkins Review, VI (Fall), 5-15.
The "Southern temper" involves simultaneous awareness of and sensitivity to the concrete, the elemental, the ornamental, the representative, and the totality. Porter shares this temper with such writers as Faulkner, Warren, Wolfe, Welty, and Gordon.
Reprinted in South: Modern Southern Literature in Its Cultural Setting (1961.B10).

8   HOBSON, LAURA Z. "Tradewinds," SatR, XXXV (13 September), 6, 8.
Porter is clearly one of the most subtle and most skillful American writers. Her forthcoming collection of essays, The Days Before, should be a book for the intelligent reader.

9   JACKSON, KATHERINE GAUSS. Review of The Days Before, Harper's Magazine, CCV (December), 108.
In The Days Before Porter opens up "new worlds to mind, heart, and spirit." The graceful, flawlessly written essays are sharp, wise, compassionate, and moving.

10 MATTHIESSEN, F. O. "That True and Human World," in The Responsibilities of the Critic: Essays and Reviews by F. O. Matthiessen, sel. by John Rackliffe. New York: Oxford, pp. 67-71.
Reprinted from Accent (1945.B4).

1952

11   McDONALD, GERALD D. Review of The Days Before, LJ, LXXVII
      (15 October), 1807-08.
           Some of the essays in The Days Before are potboilers,
      but all the essays have Porter's invariable intelligence
      and grace. The essays on James, Woolf, Mansfield, Stein,
      Forster, and Rilke are of permanent value.

12   NATHAN, PAUL S. "Rights and Permissions," Publishers Weekly,
      CLXII (22 November), 2098.
           Porter's screenplay for "Young Bess" may finally be put
      into production, although her scenario about Madame Sans-
      Gêne continues to rest in limbo. Porter is now living in
      New York and hopes to complete her novel. She is "rather
      shocked" at some radio adaptations of her stories.

13   POORE, CHARLES. "Books of the Times," New York Times
      (23 October), p. 29.
           The Days Before contains fine pieces of strong opinion
      and "singing clarity."

14   ROLO, CHARLES J. "Reader's Choice," Atlantic, CXC (December),
      97-98.
           Far from being a potpourri, The Days Before is very
      nearly a self-portrait witnessing to Porter's esteem for
      the artist's unique vocation. The book is intelligent,
      sane, and charming.

15   SCHORER, MARK. "Biographia Literaria," New Republic, CXXVII
      (10 November), 18-19.
           Porter's critical essays are the best writings in The
      Days Before, particularly the essays on James, Hardy,
      Cather, and Stein. The essays of the second and third
      sections of the book are too frequently dull, however, and
      a few are even vulgar.

16   SCHWARTZ, EDWARD. "Miss Porter's Essays," Nation, CLXXIII
      (15 November), 452-53.
           The essays in The Days Before are unified by an implicit
      set of values that runs through them. Again and again,
      Porter returns to her favorite themes: that the artist
      must be objective and that he must interest himself in the
      individual; that man is a victim of the irrational and yet
      must strive to be rational; that abstract solutions are
      suspect and that the inquisitive spirit must be tolerated.
      One regrets only that the Mather essays are not included
      in the collection.

17 STALLINGS, SYLVIA. "Deft Touch," New York Herald Tribune Book Review (2 November), sec. vi, p. 8.
    Porter's sharp eye and command of language do not fail her in The Days Before. Her essays on famous writers are particularly incisive, and her political essays are "triumphant." Most of the Mexican pieces, however, are slight in their effect.

18 SULLIVAN, RICHARD. "More Distinguished Prose from a Fascinating Mind," Chicago Sunday Tribune (26 October), sec. iv, p. 4.
    The considerable range and the general quality of the essays collected in The Days Before reveal the mind of their maker as fascinating, unwavering, independent, and honorable. Porter is sometimes indecisive about the proper allegiances of the mind and heart, but she is clearly capable of great love and generosity.

19 WEST, RAY B., JR. "Katherine Anne Porter and 'Historic Memory,'" Hopkins Review, VI (Fall), 16–27.
    Porter's characters usually have qualities or experiences which have some point of resonance with her own character and experiences. This accounts both for the restricted quantity of her work and for its high level of competence. Indeed, Porter's memory is "historic," reaching back beyond her personal past to legend and myth. The Miranda of "Old Mortality" is Porter, seeking definition through knowledge of her past.
    Reprinted in Southern Renaissance: The Literature of the Modern South (1953.B13) and in South: Modern Southern Literature in Its Cultural Setting (1961.B10). Partially reprinted in A Library of Literary Criticism (1969.B2) and expanded in Katherine Anne Porter (1963.B23).

20 _____. "Katherine Anne Porter: Symbol and Theme in 'Flowering Judas,'" in Critiques and Essays on Modern Fiction: 1920–1951, edited by John W. Aldridge. New York: Ronald Press, pp. 217–23.
    Reprinted from Accent (1947.B4).

21 _____. The Short Story in America: 1900–1950. Chicago: Henry Regnery, pp. 72–76.
    Porter is among the best of the Southern writers, and no other writer of her kind has maintained so consistently fine an achievement. She is particularly skillful in introducing her themes through mythical concepts. "Flowering Judas," "Pale Horse, Pale Rider," "Old Mortality," and "María Concepción" are her most popular and characteristic stories.

1953

1953 A BOOKS - NONE

1953 B SHORTER WRITINGS

1   ALLEN, CHARLES. Review of The Days Before, ArQ, IX (Spring),
     71-73.
         The Days Before reveals Porter's divided sensibility.
     She sees love and hate clearly, yet she cannot explain
     them; she is an intelligent humanist, yet she thinks men
     desire to suffer; she is indebted to male writers, yet she
     is femininely shy of them.

2   ANON. "A Writer's Reflections," TLS (16 October), p. 663.
         The essays in The Days Before have the same intellectual
     acuity and perception that marks Porter's stories, al-
     though some of the essays in the second section substitute
     a vague liberalism for systematic thought.

3   CASSINI, IGOR. "The New 400," Esquire, XXXIX (June), 48.
         On the basis of her being a loyal American, a leader in
     her field, a person of excellent character, a woman of
     culture and taste, and a "whole" woman, Porter is listed
     among "the aristocracy of achievement" in America.

4   FIEDLER, LESLIE A. "Love Is Not Enough," YR, XLII (Spring),
     456, 458-59.
         Porter argues that a writer in search of a master should
     choose according to his own needs and from a broad field,
     but she does not realize that a writer is not free in such
     matters, as her own allegiance to Henry James demonstrates.

5   HARTLEY, LODWICK. "The Lady and the Temple: The Critical
     Theories of Katherine Anne Porter," CE, XIV (April),
     386-91.
         The Days Before illumines Porter's critical tenets and
     some of her limitations, revealing her as a classicist in
     the Greek mode both in practice and in theory. Her dis-
     taste for dogma and authority causes her to dislike neo-
     classicism, and she is generally contemptuous of experi-
     ment. Art is wholly above the ordinary, she thinks, and
     on the basis of that position she will probably continue
     to be regarded as a high priestess of Art despite her in-
     sistence that the artist has a serious social responsi-
     bility.
         Reprinted in Katherine Anne Porter: A Critical Symposium
     (1969.A1).

6   McDOWELL, FREDERICK P.   "An Autobiography of an Artist's
        Mind," WR, XVII (Summer), 334-37.
            The essays of The Days Before are most valuable for
        their relevance to the themes of Porter's fiction, partic-
        ularly for illumining the polarities which she unsenti-
        mentally allows to exist together. The more general es-
        says are the best in the collection.

7   MIZENER, ARTHUR. "A Literary Self-Portrait," PR, XX (March-
        April), 244-46.
            The Days Before is valuable for its revelation of a fine
        mind, working informally, and yet ordering its tastes and
        ideas with great elegance. Porter's hero is apparently
        Henry James and her favorite writer, E. M. Forster.

8   PARRISH, STEPHEN MAXFIELD. "Critics Academic and Lay," VQR,
        XXIX (Winter), 158-59.
            More about writers than writing, the critical studies of
        The Days Before are vivid, informed and piercing. A por-
        trait of Porter herself is what principally emerges from
        the volume.

9   SCHWARTZ, EDWARD. "Katherine Anne Porter: A Critical Bibli-
        ography," BNYPL, LVII (May), 211-47.
            The first part of this bibliography attempts a compre-
        hensive listing of Porter's books, stories, poems, essays,
        and book reviews; it lists the first appearance of stories
        and poems together with some important reprints; and it
        either abstracts or describes many of the essays, comments,
        and book reviews. The second part lists critical articles
        and reviews of Porter's work, dividing the material into
        general comment and comment about individual works, and
        abstracting (largely by means of quotation) the more im-
        portant items. Porter read and corrected the manuscript
        of the bibliography.

10   SMITH, HARRISON. "Writers as Readers," SatR, XXXVI
        (28 November), 64.
            Porter's recording of "Flowering Judas" for Columbia
        Records is the most successful in their LP series record-
        ing famous writers. This is because "Flowering Judas" is
        "an intense and oddly disturbing story" with a flavor of
        poetry and mysticism that is more appropriate to the re-
        cording medium than the heavily plotted stories of some
        other writers in the series.

1953

11   SPILLER, ROBERT E.   "Wiles & Words," <u>SatR</u>, XXXVI (10 January),
       12.
          Most collections of an author's magazine pieces fail,
       but <u>The Days Before</u> succeeds because of Porter's interest-
       ing and unchanging personality and because of her unified
       point of view. In these writings that spread over thirty
       years, she is consistently wise, sane, original, and
       delightful.

12   WARREN, ROBERT PENN.   "Introduction" to "Katherine Anne Por-
       ter: A Critical Bibliography" by Edward Schwartz, <u>BNYPL</u>,
       LVII (May), 211-16.
          Porter should be praised not only for the purity of her
       English and for her artistry, but also for her "vivid and
       significant images of life." Porter's imagination is es-
       sentially austere and her prose is a "bright, indicative
       poetry," as a passage from "Noon Wine" illustrates. All
       of Porter's work is concerned with the necessity for and
       difficulty of moral definitions.

13   WEST, RAY B., JR.   "Katherine Anne Porter and 'Historic
       Memory,'" in <u>Southern Renaissance: The Literature of the</u>
       <u>Modern South</u>, edited by Louis D. Rubin and Robert D.
       Jacobs. Baltimore: Johns Hopkins, pp. 278-89.
       Reprinted from <u>Hopkins Review</u> (1952.B19)

<u>1954 A   BOOKS - NONE</u>

<u>1954 B   SHORTER WRITINGS</u>

1   ANON. "Katherine Anne Porter," in <u>Six Great Modern Short</u>
       <u>Novels</u>. New York: Dell, p. 156.
          Biographical note and list of publications.

2   GRAVES, ALLEN WALLACE. "Difficult Contemporary Short Stories:
       William Faulkner, Katherine Anne Porter, Dylan Thomas,
       Eudora Welty, and Virginia Woolf." Ph.D. dissertation,
       University of Washington.
          "Flowering Judas" and "Pale Horse, Pale Rider" are dif-
       ficult stories and cannot be analyzed in such terms as
       "atmosphere," "character," and "conflict." They must be
       analyzed word by word, particularly at those moments when
       some obscurity halts the narrative flow. "He," on the
       other hand, is a very easy story, without any narrative
       "stops" at all.

3   SCHWARTZ, EDWARD. "The Way of Dissent: Katherine Anne Por-
        ter's Critical Position," WHR, VIII (Spring), 119-30.
        Porter belongs to the great tradition of dissent and
     free inquiry. She rejected at an early age the orthodox
     religious beliefs and social beliefs of her family, and in
     her literary criticism she has written often of the need
     for a skeptical attitude toward life and all human insti-
     tutions. Yet Porter's position is also somewhat paradoxi-
     cal: always a champion of realism, she likes to insist
     that an artist must deal hard-headedly with his "familiar
     country"; her devotion to art has a distinctly religious
     quality to it; and she is a traditionalist in many of her
     views.
     Reprinted in Katherine Anne Porter: A Critical Symposium
     (1969.A1).

1955 A   BOOKS - NONE

1955 B   SHORTER WRITINGS

1   BOGAN, LOUISE. Selected Criticism. New York: Noonday,
        pp. 33-35.
        Reprinted from New Republic (1930.B2).

2   WYKES, ALAN. A Concise Survey of American Literature. Lon-
        don: Arthur Barker, p. 175.
        Porter tends to sacrifice the essentials of narrative to
     psychological detail and to gain atmosphere at the expense
     of strength.

1956 A   BOOKS - NONE

1956 B   SHORTER WRITINGS

1   ALLEN, CHARLES A. "Katherine Anne Porter: Psychology as
        Art," SWR, XLI (Summer), 223-230.
        Porter's favorite theme is the manner in which the
     frustration of physical and social needs leads to a
     hostility which is a betrayal of life. She explores the
     childhood beginnings of hostility in "The Downward Path to
     Wisdom," and she views its adult manifestations in "The
     Cracked Looking-Glass" and "María Concepción." She uses a
     symbolistic method to explore Granny's betrayal in "The
     Jilting of Granny Weatherall," and she merges the elements
     of symbol, tone, atmosphere, point of view, language,

1956

(ALLEN, CHARLES A.)
character, and theme to explore the theme of betrayal in
"Flowering Judas." "Hacienda," on the other hand, sati-
rizes our defensive need for self-importance when faith
and love have gone.

2   HALL, JAMES B., and JOSEPH LANGLAND, eds. The Short Story.
New York: Macmillan, pp. 381-82.
"Theft" is patterned on a series of different kinds of
theft. Every encounter in the story is a kind of theft,
costing someone something.

3   HOFFMAN, FREDERICK J. "Katherine Anne Porter's 'Noon Wine,'"
CEA, XVIII (November), 1, 6-7.
"Noon Wine" is a tragedy of inadequate self-awareness.
Thompson defends himself by killing Hatch, yet he does not
know the self he is defending. Thus, his suicide is "an
act of violent supererogation."

4   O'CONNOR, WILLIAM VAN. "The Novel of Experience," Crit, I
(Spring), 37-44.
Like Willa Cather, Porter often deals with the contrast
between dreams and facts, notably so in "Old Mortality"
and "Pale Horse, Pale Rider."

5   PORTER, KATHERINE ANNE. "'Noon Wine': The Sources," YR, XLVI
(September), 22-39.
The sources of "Noon Wine," Porter says, are in her
whole life and her whole society: the story is made of
thousands of real events which grouped themselves in her
mind over the years until they assumed meaning. The
scenes in which the killing is heard and in which the
Thompsons visit neighboring farms and the physical appear-
ances of the characters have particularly clear sources in
her memory. Porter sees the story as full of "the most
painful and emotional confusion," everyone trying to do the
right thing according to his level of virtue.
Reprinted in Understanding Fiction (1959.B3), in The Art
of Writing Fiction (1968.B4), and in Reading the Short
Story (1968.B5).

1957 A BOOKS

1   MOONEY, HARRY J., JR. The Fiction and Criticism of Katherine
Anne Porter. Critical Essays in Modern Literature, no. 2.
Pittsburgh: University of Pittsburgh Press.

(MOONEY, HARRY J., JR.)
   The Days Before is an uneven book, containing both criticism of the first rank and ephemeral writings that
hardly deserve to be collected. The six Miranda stories,
taken as a whole, are Porter's best work. The grandmother
and Miranda represent the spirit of endurance in the face
of tragedy, and the cycles of the two women's lives are
neatly related as the grandmother passes her spirit on to
Miranda. In Porter's longer narratives, however, that
spirit is viewed differently. In "Noon Wine," "Hacienda,"
and "The Leaning Tower," it is killed by hostile forces
that it does not understand, and in "The Cracked Looking-
Glass" it is preserved only when its value comes to be
appreciated. Porter's other short stories are variable in
attitude, range, tone, and achievement, but her passion
for the common man is clear in them, too. Ship of Fools
(rev. ed.) is one of the great novels of our time, but it
is unsatisfactory as Porter's "final" statement, for it is
misanthropic in a way that the body of the work is not.
Indeed, the determinedly anti-heroic stance of the novel
restricts its innate value and it falls short of the
greatness we had expected.
   Reprinted with a new chapter on Ship of Fools in 1962
(1962.A1).

1957 B   SHORTER WRITINGS

1   ANGOFF, ALLEN. "Katherine Anne Porter: Pale Horse, Pale
       Rider," in American Writing Today: Its Independence and
       Vigor. New York: New York University Press, pp. 399-401.
       Reprinted from TLS (1939.B3).

2   STEGNER, WALLACE, and MARY STEGNER. Great American Short
       Stories. New York: Dell, p. 27.
          Porter's stories illustrate the worthiness of the short
       story as art. They combine the influences of James,
       Southern Gothicism, and female sensibility, while avoiding
       the excesses of each.

1958 A   BOOKS - NONE

1958 B   SHORTER WRITINGS

1   POSS, S. H. "Variations on a Theme in Four Stories of Kath-
       erine Anne Porter," TCL, IV (April-July), 21-29.
          "The Circus," "Old Mortality," "Pale Horse, Pale Rider,"
       and "The Grave" all explore the theme of "what is worth

1958

(POSS, S. H.)
belonging to" and together they form a sort of <u>Bildungs-roman</u>. "The Circus" and "Old Mortality" depict the world as failing Miranda's hope for an ideal state; "Pale Horse, Pale Rider" depicts a similar failure mitigated by the momentary intuition of an ideal state; and "The Grave" presents real and ideal states as irreconcilable. Progressing from cognition to ratiocination to myth, Miranda finally learns what Leopold Bloom came to know--that the "longest way round is the shortest way home."

2 WARREN, ROBERT PENN. "Irony with a Center: Katherine Anne Porter," in <u>Selected Essays</u>. New York: Random House, pp. 136-56.
Reprinted from <u>Kenyon Review</u> (1942.B12).

1959 A BOOKS - NONE

1959 B SHORTER WRITINGS

1 JOHNSON, JAMES WILLIAM. "The Adolescent Hero: A Trend in Modern Fiction," <u>TCL</u>, V (April), 3-11.
The Miranda of "Pale Horse, Pale Rider" and "Old Mortality" goes through a process similar to McCullers' Frankie Addams, evolving from an asexual childhood to a bisexual adolescence to a feminine maturity.

2 KAPLAN, CHARLES. "True Witness: Katherine Anne Porter," <u>ColQ</u>, VII (Winter), 319-27.
Porter's goal in her fiction has always been to see and to understand the world around her as fully and as honestly as possible. She does this, she says, "by a constant exercise of memory." The stories printed in Harcourt Brace's "Harvest" collection particularly illumine this method of understanding, each story turning either on an illumining intrusion of the past into the present or on a way of understanding the past.

3 PORTER, KATHERINE ANNE. "'Noon Wine': The Sources," in <u>Understanding Fiction</u>, ed. Cleanth Brooks and Robert Penn Warren. New York: Appleton-Century-Crofts, pp. 610-20.
Reprinted from <u>YR</u> (1956.B5).

4 YOUNGBLOOD, SARAH. "Structure and Imagery in Katherine Anne Porter's 'Pale Horse, Pale Rider,'" <u>MFS</u>, V (Winter), 344-52.

KATHERINE ANNE PORTER: A REFERENCE GUIDE

1960

(YOUNGBLOOD, SARAH)
"Pale Horse, Pale Rider" is structured in three movements, each movement presenting a more intensely psychological action in a new setting. War dominates the theme
of the story, confusing appearance and reality, fostering
the need for a personal "code," and isolating the characters one from another. Miranda's death-wish dominates the
psychological level of the story, and the influenza that
endangers her life is both a religious manifestation to
her and the appropriate manifestation of a society at war.
Reprinted as "Structure and Imagery in 'Pale Horse, Pale
Rider'" in Katherine Anne Porter: A Critical Symposium
(1969.A1).

1960 A BOOKS - NONE

1960 B SHORTER WRITINGS

1   ALDINGTON, RICHARD. "A Wreath for Lawrence?" Encounter, XIV
        (April), 51-54.
            Porter's essay on Lawrence, "A Wreath for the Gamekeep-
        er," is foolish and wrong-headed. It matters little
        whether Porter thinks Lawrence was right or wrong about
        sex, and Porter's objection to Lady Chatterley's "dreary,
        hopeless situation" quarrels with Lawrence's subject.
        Porter has missed the life-giving quality of Lawrence
        completely.

2   BROOKS, CLEANTH, and ROBERT PENN WARREN. The Scope of Fic-
        tion. New York: Appleton-Century-Crofts, pp. 227, 326.
            "Theft" is the story of a woman who realizes she is her
        own thief.

3   JOHNSON, JAMES WILLIAM. "Another Look at Katherine Anne
        Porter," VQR, XXXVI (Autumn), 598-613.
            Porter is concerned with six broad themes: "the work-
        ings of the human heart; appearance and reality; the epi-
        phanic apperception of truth; the subterranean rills of
        individual emotion which produce the emotional torrents of
        an historical era; [and] self-delusion and its conse-
        quences." Her more specific themes include "the individu-
        al within his heritage" (as in "Old Mortality," "The Old
        Order," "The Source," "The Witness," and "The Last Leaf"),
        "cultural displacement" ("The Leaning Tower" and "Flower-
        ing Judas"), "unhappy marriages and the self-delusion at-
        tendant upon them" ("Rope," "That Tree," "A Day's Work,"
        "Cracked Looking-Glass"), "the death of love and the

1960

(JOHNSON, JAMES WILLIAM)
survival of individual integrity" ("Pale Horse, Pale
Rider," "The Downward Path," "Theft," "The Circus," "The
Grave," and "The Fig Tree"), "man's slavery to his own nature and subjugation to a human fate which dooms him to
suffering and disappointment" ("Noon Wine," María Concepción," "Magic," "He," "Granny Weatherall"). "Hacienda" is
a compendium of all of Porter's themes. In consort with
carefully executed symbols, these themes add up to a
vision of the world as bleak and tragic and to a complete
"fictional" philosophy.
Reprinted in Katherine Anne Porter: A Critical Symposium
(1969.A1) and partially reprinted in A Library of Literary
Criticism (1969.B2).

4   PRAGER, LEONARD. "Getting and Spending: Porter's 'Theft,'"
Perspective, XI (Winter), 230-34.
"Theft" is about a woman facing the emptiness of her existence and realizing that she has been her own worst ene-
my in avoiding human feeling and human commitment. The
stolen purse is symbolic of her loss of selfhood, and the
central irony of the story is that the theft of self is
consequent upon a failure to give oneself.

5   RYAN, MARJORIE. "Dubliners and the Stories of Katherine Anne
Porter," AL, XXXI (January), 464-73.
While some of Porter's stories owe little or nothing to
Joyce, the "moral paralysis" theme of Dubliners is a domi-
nant theme in her work, and stories such as "A Day's
Work," "The Downward Path," and "The Cracked Looking-
Glass" are Joyceian in technique as well as in theme.
"Theft," "That Tree," and "Rope" are variations on Dub-
liners' theme, but they are all Joyceian in situation.
"Noon Wine," "Pale Horse, Pale Rider," and "The Leaning
Tower" fail to resemble Joyce's stories in that they involve oddly cold and threatening persons and are sympathetic to those who must confront them. While she is in-
debted to Joyce, then, and has acknowledged her indebted-
ness, Porter is both more comprehensive in her view and
more sympathetic with her characters than Joyce.

6   SCHWARTZ, EDWARD G. "The Fictions of Memory," SWR, XV (Summer), 204-15.
The drama of recovering one's lost freedom by discover-
ing one's burden and destiny is the major theme of Porter's stories. "The Circus," "Old Mortality," "Pale
Horse, Pale Rider," and "The Grave" are particularly
central to her work in recording Miranda's initiation,
conflict, and survival in a world blighted by Time's

1961

(SCHWARTZ, EDWARD G.)
wintery hand. Miranda's quest suggests Porter's relationship to her art: Miranda survives and recovers a lost
sense of order through her commitment to awareness, and
Porter's art achieves its order through a similar commitment.
Reprinted in Katherine Anne Porter: A Critical Symposium
(1969.A1).

7   STEIN, WILLIAM BYSSHE. "'Theft': Porter's Politics of Modern
Love," Perspective, XI (Winter), 223-28.
The protagonist of "Theft" suffers from a "dissociation
of sensibility," having substituted passion for love, and
careerism for marriage and motherhood. The five flashbacks make clear her failure to be a natural woman and
evoke both psychological and religious frames of reference
to illumine her failure.

8   WALTERS, DOROTHY JEANNE. "The Theme of Destructive Innocence
in the Modern Novel: Greene, James, Cary, Porter." Ph.D.
dissertation, University of Oklahoma.
"Destructive innocence" is a major theme in the modern
novel, informing such varied works as The Quiet American,
The Golden Bowl, The Horse's Mouth, and "Noon Wine." Olaf
Helton, in Porter's "Noon Wine," is a passive agent of
destruction, provoking evil simply by his presence.

1961 A   BOOKS - NONE

1961 B   SHORTER WRITINGS

1   ANON. "First Novel," Time, LXXVIII (28 July), 70.
Ship of Fools tells in parable form of the human climate
that permitted the rise of fascism. It is in the Grand
Hotel mode and is the product of twenty years of work.

2   ANON. "The Best Years," Newsweek, LVIII (31 July), 78.
Porter's general reputation is unassailable, and Ship of
Fools will almost certainly be praised when it is pub-
lished. Begun thirty years ago as a letter to Caroline
Gordon, the novel has been worked on at Yaddo, at Colorado
University, in Connecticut, and finally on Cape Ann.

3   BOOTH, WAYNE C. The Rhetoric of Fiction. Chicago: University
of Chicago Press, pp. 274-77.
The peculiar intensity and poignancy of "Pale Horse, Pale
Rider" is due largely to Miranda's point of view. Any
other narrator would violate Miranda's aloneness.

1961

4   FLOOD, ETHELBERT, O.F.M. "Christian Language in Modern
      Literature," Culture, XXII n. s. (March), 28-42.
         Christian tradition is an important part of the language
      in "Flowering Judas" but it is not in itself a subject of
      the story. Rather, the interweaving of Laura's story with
      the story of Christ's final hours is basically ironic,
      underlining the inadequacy of Laura's attempt to save
      Eugenio.

5   GOLD, HERBERT, and DAVID L. STEVENSON. Stories of Modern
      America. New York: St. Martin's Press, pp. 294, 306.
         Laura's character is the essence of "Flowering Judas."
      She thinks of herself as alive, yet she cannot give her-
      self to any person or cause.

6   GREENE, GEORGE. "Brimstone and Roses: Notes on Katherine
      Anne Porter," Thought, XXXVI (Autumn), 421-40.
         Although Porter was born in the same decade as Heming-
      way, Faulkner, Wilder, Fitzgerald, and Marquand, she re-
      sists alignment with them. The reason for this is not
      that her work is inferior to theirs; the reasons are
      rather to be found in the manner in which she developed,
      in the writers for whom she early developed a taste, in
      the catholicity of her interests, and, most importantly,
      in her determination to explore the nature of human love.
      Unlike her contemporaries, she seems convinced that "in a
      world perilously balanced between a defunct past and inde-
      terminate future, the reality of love . . . remains ulti-
      mately dissatisfying and, what is worse, indefinable."
      Indeed, all of Porter's fiction represents a challenging
      of the uncertainties that her generation grimly accepted.

7   JOHNSON, SHIRLEY E. "Love Attitudes in the Fiction of Kath-
      erine Anne Porter," WVUPP, XIII (December), 82-93.
         Porter seems to think that women understand the falla-
      cies of romantic love. In most of her stories, in "Virgin
      Violeta" and the Miranda stories especially, she presents
      women as already disillusioned with romantic love or in
      the process of being disillusioned. Marriages usually
      survive severe strain in Porter (as in "Rope," "The Down-
      ward Path," "A Day's Work," "The Cracked Looking-Glass,"
      and "María Concepción"), but she sees the drudgery and the
      dullness in them, never the reconciliations and reciproci-
      ty that are possible. Porter's widows are free externally
      but not internally from the obligations imposed upon them
      by men, and her spinsters (as in "Old Mortality," "Flower-
      ing Judas," and "Theft") are resigned to living incomplete
      lives.

8   MALE, ROY R. "The Story of the Mysterious Stranger in Ameri-
        can Fiction," Criticism, III (Fall), 283, 286-87.
            "Noon Wine" employs the theme of the mysterious stranger
        in ways analogous to Harte's "The Luck of Roaring Camp,"
        Warren's "Blackberry Winter," Hawthorne's "The Gray
        Champion," Melville's "The Lightning-Rod Man," Twain's
        "The Mysterious Stranger," and Howell's "A Traveller from
        Altruria."

9   PIERCE, MARVIN. "Point of View: Katherine Anne Porter's
        'Noon Wine,'" Ohio University Review, III (1961), 95-113.
            The manipulations of point of view in "Noon Wine" help
        to make clear the story's tragic theme. Shifting among
        several third-person-limited points of view and an omnis-
        cient point of view, the story probes Thompson's charac-
        ter as it is revealed both to himself and to others.
        Thus, we are enabled to appreciate the difference between
        what Thompson is and what he might be--an essential com-
        ponent of the tragic vision.

10   RUBIN, LOUIS D., JR., and ROBERT D. JACOBS. South: Modern
        Southern Literature in Its Cultural Setting. Garden City:
        Doubleday, pp. 291-313.
            Essays reprinted from Hopkins Review (1952.B7) and
        (1952.B19).

11   SLOCUM, KATHLEEN. "Katherine Anne Porter: A Fiercely Burning
        Particle," Censor, IV (Fall), 5-15.
            Porter's stories about Miranda center on Miranda's dis-
        covery of her own identity, while her non-Miranda stories
        are concerned with individuals who are caught up in social
        and political upheavals.

12   SNELL, GEORGE. The Shapers of American Fiction: 1798-1947.
        New York: Cooper Square, p. 301.
            Hawthorne's shadows and love of allegory are evident in
        Porter's work, as well as James' sensitivity and involu-
        tion. Porter seems "still on the threshold of real
        achievement," however.

*13   STALLMAN, ROBERT, and ARTHUR WALDHORN, eds. American Liter-
        ature: Readings and Critiques. New York: Putnam,
        pp. 767-70.
            Cited in A Bibliography of the Works of Katherine Anne
        Porter and A Bibliography of the Criticism of the Works of
        Katherine Anne Porter (1969.A2), p. 128.
        Reprinted from Accent (1947.B4).

1961

14   YOSHA, LEE WILLIAM. "The World of Katherine Anne Porter."
      Ph.D. dissertation, University of Michigan.
         Porter is concerned with four major situations: the
      person in conflict with the past, the person in conflict
      with the family, the woman in conflict with a male-
      constructed world, and the person in conflict with "for-
      eign" attitudes. Porter's work brings the art of the
      short story to its consummation, and it is concerned more
      than any other body of work with the strengths and weak-
      nesses of human faculties.

1962 A   BOOKS

1   MOONEY, HARRY J., JR. The Fiction and Criticism of Katherine
     Anne Porter. Rev. ed. Critical Essays in Modern Litera-
     ture, no. 2. Pittsburgh: University of Pittsburgh Press.
        Reprinted with a new chapter on Ship of Fools. See
     item (1957.A1).

1962 B   SHORTER WRITINGS

1   ALLEN, CHARLES A. "The Nouvellas [sic] of Katherine Anne Por-
     ter," University of Kansas City Review, XXIX (Winter), 87-93.
        While Porter's short stories focus usually on the hos-
     tility of the individual, her nouvelles focus on the in-
     dividual as the victim of a hostile society. In "Noon
     Wine" Hatch plays on Thompson to bring about the murder,
     and Thompson is driven to suicide by his wife, sons, and
     neighbors; in "Old Mortality" Amy has a death-charm for
     both Gabriel and Honey, and Miranda is destined to be a
     second Amy; in "Pale Horse, Pale Rider" the forces of
     death and evil are clearly dominant and Miranda is led to
     denounce the world; and in "The Leaning Tower" the empha-
     sis is on the destructive traits in the German character
     which threaten Charles Upton.

2   ANON. Review of Ship of Fools, The Booklist and Subscription
     Books Bulletin, LVIII (April), 565.
        Despite its length and absence of plot, Ship of Fools is
     continually fascinating, particularly in its
     characterizations.

3   ANON. "The Longest Journey," Newsweek, LVIX (2 April), 88-89.
        Ship of Fools is "a work of rugged power and myriad in-
     sights, a book of the highest relevance to the bitterness
     and disruption of modern civilization."

4   ANON. "Speech After Long Silence," Time, LXXIX (6 April), 97.
        Ship of Fools is filled with despair, although of an
    objective and unemotional kind. Porter sees ignorance and
    evil ruling the world, but she is subtle enough to see
    that the wicked are as weak as the good.

5   ANON. Review of Ship of Fools, Bookmark, XXI (May), 224.
        Ship of Fools is "a finely written, allegorical novel
    presaging World War II." The passengers are delineated
    with extraordinary precision.

6   ANON. Cover note, Jubilee, X (May), 1.
        Biographical note.

7   ANON. Review of Ship of Fools, Wisconsin Library Bulletin,
    LVIII (May-June), 178.
        Although Ship of Fools is superbly written and master-
    fully crafted, its characters are repugnant in every way
    and its vision is despairing: the allegory suggests that
    each of us sails on his own ship of truth, carrying a car-
    go of folly.

8   ANON. Review of Ship of Fools, VQR, XXXVIII (Summer), lxxii.
        With uncommon skill, Porter gives us a world of unre-
    lieved pessimism and utter cynicism somewhat out of key
    with her image of a ship on the way to eternity.

9   ANON. "Katherine Anne Porter Cited for Writings," The New
    York Times (11 October), p. 45.
        Porter has received the Emerson-Thoreau Medal of the
    American Academy of Arts and Sciences for her contribu-
    tions to prose fiction, particularly for Flowering Judas
    and Pale Horse, Pale Rider.

10 ANON. "On the Good Ship Vera," TLS (2 November), p. 837.
        The origin of contemporary evil is the awesome theme of
    Ship of Fools, but the novel itself is "a drastic fail-
    ure." The characters are stereotypes, the episodes are
    uncoordinated "set-pieces," the allegory is too naive to
    contain the theme, and the structure is too mechanical.
    One wonders if Porter brought enough knowledge to the
    writing of the book and if the knowledge she brought had
    really penetrated her feelings.

1962

11   ARIMOND, CARROLL.   Review of Ship of Fools, Extension, LVII
         (August), 25.
            Ship of Fools is "a masterly study of many-sided per-
         sonalities," and Porter is one of the great novelists of
         our time. The ship is infested with evil, and the voyage
         changes no one.

12   AUCHINCLOSS, LOUIS.   "Bound for Bremerhaven--and Eternity,"
         New York Herald Tribune Books (1 April), sec. vi, p. 3.
            Ship of Fools fulfills all that was expected of it. The
         characters may be unappealing and little may happen in the
         story, but our interest is held by the general intelli-
         gence and humor. Porter never disguises sentimentality as
         compassion: if her characters cannot communicate, it is
         because they spurn communication, and if they are not even
         pitied, it is because selfishness and egoism are not
         pitiable.

13   BECK, WARREN.   "Masterly Novel Crowns Author's Notable Career,"
         Chicago Sunday Tribune (1 April), sec. iv, p. 1-2.
            The overlapping and interlocking events of Ship of Fools
         are a "triumph of story-telling." The novel has both the
         elegant style and the psychological deftness of Porter's
         short fiction, and it maintains a fine balance of event-
         fulness and insight. It is the crown of Porter's career.

14   BEDFORD, SYBILLE.   "Voyage to Everywhere," Spectator
         (16 November), pp. 763-64.
            The Great American Novel has appeared and it is a great
         universal novel. The theme is a condemnation of the human
         condition, and every scene is convincingly alive. Porter
         can be faulted only for her excessive length, for her
         "rather too much insistence on armpits, smells, and fat,"
         and for her obsession with grotesques.

15   BERG, PAUL.   "Celebrating a Celebrated Author," St. Louis
         Post-Dispatch Pictures (22 April), pp. 4-6.
            Biographical sketch and account of the writing of Ship
         of Fools.

16   BODE, CARL.   Review of Ship of Fools, WSCL, III (Fall), 90-92.
            Ship of Fools is "an honest, disheartening book," not so
         much over-written as revised downward. It lacks the fin-
         ished surface of Porter's earlier work, together with the
         elegant symbolism and sureness of tone. Two generaliza-
         tions about evil can be deduced from the book: that the
         young are more wicked than the old, and that men are more
         wicked than women.
         Reprinted in The Half-World of American Culture (1965.B8).

17 BOOTH, WAYNE C. "Yes, But Are They Really Novels?" YR, LI
    n.s. (Summer), 632-34.
        Ship of Fools is an admirable book, but it is disap-
    pointing at the same time. In attempting a canvas large
    enough to defeat a Shakespeare, Porter has given us a
    fragmented and diluted narration in which her unity is
    based on concept rather than on action. Such a work de-
    mands the complete success of every part if it is to be
    successful, and too many parts of the book lack that suc-
    cess. One is tempted to protest that this is not the
    Porter we know, for the conciseness, the economy, and the
    simplicity we have admired in her earlier work are absent
    here.

18 BRADBURY, MALCOLM. Review of Ship of Fools, Punch, CCXLIV
    (21 November), 763-64.
        Ship of Fools is perhaps too ambitious a novel for our
    contemporary taste, but it is a very fine book which con-
    veys objectively and detachedly the variety of ways of be-
    ing human. Occasionally, the book is mechanical and
    repetitive.

19 COPELAND, EDITH. Review of Ship of Fools, BA, XXXVI (Summer),
    322-23.
        Ship of Fools is a parable illustrating that persons
    bring destruction upon themselves and others because of
    what they are and are not--particularly because of the
    evil hidden in their hearts and the cruelties they dis-
    guise as love. Such an imposing novel probably does not
    come more than once in a generation.

20 COWSER, ROBERT G. "Porter's 'The Jilting of Granny Weather-
    all,'" Expl, XXI (December), item 34.
        "The Jilting of Granny Weatherall" has an ambiguous
    title. It refers both to the time when Granny was jilted
    by her intended bridegroom and to her betrayal by death
    when it fails to bring her any sign of assurance. The
    second is the crucial jilting in the story.

21 CYR, ANNE. "Ship of Fools," Sign, XLI (July), 63.
        Ship of Fools is a "sprightly" novel on the surface, but
    there is hardly a likeable character in it and the reader
    is relieved when the "joyless debauchery" is over.

1962

22 DANIELS, SALLY. "The Foundering of Ship of Fools, I," MinnR,
    III (Fall), 124-27.
        While Porter has a fuller knowledge of the human condi-
    tion than any other living writer, Ship of Fools fails in
    some crucial ways. Neither the plot nor the characters
    develop adequately, and the "climax" of the ship's party
    is "trumped up and mechanical."

23 DE VRIES, PETER. "Nobody's Fool," NY, XXXVIII (16 June),
    28-29.
        A parody of Ship of Fools and of its twenty-year writing.

24 DOLBIER, MAURICE. "I've Had a Good Run for My Money," New
    York Herald Tribune Books (1 April), sec. vi, p. 3.
        [Interview] Porter compares the making of Ship of Fools
    to the weaving of a tapestry. She affirms that O. Henry
    was her father's first cousin and that she is descended
    from Daniel Boone's younger brother Jonathan. She de-
    spises Sartre for attempting to Germanize French thought,
    and she finds Simone de Beauvoir's Second Sex a "stupid"
    book.

25 DRAKE, ROBERT. "A Modern Inferno," National Review, XII
    (24 April), 290.
        The Inferno-like Ship of Fools is a very distinguished
    effort, but it is practically a textbook on the pathology
    of sin, and it is dull to that degree. Porter remains a
    short story writer.

26 DUCHENE, ANNE. "Twenty Years Agrowing," Manchester Guardian
    (2 November), p. 12.
        Ship of Fools is elephantine and lacks the nervous pulse
    of Porter's earlier work. The portraits are admirable,
    but there is no discovery in the book, no cathartic re-
    lease, no insights.

27 ENGLISH, CHARLES. "A Long-awaited Masterpiece," Jubilee, X
    (May), 46-48.
        Ship of Fools reminds us that a whole world crashed
    thirty years ago. Porter's writing is economical, humor-
    ous, and magnificently stylized.

28 FEFFERMAN, STAN. Review of Ship of Fools, Canadian Forum,
    XLII (August), 115.
        Ship of Fools is a pessimistic book, charting the effort
    of nearly fifty characters to preserve their identities
    and their consequent failure to reach human community.
    The fable is especially portentious for being set in 1931.

29   FINKELSTEIN, SIDNEY. "Ship of Fools," Mainstream, XV
          (September), 42–48.
             Ship of Fools is stylistically impeccable, but notional-
          ly disturbing: its author stands coldly aloof from her
          characters; she attacks only small-fry in this book about
          fascism and anti-Semitism; and her concept of a "national
          character" supports the very forces she claims to despise.
          Given her picture of history, we wonder how fascism was
          ever destroyed.

30   FINN, JAMES. "On the Voyage to Eternity," Commonweal, LXXVI
          (18 May), 212–13.
             Ship of Fools is an important, formidable study of man
          as an irrational, yet rationalizing, animal. Porter re-
          fuses to give us an easy optimism and remains true to her
          "harsh, clear vision."

31   GARDINER, HAROLD C. Review of Ship of Fools, America, CVII
          (26 May), 54.
             Ship of Fools is a boring series of character sketches
          rather than a novel, and Porter is untrue to human nature
          in offering no positive vision.

32   GARDNER, JOHN, and LENNIS DUNLAP. The Forms of Fiction. New
          York: Random House, pp. 40–41.
             Having no plot, "The Witness" is not a short story but a
          sketch. The characterization of Jimbilly seems to be Por-
          ter's chief concern.

33   GIRSON, RICHELLE. "The Author," SatR, XLV (31 March), 15.
             [Interview.] Porter says that Ship of Fools is a story
          of "the criminal collusion of good people" that she saw in
          the rise of European fascism. She does not identify with
          any one of the characters in the story but rather with all
          of them, and she does not think of the book as pessimistic
          so much as summarizing what she knows of nature, life, and
          human relationships.

34   GOLDSBOROUGH, DIANA. "The Ship and the Attic," TamR, XXIV
          (Summer), 104–07.
             Ship of Fools is a marvelous accomplishment, but it
          would have been even greater and more useful had it ap-
          peared in 1938. Porter distributes her misanthropy im-
          partially among the various nationalities in the book.

1962

35 GREENE, MAXINE. "Beyond Compassion," The Humanist, XXII
    (November–December), 197.
        The jaundiced view of life and human nature in Ship of
    Fools may be offensive to humanists, but Porter is truth-
    ful about what she sees and invites us to compassionate
    with the world of fools.

36 HAFLEY, JAMES. "'María Concepción': Life Among the Ruins,"
    Four Quarters, XII (November), 11–17.
        The achievement of "María Concepción" demonstrates how
    meaning in fiction is based on "achieved verbal form"
    rather than on plot or objects. The events of the story
    are misleading when abstracted in themselves and suggest
    the triumph of duty; the verbal form of the story (and
    particularly the images related to walking), on the other
    hand, suggests that the story says "life beats death, how-
    ever clumsily it may sometimes do so." The introduction
    to Flowering Judas is curiously inconsistent with the sto-
    ry's achieved meaning.

37 HAGOPIAN, JOHN V. "Katherine Anne Porter: Feeling, Form, and
    Truth," Four Quarters, XII (November), 1–10.
        "Old Mortality," "Pale Horse, Pale Rider," "Flowering
    Judas," "The Jilting of Granny Weatherall," and "Holiday"
    suggest that Porter is expert in a number of technical
    areas. In these stories the detail is extraordinarily
    sensitive, the characters are carefully individuated, and
    the symbolism is both masterful and subtle. Self-discovery
    is the basic subject of her stories.

38 HEILMAN, ROBERT B. "Ship of Fools: Notes on Style," Four
    Quarters, XII (November), 46–55.
        The style of Ship of Fools is "a window of things and
    people, not a symbolic aggression of ego upon them." The
    singular, the mannered, and the self-indulgent have no
    place in the prose, and yet it embraces a wide spectrum of
    tones and attitudes. It is a style that evokes the writ-
    ings of Jane Austen and George Eliot, and it establishes
    Porter as a traditionalist in the very best sense.
    Reprinted in Katherine Anne Porter: A Critical Symposium
    (1969.A1).

39 HENDRICK, GEORGE. "Katherine Anne Porter's 'Hacienda,'" Four
    Quarters, XII (November), 24–29.
        "Hacienda" is a brilliantly written story about spiritu-
    al, physical, moral, and psychological isolation. To be
    appreciated, it must be read in the light of Porter's Mex-
    ican writings, her 1940 preface to Flowering Judas, and the

(HENDRICK, GEORGE)
  filming of Eisenstein's ¡Que Viva Mexico!
  Reprinted in revised form as part of Katherine Anne Porter
  (1965.A1).

40 HICKS, GRANVILLE. "Voyage of Life," SatR, XLV (31 March),
    15-16.
      Ship of Fools is neither a masterpiece nor a disappoint-
    ment. Its subjects are national, religious, and sexual
    chauvinism, and Porter is both lucid and intelligent in
    representing these as unchanging modes of arrogance. Had
    the novel been published in the thirties, it would have
    been read as an attack on fascism, but it seems today to
    attack human possibility itself, and for that reason it
    seems both cold and remote.

41 HOGAN, WILLIAM. "A Devil's Mix From a Blender," San Francisco
    Sunday Chronicle (1 April), p. 28.
      Ship of Fools is a large, complex montage that throbs
    with life but which seems to be more a blend of short sto-
    ries than a novel. A dazzling performance, it nevertheless
    leaves one wondering what it was all about.

42 _____. "The Porter Novel Will Create News," San Francisco
    Chronicle (23 March), p. 3-E.
      Ship of Fools will be published next week after a
    twenty-year delay. Porter is a stylist of almost legend-
    ary reputation.

43 HUTCHENS, JOHN K. "Ship of Fools," New York Herald Tribune
    (2 April), p. 19.
      Ship of Fools lacks the dazzling perfection of Porter's
    short stories: it offers no revelation; the state of af-
    fairs at the end is foreseen by mid-book; the dramatic
    irony is less striking than obvious; and the style is too
    often flabby. The novel should be regarded as a series of
    short stories related to each other through interwoven
    character sketches.

44 HYMAN, STANLEY. "Archetypal Woman," New Leader, XLV (2 April),
    23-24.
      Ship of Fools is better than its structure or its title
    suggests, for its scenes are frequently powerful and its
    language is always distinguished; in the last analysis,
    however, the novel disgusts us more than it moves us.

1962

45   JANEWAY, ELIZABETH. "For Katherine Anne Porter, Ship of Fools
      Was a Lively Twenty-Two Year Voyage," New York Times Book
      Review (1 April), sec. vii, pp. 4-5.
         [Interview.] Porter considers her talent her one im-
      portant possession and her one care. Her education did
      little to foster it, but it is a sort of compulsion with
      her, and she thinks of herself as "obstinate," "persist-
      ent," and "willful" as a writer. Although she sometimes
      had to delay the writing of a scene until it came clear to
      her, Ship of Fools was a vital project with her since its
      inception and the plan of the book was never altered
      substantially.

46   JOSEPHSON, MATTHEW. Life Among the Surrealists. New York:
      Holt, Rinehart, and Winston, pp. 352-54.
         Account of Josephson's interest in and advice to Porter
      when he was the book editor of the Macaulay Company and
      she was a beginning writer.

47   KASTEN, MAURICE. Review of Ship of Fools, Shenandoah, XIII
      (Summer), 54-61.
         Ship of Fools has very real victories as a novel, but it
      is not a convincing allegory. Nothing enables the reader
      to see the characters in an intensely symbolic way, and
      the ship is "too palpable a microcosm to be accepted also
      as a macrocosm."

48   KAUFMANN, STANLEY. "Katherine Anne Porter's Crowning Work,"
      New Republic, CXLVI (2 April), 23-25.
         We had expected so much of Ship of Fools that it cannot
      help but be a disappointment. Its style is more labored
      and less certain than Porter's accustomed style; the
      tapestry structure seems to rotate our attention compul-
      sively; the characters are too static and represent too
      narrow a range of men; and profundity is wholly lacking.
      The book is more satiric than tragic, and it falls into
      misanthropy.

49   KIRSCH, ROBERT R. "The Long-Awaited Ship of Fools Founders,"
      Los Angeles Times (25 March), p. 22.
         Ship of Fools fails both to interest and to generate
      excitement. One cannot quarrel with the bleak theme as
      such, but one can ask that a more engrossing story support
      it.

50 LALLEY, J. M. "Gaudeamus Omnes!" Modern Age, VI (Fall), 440-52.
   The theme of Ship of Fools is sin. Porter's theology is Jansenistic, and she sees her characters as totally, inescapably depraved. Thus, the effect of her book is tedious, as an unrelieved study of vice is always tedious.

51 LEHAN, RICHARD. "Under the Human Crust," Austin, Texas American Statesman (8 April), p. E-8.
   Ship of Fools is wholly convincing and a devastating performance.

52 MADDOCKS, MELVIN. "Miss Porter's Novel," Christian Science Monitor (5 April), p. 13.
   Ship of Fools is Porter's magnum opus and it makes other contemporary novels seem trivial and amateurish. There is no plot in the novel, no premises and no conclusion, no condemnations and no forgiveness, but Porter's study of human foolishness is neatly and tightly finished.

53 MARTY, MARTIN E. Review of Ship of Fools, Christian Century, LXXIX (18 April), 492.
   Ship of Fools "appears to be a stylistically flawless work short on plot but long on perceptive character studies."

54 McDONNELL, THOMAS P. Review of Ship of Fools, CathW, CXCV (June), 180-81, 184.
   Ship of Fools is indisputably a masterpiece. It uses the ancient structure of the journey to develop both a panorama and a microcosm of the modern world, and it is one of the few great books in American literature to come to terms with Europe. Those who will see it as a "floating Grand Hotel" and those who will demand of it a simple story line will both be disappointed, for Porter has "neither the artificiality of the one nor the easy condescension of the other."

55 MOLZ, KATHLEEN. "Presenting a Fellow Passenger--Katherine Anne Porter," PLA Bulletin, XVIII (Summer), 9.
   Biographical sketch touching on Porter's family, her publications, university career, and awards, coupled with an announcement that she is to speak to the Pennsylvania Library Association Conference on October 6, 1962.

1962

56   MORSE, J. MITCHELL. Review of Ship of Fools, HudR, XV
        (Summer), 292-94.
            Ship of Fools is a merely good novel when we had ex-
        pected a great one. Porter lacks a suitable technique in
        the novel; she falsifies her material; and she fails to
        achieve verisimilitude, intellectual tautness, and her
        usual level of style.

57   MOSS, HOWARD. "No Safe Harbor," NY, XXXVIII (28 April),
        165-73.
            The main focus of Ship of Fools is the German ethos that
        preceded Hitler's rise to power, but it is a human comedy
        and a moral allegory as much as a political novel. Its
        texture is "a series of mishaps" in which intention and
        lack of intention are equally disastrous. All of the
        characters need to feel they "belong" and that very need
        turns them into fools, innocent only in their ignorance.
        Only "a hero and a heroic extravagance" are lacking.

58   MURPHY, EDWARD. Review of Ship of Fools, Ramparts, I
        (November), 88-91.
            Porter has been rebuked for her harsh view of man in
        Ship of Fools, but a close reading of the text suggests
        that she is closer to Erasmus than to Brant. Indeed, Dr.
        Schumann embodies Porter's perception of the highest
        Christian values.

59   MURRAY, JAMES G. Review of Ship of Fools, Critic, XX (June-
        July), 63-64.
            Ship of Fools is admirable in many ways, but it is not
        completely satisfying. Its allegory and realism do not
        mix well, its intention and achievement are at odds, and
        its tragedy is too often comic.

60   O'BRIEN, JOHN H. "Katherine Porter's Latest: An Allegory in
        Search of a Symbol," Detroit News (8 April), p. F-3.
            Ship of Fools teases the reader with the possibility of
        allegories and symbols that he must uncover for himself.
        Its writing is "beyond reproach."

61   PARKER, DOROTHY. Review of Ship of Fools, Esquire, LVIII
        (July), 129.
            Ship of Fools is admirably clear as an allegory and its
        portraits are finely drawn.

62   PICKREL, PAUL. Review of Ship of Fools, Harper's Magazine,
         CCIV (April), 84, 86.
              Instead of a plot, Ship of Fools uses an elaborate in-
         terplay of characters, evocative of the Freudian superego,
         ego, and id. The novel is a masterpiece.

63   POORE, CHARLES. "Books of the Times," New York Times
         (3 April), p. 37.
              Porter's favorite word in the "miraculously brilliant"
         Ship of Fools is "bitter"; the novel is a "cathedral for
         the damned" and its characters are in sharp, unsparing
         focus.

64   POWERS, JAMES. "She Stands Alone," Four Quarters, XII
         (November), 56.
              One should not compare Porter with other writers. She
         has come closer to giving us reality than any other Ameri-
         can writer of fiction, and she has always known what she
         was doing.

65   RYAN, MARJORIE. "Katherine Anne Porter: Ship of Fools,"
         Crit, V (Fall), 94-99.
              It is clear that disaster haunts us in Ship of Fools,
         that primitive violence and egoism are part of our nature,
         and that neither codes of conduct nor self-imposed isola-
         tion can govern our tendencies toward violence. It is not
         clear, however, whether Porter sees these things satiri-
         cally, ironically, or pessimistically. We must await
         further study of the novel before we can decide upon its
         tone.
              Partially reprinted in A Library of Literary Criticism
         (1969.B2).

66   SCHORER, MARK. "Katherine Anne Porter," afterword to Pale
         Horse, Pale Rider. New York: New American Library,
         pp. 167-75.
              The stories of Pale Horse, Pale Rider ask in turn the
         three questions that dominate Porter's fiction: "What
         were we? What are we? What will we be?" In "Old Mor-
         tality" the present and the past are always merging, and
         the unknown future looms ahead. In "Noon Wine" the pres-
         ent is a "horror" which cannot be grasped until one is
         irrevocably in it. In "Pale Horse, Pale Rider" Miranda
         learns that the past, present, and future are inseparable
         --that each decrees the other backward and forward. Ulti-
         mately, Porter makes us know "that with every present
         creation the artist dies into his past in order to bring
         forth another creation."
              Reprinted in The World We Imagine (1968.B6).

1962

67 SCHORER, MARK. "We're All on the Passenger List," New York
Times Book Review (1 April), sec. vii, pp. 1, 5.
Like Brant's Das Narrenschiff, Ship of Fools moves from
character to character, but Porter adds to this a constant, ironical point of view that has complete authority.
This gives her the freedom to move into allegory without
violence to her work. Imaginative sympathy is offered to
every character, and there is a good deal of comedy in the
book. It is the Middlemarch of our day.

68 SHERMAN, THOMAS B. "Reading and Writing," St. Louis Post-
Dispatch (22 April), p. 4-C.
Ship of Fools is a "long and juicy" success because its
characters are interesting as individuals at the same time
that they are representative of types.

69 SOLOTAROFF, THEODORE. "Ship of Fools and the Critics," Commentary, XXXIV (October), 277-86.
The favorable reviews of Ship of Fools, having been inspired more by Porter's reputation and by the twenty-year
history of her manuscript than by a considered attention
to the novel's art, have been singularly imperceptive.
The novel is actually tedious in its method and stupid in
its ideas. All of the characters are caricatures and
their behavior is boringly repetitive. Having no longer
the talent she displayed in "Noon Wine," Porter has chosen
in a merely bilious spirit to quarrel incessantly with
human nature.
Reprinted as "Ship of Fools: Anatomy of a Best Seller" in
The Red Hot Vacuum (1970.B12) and partially reprinted in A
Library of Literary Criticism (1969.B2).

70 SOUTHERN, TERRY. "When Film Gets Good ...," Nation, CXCV
(17 November), 330.
Almost everything done in Ship of Fools could have been
done with more grace and drama by a film-maker. It is a
good novel, but it is insufficiently aware of the possibilities for contemporary fiction, and to that extent it
is not a good book.

71 STALLMAN, R. W. "Collecting Katherine Anne Porter," Four
Quarters, XII (November), 56.
While a lecturer at the University of Connecticut Writers' Conference, Porter expected to be escorted from her
dormitory to her lectern. She was able to improvise an
amusing lecture when told that she should not read from
her works.

72 TAUBMAN, ROBERT. "A First-Class Passenger," New Statesman,
       LXV (2 November), 619-20.
          Ship of Fools is not the masterpiece that was promised
       us, and it suggests that Porter is a merely popular novel-
       ist with some special gifts. The journey structure of the
       book must assimilate an interesting selection of charac-
       ters if it is to be successful, and Porter gives us merely
       a clutter of banal types. Her analysis of folly is mar-
       ginal, her feeling for anti-Semitism is dated, and her
       too-frequent lapse into phrase-making shows the proximity
       of her liberal, humanistic stance to the merely
       dilettantish.

73 THOMPSON, JOHN. "The Figure in the Rose-Red Gown," PR, XXIX
       (Fall), 608-12.
          Despite the excessive advertising, Ship of Fools is not
       really a bad book. In being almost pure statement, how-
       ever, it departs from the earlier, symbolist mode of Por-
       ter's work. The statement of the book is an honest and
       spirited curse, and all of its characters are devils.

74 WATKINS, SUE. "Finally Comes the Novel," Austin, Texas Ameri-
       can Statesman (8 April), p. E-7.
          Porter has finally written the novel that she warned
       Eudora Welty against writing.

75 WEBER, BROM. "The Foundering of Ship of Fools, II," MinnR,
       III (Fall), 127-30.
          Respect for Porter's previous work and Porter's status
       in American letters has caused many reviewers to praise
       Ship of Fools unwarrantedly. The novel is "a naturalistic
       allegory which laboriously blends stereotyped characters
       and pre-conceived judgments while failing to achieve in-
       tensity or to offer revelations." The novel's greatest
       flaw is its long-windedness.

76 WESCOTT, GLENWAY. "Katherine Anne Porter: The Making of a
       Novel," Atlantic Monthly, CCIX (April), 43-49.
          Porter's life has been a struggle in many ways, embrac-
       ing serious illnesses, abortive careers in Hollywood and
       in the universities, and occasional poverty. Yet Porter's
       letters are uniquely spirited and subjective, contrasting
       with the extreme objectivity of her fiction (and perhaps
       making that objectivity possible). Ship of Fools is in
       the tradition of her stories, if it is more varied than
       they, and everything in it supports the engrossing gallery
       of portraits and themes, the philosophy, and the tale.

1962

(WESCOTT, GLENWAY)
Reprinted in revised form under the title "Katherine Anne
Porter Personally" in Images of Truth: Remembrances and
Criticism (1963.B22) and in Katherine Anne Porter: A
Critical Symposium (1969.A1), and partially reprinted in
A Library of Literary Criticism (1969.B2).

77 WIESENFARTH, BR. JOSEPH, F.S.C. "Illusion and Allusion:
Reflections in 'The Cracked Looking-Glass,'" Four
Quarters, XII (November), 30-37.
"The Cracked Looking-Glass" depicts "a woman's making
her life meaningful almost at the moment she realizes how
much of it has been otherwise." She achieves this by ac-
commodating her illusion to reality, having formerly
sought refuge from reality in her illusions. Indeed, the
story is structured upon a series of movements from reality to illusion and back to reality. The symbol of the
cracked looking-glass evokes the use of that symbol in
Ulysses, in "The Lady of Shalott," and in 1 Corinthians
13:12.
Reprinted as "Reflections in 'The Cracked Looking-Glass,'"
in Katherine Anne Porter: A Critical Symposium (1969.A1).

78 WILSON, ANGUS. "The Middle-Class Passenger," London Observer
(28 October), p. 27.
Ship of Fools is "no more than a middling good sort of
novel," evoking the best-sellers of Vicki Baum and Louis
Bromfield. All of Porter's art cannot redeem her middle-
brow formula or the superfluous sexuality of the book.
She might better have made a short story of her material.

79 YANITELLI, VICTOR R., S.J. Review of Ship of Fools, Best
Sellers, XXII (15 April), 25-26.
Ship of Fools is not the achievement in American letters
that it might have been. While its symbols are expertly
blended and its characters are vividly developed, its narrative is inadequately sustained and its power is too
diluted.

80 YLVISAKER, MIRIAM. Review of Ship of Fools, LJ, LXXXVII
(15 March), 1152.
Ship of Fools is a rich, complex, ironical novel whose
theme is human foolishness. It effectively expands and
codifies the themes of the short stories.

KATHERINE ANNE PORTER: A REFERENCE GUIDE

1963 A   BOOKS - NONE

1963 B   SHORTER WRITINGS

1   ABRAHAMS, WILLIAM. "Progression Through Repetition," MR, IV
     (Summer), 805-09.
          Porter is as much an allegorist in Ship of Fools as Tur-
     genev, Flaubert, or James, and no more of one. Indeed,
     the novel balances ideas and their authentication exqui-
     sitely. If there is no development in the characters, it
     is because the characters are their qualities: their re-
     petition is a way of getting at the truth.

2   AMORY, CLEVELAND. "Celebrity Register," McCalls, XC (April),
     184.
          Biographical note.

3   BRADBURY, JOHN M. Renaissance in the South: A Critical His-
     tory of the Literature, 1920-1960. Chapel Hill: Univer-
     sity of North Carolina Press, pp. 70-74.
          Porter belongs to the symbolic naturalist tradition in
     Southern literature, although her search for modern values
     has taken her to both Mexico and Europe. Porter rejects
     the conservative agrarian ideology, however, and she de-
     picts Southern heritage as a compound of hypocrisy, weak-
     ness, and cruelty. The major goal of her work is to sound
     the social and political troubles of of our time.

4   BRIDE, SISTER MARY, O.P. "Laura and the Unlit Lamp," SSF, I
     (Fall), 61-63.
          "Flowering Judas" does not condemn Laura's chastity, but
     condemns rather her rejection of love and life. She is
     unable to make a choice between good and evil and so at-
     tempts to substitute conformity for commitment. Braggioni
     is really a more admirable character than she is in that
     he can both love and inspire love.

5   CURLEY, DANIEL. "Katherine Anne Porter: The Larger Plan,"
     Kenyon Review, XXV (Autumn), 671-95.
          The failure of Ship of Fools illumines Porter's real
     talents and real limitations. We see that she is at her
     best when treating human beings simply as human beings (as
     in the Miranda stories and in "Flowering Judas") and that
     when she attempts a broader context (as in "The Leaning
     Tower") she mistakenly wages "a frontal attack on the
     universal." She is at her best, too, when she writes
     autobiographically, as she does in the Miranda stories and
     the stories related to her personal experience. When she

(CURLEY, DANIEL)

moves away from her experience, her sense of irony and point of view fail her: thus, the irony in Ship of Fools is absurdly heavy and the point of view lacks authority.

6 _____. "Treasure in 'The Grave,'" MFS, IX (Winter), 377-84.

"The Grave" is based on the concepts that the writer's mind is a grave of the past and that in his art the writer resurrects his buried past. By proceeding chronologically rather than by making use of flashbacks, Porter has analyzed the artist's experience from the point of view of the developing person. The prologue, body, and final epiphany of the tale all tell the same story of burial, suggesting thereby that it is a collective experience. Indeed, "The Grave" offers a key to the rest of Porter's work inasmuch as it sets down her essential fable.

7 DEASY, BR. PAUL FRANCIS, F.S.C. "Reality and Escape," Four Quarters, XII (January), 28-31.

Porter's "He" is informed at every level by the principle that frustration results from a failure to face reality.

8 HARTLEY, LODWICK. "Dark Voyagers: A Study of Katherine Anne Porter's Ship of Fools," University Review, XXX (Winter), 83-94.

Like Kafka, Porter shows reality to be a nightmare of rather flat design. Her characters skirt both tragedy and greatness, both love and happiness, and we see the terror of human failure rather than its majesty. Placed in the context of Porter's other work, Ship of Fools seems a choric expression of her continuing concern with the failures of Western man.

Reprinted in Katherine Anne Porter: A Critical Symposium (1969.A1).

9 HENDRICK, GEORGE. "Hart Crane Aboard the Ship of Fools: Some Speculations," TCL, IX (April), 3-9.

Porter seems to have apportioned certain of Hart Crane's characteristics and acts among three different men in Ship of Fools. Specifically, Denny's obsession with venereal disease and his drunken banging of Mrs. Treadwell's door, Echegaray's rescue of the bulldog, his artistic incapacitation and his self-destructive impulse, and Baumgartner's alcoholism and temptations to suicide suggest the Hart Crane whom Porter knew. Her treatment of Crane in the three characters suggests that Porter feels ambivalently about Crane.

(HENDRICK, GEORGE)
> Reprinted in expanded form as part of <u>Katherine Anne Por-
ter</u> (1965.A1).

10 HOLMES, THEODORE. "The Literary Mode," <u>Carleton Miscellany</u>,
>   IV (Winter), 124-28.
>   <u>Ship of Fools</u> is inferior to Warren's <u>The Cave</u>, for Por-
>   ter has mistaken art for life.

11 JOSELYN, SISTER M., O.S.B. "Animal Imagery in Katherine
>   Anne Porter's Fiction," in <u>Myth and Symbol; Critical Ap-
>   proaches and Applications</u>, edited by Bernice Slote.
>   Lincoln: University of Nebraska Press, pp. 101-115.
>   "Flowering Judas," "Pale Horse, Pale Rider," "The Down-
>   ward Path to Wisdom," "The Circus," "The Leaning Tower,"
>   and <u>Ship of Fools</u> all employ elaborate animal imagery for
>   the purposes of characterizing, of defining and limiting
>   the terms of conflict, of establishing tone, and of con-
>   cretizing and dramatizing value judgments.

12 KIELY, ROBERT. "The Craft of Despondency--The Traditional
>   Novelists," <u>Daedalus</u>, XCII (Spring), 220-37.
>   Waugh, Greene, and Porter are "traditional" novelists in
>   their valuing of coherence, economy, and literateness, but
>   their stories of men reduced to a brutish level are pe-
>   culiarly modern allegories in their lack of suggestiveness
>   and unrelieved morbidity. <u>Ship of Fools</u> is richer and
>   more feminine than Waugh's novels, but it is as insistent
>   upon morbidity and brutishness as anything in Waugh.
>   These writers differ from their contemporaries by inform-
>   ing their disaffection with humanity with a sense of
>   Christian tradition. They tend to ask Catholic questions
>   and to imply non-conformist answers.

13 KIRKPATRICK, SMITH. "<u>Ship of Fools</u>," <u>SR</u>, LXXI (Winter),
>   94-98.
>   <u>Ship of Fools</u> is "a lament for us all," because we are
>   all foolish enough to hide our love behind masks. Some-
>   times the masks are pathetically simple (Frau Baumgartner)
>   and sometimes very intricate (Mrs. Treadwell). Usually,
>   however, the masks shift rapidly (Jenny and David) and for
>   this reason their wearers tend towards caricature (Amparo,
>   Pepe, Arne Hanson). The Germanic mask of discipline and
>   family is particularly ineffectual.

14   McINTYRE, JOHN P.   "Ship of Fools and Its Publicity," Thought,
     XXXVIII (Summer), 211-20.
          The uneven critical reception of Ship of Fools illus-
     trates the reviewers' ignorance of critical techniques.
     They fail especially to appreciate that the novel is con-
     structed in an ironic mode, but they fail also to see that
     the fear of rationalism in the book descends from the ma-
     jor novels of Hawthorne and that the theme and structure
     of the book descend from Melville's Confidence Man.

15   PLANTE, PATRICIA R.   "Katherine Anne Porter: Misanthrope
     Acquitted," XUS, II (December), 87-91.
          Porter's despair with the evil in both man and the world
     is founded on "an intellectual vision of divine possibili-
     ty and promise."   That vision is rooted in her religious
     background and it emerges in Ship of Fools.

16   RUBIN, LOUIS D., JR.   "We Get Along Together Just Fine ...,"
     Four Quarters, XII (March), 30-31.
          Although the characters in Ship of Fools are shown at
     their worst, Porter does not satirize them so much as gaze
     at them objectively and with implicit compassion.   Aware
     of how difficult it is to believe in God and to love, Por-
     ter has given us a religious novel.

17   RUOFF, JAMES.   "Katherine Anne Porter Comes to Kansas," MQ, IV
     (Summer), 305-14.
          [Interview.]   Porter finds that her material comes to
     her--she does not go out looking for it.   She respects
     Hemingway, Conrad, Welty, Joyce, the early Mary McCarthy,
     and Sterne, and she has difficulty with Saroyan and Fitz-
     gerald.   She is a "first-draft" writer but can occasional-
     ly revive abandoned manuscripts.   Symbols take care of
     themselves in her writing.   She permits a writer to be
     obscure, but not to be isolated from society or to become
     so involved with one aspect of society as to lose his per-
     spective.   She experienced great difficulty with Ship of
     Fools because she didn't really want to write it in the
     form of a novel.
          For a partial transcription of this interview, see item
     (1963.B18).

18   RUOFF, JAMES, and DEL SMITH.   "Katherine Anne Porter on Ship
     of Fools," CE, XXIV (February), 396-97.
          [Interview.]   Porter comments at the University of
     Wichita in September, 1961, that Ship of Fools ends exact-
     ly the way she had planned and that it had its inspiration
     in her own voyage to Bremerhaven in 1931.   She experienced

(RUOFF, JAMES, and DEL SMITH)
> great difficulty with the work, not really wanting to write
> it in the novel form that the material required. She
> thinks of the book as illustrating the general "collusion
> in evil" that allows tyrants to exist.
> This is a partial transcript of the interview summarized
> in item (1963.B17).

19   SPILLER, R. E., et al. Literary History of the United States.
>   3rd ed., rev. New York: Macmillan, pp. 1297, 1314,
>   1387.
>   Porter's technical virtuosity in prose is the equivalent
>   of Elinor Wylie's virtuosity in verse. She escapes the
>   genteel tradition by a boldness and talent greater than
>   Elizabeth Madox Roberts'.

20   THOMPSON, BARBARA. "Katherine Anne Porter: An Interview,"
>   Paris Review, XXIX (Winter–Spring), 87–114.
>   [Interview.] Porter comments upon her youthful reading,
>   the influence of various writers upon her, and her opinion
>   of several writers; upon her family history, her feelings
>   toward the South, and her early adulthood; upon the obli-
>   gations of an artist, the nature of art, and her writing
>   experiences; upon the origin and method of "Flowering
>   Judas," the origin and meaning of Ship of Fools, and her
>   reputation as a stylist.
>   Reprinted in Writers at Work (1965.B29) and in Katherine
>   Anne Porter: A Critical Symposium (1969.A1).

21   WALSH, CHAD. "A Medley of Versemakers," Chicago Sun Bookweek
>   (29 December), p. 10.
>   Ship of Fools does not merit the praise it has received.
>   It has neither the profundity nor the cosmic scope that
>   has been claimed for it.

22   WESCOTT, GLENWAY. "Katherine Anne Porter Personally," in
>   Images of Truth: Remembrances and Criticism. London:
>   Hamish Hamilton, pp. 25–58.
>   Reprinted in revised form from Atlantic Monthly
>   (1962.B76).

23   WEST, RAY B., JR. Katherine Anne Porter. UMPAW, no. 28.
>   Minneapolis, University of Minnesota Press.
>   As a non-practicing Catholic and liberal Southerner,
>   Porter is interested in the relationship between fixed
>   social and moral positions and a changing world. Thus,
>   her stories deal with a threat to Christian morality and
>   traditional values and with the inability of man to fulfill

1963

(WEST, RAY B., JR.)
his dreams. All of Porter's characters are drawn from her
own experience, and she treats her memories as almost
mythical events; indeed, the rendering of myth is frequently both her matter and her method. Although Ship of
Fools is necessarily more rich and more technically intri-
cate than the stories, it is related to them in both matter and technique. As a literary critic, Porter is more
European than American, but as a literary figure she belongs to the second American Renaissance.
Partially reprinted in revised form from Hopkins Review
(1952.B19).

1964 A BOOKS

1   NANCE, WILLIAM L. Katherine Anne Porter & the Art of Rejec-
        tion. Chapel Hill: University of North Carolina Press.
        Porter's work is unified by a "rejection" theme and can
     be divided into semi-autobiographical stories and non-
     autobiographical stories. The autobiographical protago-
     nists (Miranda, Laura, Granny Weatherall, Charles Upton,
     Sophia Jane, and the narrator of "Hacienda") see every hu-
     man relationship as oppressive and have the power to es-
     cape oppressive unions through an act of rejection. Non-
     autobiographical protagonists have no such power and suf-
     fer mutually destructive relationships. The rejection
     theme is not always the explicit theme of the stories, but
     it always governs their emotional effects.

1964 B SHORTER WRITINGS

1   ANON. "Clear Colours," TLS (9 January), p. 21.
        "Old Mortality" is the best of The Collected Stories and
     its nostalgia for the past is typical of Porter's other
     pieces about the South. Porter is neither a political
     writer nor a Southern writer, however. Calculatedly in-
     dependent of all schools and influences, her work seems
     directed only by her fresh-flowing sympathies.

2   BLUEFARB, SAM. "Loss of Innocence in 'Flowering Judas,'"
        CLAJ, VII (March), 256-62.
        In the usual initiation story, loss of innocence is fol-
     lowed by a period of temporary paralysis which leads in
     its turn to action. In "Flowering Judas," however, Laura
     does not really emerge from her paralysis, for her dedica-
     tion at the end is that of the zombie. She is caught be-
     tween a rejected, childhood faith and an inadequate poli-
     tical faith, with all of her idealism gone sour.

3   BURGESS, ANTHONY. "A Long Drink of Porter," Spectator, CCXII
    (31 January), 151.
       Porter will be remembered for her Collected Stories
    rather than for Ship of Fools. The secret of her stories
    is a flow checked only by the solidity of a symbol. The
    Pale Horse, Pale Rider trilogy is the triumph of the
    collection.

4   BURNETT, WHIT, and HALLIE BURNETT. The Modern Short Story in
    the Making. New York: Hawthorn, pp. 404-05.
       Biographical note and a statement from Porter about
    "Noon Wine" as a "long story."

5   CURRENT-GARCIA, EUGENE, and WALTON R. PATRICK. American Short
    Stories: 1820 to the Present. Rev. ed. Chicago: Scott,
    Foresman, pp. 423-24.
       "Flowering Judas" displays Porter's metaphorical rich-
    ness and symbolism at their best and as organically relat-
    ed to all of the story's elements.

6   HERTZ, ROBERT NEIL. "Rising Waters: A Study of Katherine
    Anne Porter." Ph.D. dissertation, Cornell University.
       Both the essays and the stories of Porter are concerned
    with the conflict between selflessness and self love, and
    Ship of Fools is fully philosophic in this regard. Porter
    insists throughout her work that we must reserve judgment
    on most moral questions, but, nonetheless, that we must
    censure those who live solely by evil.
    Partially reprinted in MQ, (1965.B14).

7   JOSELYN, SISTER M., O.S.B. "'The Grave' as Lyrical Short
    Story," SSF, I (Spring), 216-21.
       "The Grave" is a "lyrical" short story in that it coun-
    terpoints a syllogistic plot with a "hovering" conscious-
    ness which exploits the symbols of the grave, the ring,
    the dove, and the rabbits, and in that it employs a ba-
    sically elegiac tone.

8   _____. "On the Making of Ship of Fools," SDR, I (May), 46-52.
       The content of the eleven previously published chapters
    of Ship of Fools is almost unchanged in the final version,
    although the chapters are rearranged and the diction and
    style are improved. Twenty-eight "bridges" connect the
    chapters now, and the concluding section is new. These
    alterations to the set of original chapters add new stress
    to the allegory, improve the chronology, create several
    climaxes, and add emphasis to several characters.

1964

9   PRITCHETT, V. S.   "Stones and Stories," New Statesman, LXVII
     (10 January), 47-48.
        Porter's stories merit their high reputation. She
     writes from the inside of situations and characters, and,
     classically, she tests her characters against the element-
     al and the ineluctable. They discover, almost always and
     to their shock, something violent or rock-like in them-
     selves, in others, and in situations. Porter's gift is
     for exploring whole consciousnesses, and her short stories
     are completely satisfying.

10   RYAN, MARJORIE.   "Katherine Anne Porter: Ship of Fools and
     the Short Stories," BuR, XII (March), 51-63.
        The view of life in Porter's short stories is no less
     grim than that in Ship of Fools, but the stories are al-
     most always from the point of view of a suffering or ter-
     rified consciousness, whereas the point of view in the
     novel is more remote. Indeed, the ironic and satiric note
     that underlies the stories has become dominant in the
     novel, and the poetic tones that dominate the stories have
     become undertones in the novel.

1965 A   BOOKS

1   HENDRICK, GEORGE.   Katherine Anne Porter.   TUSAS.   New York:
     Twayne.
        Porter's use of Mexican culture in her stories shifts
     from an inside view in "María Concepción," her first story,
     to an alienated view in "That Tree," her last Mexican sto-
     ry. Her grandmother stories and Miranda stories are
     largely autobiographical, with both the grandmother and
     Southern society influencing Miranda to enter her "brave
     new world." In all of her stories, and in Ship of Fools
     as well, Porter is in complete command of her craft and a
     conscious artist in the tradition of James and Joyce.
     (The book includes explications of all of Porter's stories
     and comments upon her non-fiction. A biographical essay
     and chronological chart preface the book).
     Sections of this book reprinted in revised form from Four
     Quarters (1962.B39) and TCL (1963.B9). Partially reprint-
     ed in A Library of Literary Criticism (1969.B2).

1965 B SHORTER WRITINGS

1   ADAMS, ROBERT HICKMAN. "The Significance of Point of View in
     Katherine Anne Porter's Ship of Fools." Ph.D. disserta-
     tion, University of Southern California.
        Porter manipulates point of view in Ship of Fools to
     create suspense and humor, to prevent sentimentality and
     reader identification, to create unifying parallels and
     leitmotifs, to characterize, to interpret, and to evalu-
     ate. Indeed, point of view is a theme in Ship of Fools
     as well as an aspect of its composition, and almost all of
     the characters are depicted as choosing and limiting their
     points of view according to their individual needs.

2   ANON. "Misanthrope," Time, LXXXVI (5 November), 122.
        Porter is one of the "grimmer misanthropes" of modern
     literature, neither the second Turgenev nor the Grandma
     Moses she is thought to be. Her output, disbursed with
     "incredible stinginess," is too small to give her the
     status of a major writer, and, as "Old Mortality" sug-
     gests, something has gone very wrong in Porter's life, re-
     sulting in "too little warmth and softness in her art" and
     climaxing in the "dead end" of Ship of Fools.

3   ANON. Review of The Collected Stories, Booklist, LXII
     (1 November), 263.
        The Collected Stories is "a convenient compilation for
     students of American literature and admirers of Porter."

4   ANON. Review of The Collected Stories, Choice, II (November),
     582-83.
        The Collected Stories is important for all libraries,
     for Porter's work is among the most important in twentieth-
     century literature.

5   ANON. Review of The Collected Stories, Playboy, XII (Decem-
     ber), 63.
        The Collected Stories is "a trunkful of gems." It con-
     tains "the agony points of much of this century, in pri-
     vate life and public affairs--along with some of the high
     points of American literature."

6   AUCHINCLOSS, LOUIS. "Katherine Anne Porter," in Pioneers and
     Caretakers: A Study of Nine American Women Novelists.
     Minneapolis: University of Minnesota Press, pp. 136-51.
        Porter is neither a regional nor a national writer. If
     the Miranda stories deal with the milieu Porter knew as a
     child, Mexican stories such as "María Concepción" show an

1965

(AUCHINCLOSS, LOUIS)
extraordinary understanding of primitive society, and German stories such as "The Leaning Tower" establish her as
an international novelist. Porter's favorite themes are
all contained in Pale Horse, Pale Rider: "Old Mortality"
deals with the questionable dignity and romance of the
American past; "Pale Horse, Pale Rider" deals with "the
presence of nightmare" in a chaotic present; and "Noon
Wine" deals with the irrefutable reality of human evil.
The third of these themes becomes increasingly dominant in
Porter's work, especially in Ship of Fools, wherein it
challenges the existence of civilization itself.
Partially reprinted in A Library of Literary Criticism
(1969.B2).

7   BELL, VEREEN M. "'The Grave' Revisited," SSF, III (Fall),
39-45.
Curley's reading of "The Grave" as a Christian fable
(1963.B6) insists that we interpret Miranda's experience
with the dead rabbits in a symbolic way, despite the realism of the passage, despite Porter's emphasis on Miranda's
"reasonless" horror, and despite Paul being an unexplained
aspect of what she sees. Like many contemporary stories,
"The Grave" does not accommodate itself so easily to the
Procrustian beds of individual critics.

8   BODE, CARL. "Miss Porter's Ship of Fools," in The Half-World
of American Culture. Carbondale: Southern Illinois University Press, pp. 220-25.
Reprinted from WSCL (1962.B16).

*9 DENHAM, ALICE. "Katherine Anne Porter, Washington's Own Lit-
erary Lioness," The Washingtonian, I (May), 33, 38-39.
Interview and biographical sketch. Cited in A Bibliography of the Works of Katherine Anne Porter and A Bibliography of the Criticism of the Works of Katherine Anne Porter (1969.A2), p. 139.

10 DONOGHUE, DENIS. "Reconsidering Katherine Anne Porter," New
York Review of Books, V (11 November), 18-19.
Porter's most memorable stories are more pictures than
narratives, structured upon static characters whose memories range about "to trouble the past, turning facts into
myths and myths into mythologies." The humanity of these
pictures is deeply affecting, and all else in the stories
is transparent beside them. Indeed, one of the main problems with Ship of Fools is that its characters have no

1965

(DONOGHUE, DENIS)
past and that they cannot, therefore, develop. Porter's
Irish stories fail similarly. "Holiday" and "Noon Wine"
are Porter's best stories.
Partially reprinted in A Library of Literary Criticism
(1969.B2).

11   FEATHERSTONE, JOSEPH. "Katherine Anne Porter's Harvest," New
Republic, CLIII (4 September), 23-26.
Ship of Fools is a great accomplishment, but Porter's
reputation rests with her short novels and stories, so
notable for their concentration, their intelligence, their
style, their portraiture, and their senses of history, na-
tionality, and society. Local-color pieces such as "María
Concepción" and "Hacienda" lack the density of the autobiographical pieces such as "Old Mortality," but they are
perfect in their own way. Political stories such as "Flowering Judas" and "The Leaning Tower" dwell on the link
between manners and politics and employ characters who
confuse emotion and form. Porter's best stories are the
initiation tales set in the Old South and Texas, but all
of her stories give compelling shape to human experience.
Reprinted as "Katherine Anne Porter's Stories" in The
Critic as Artist (1972.B3).

12   FRANKEL, HASKEL. "The Author," SatR, XLVIII (25 September),
36.
[Interview.] Porter lives a very private life,
and friends and family are important to her. Her mannerisms are Southern. She is a tough, happy person, and
has in mind completing her study of Cotton Mather and
writing a medieval mystery story.

13   GULLASON, THOMAS A. "Tragic Parables," Boston Sunday Herald
(3 October), sec. i, p. 57.
Porter's output is small, but she matured quickly after
the dull and overwritten "María Concepción," and The Collected Stories is already an established classic. Ideally,
the individual stories should be read in the full context
of Porter's several collections.

14   HERTZ, ROBERT N. "Sabastian Brant and Porter's Ship of
Fools," MQ, VI (Summer), 389-401.
In writing Ship of Fools, Porter seems to have borrowed
Brant's idea of exposing a universal folly, but, unlike
Brant, she does not denounce her characters explicitly so
much as dramatically, and, unlike Brant again, she is not
convinced that she knows the final truth about things.

1965

     (HERTZ, ROBERT N.)
       Indeed, the "philosophy" informing Ship of Fools seems to
      be that every conclusion about life is a half-truth.
      Partially reprinted from "Rising Waters" (1964.B6).

15   HICKS, GRANVILLE. "A Tradition of Storytelling," SatR,
     XLVIII (25 September), 35-36.
       With few exceptions, Porter's stories are first-rate,
     and her reputation will rest on them rather than on Ship
     of Fools. The distinguishing characteristic of her sto-
     ries is hard to define, but she knows when a story is
     right, and the reader recognizes the rightness of her
     tales. Both the Southern tradition of story-telling and
     Porter's Mexican experiences are important in her work.

16   HILL, WILLIAM B. "Review of The Collected Stories, America,
     CXIII (27 November), 686.
       Porter's output has been continually impressive, and it
     is good to have her beautiful stories collected in one
     volume.

17   KIELY, ROBERT. "Placing Miss Porter," Christian Science Moni-
     tor (24 November), p. 15.
       Porter was "placed" prematurely after the publication of
     Ship of Fools, and that novel was too readily seen as the
     culmination of her work. The Collected Stories has clear-
     ly many pieces superior to Ship of Fools: without medi-
     ocrity, sentimentality, thinness, gimmickry, self-
     conscious elegance, or solemnity, they are characterized
     by grace, irony, precision, balance, and authenticity.

18   KRAMER, DALE. "Notes on Lyricism and Symbols in 'The Grave,'"
     SSF, II (Summer), 331-36.
       The symbolism of "The Grave" is religious in part, as
     pointed out by Sister Joselyn (1964.B7), but it is also
     initiatory and psychological. The seeing of the rabbits
     is an initiation into sexual knowledge, and the irony of
     the story is that the initiation is thwarted by self-
     protective devices in Miranda's psyche both at the time of
     initiation and twenty years later.

19   LOPEZ, HANK. "A Country and Some People I Love," Harper's
     Magazine, CCXXXI (September), 58-68.
       [Interview.] Porter discusses the attraction Mexico
     holds for her, her experiences in Mexico, her Mexican
     friends, her involvement in the Obregón revolution, the
     Mexican origins of "Flowering Judas," her Mexican exhibit,
     the intellectual and cultural climate of Mexico today, the

(LOPEZ, HANK)
    writing of Ship of Fools, and her brief movie career. She
    further discusses Eudora Welty, Peter Taylor, J. F. Powers,
    Flannery O'Connor, Glenway Wescott, and Caroline Gordon as
    some of her favorite writers.

20   McDONALD, GERALD D. Review of The Collected Stories, LJ, XC
        (1 October), 4111.
          The Collected Stories is a superb collection. Since the
    publication of Ship of Fools there has been some distaste
    for Porter's doubts about "the possibility of human nobil-
    ity," but her doubts are simply one aspect of her total
    honesty.

21   MILLER, PAUL W. "Katherine Anne Porter's Ship of Fools: A
        Masterpiece Manqué," University Review, XXXII (Winter),
        151-57.
          Ship of Fools is the work of a short story writer who
    has not adequately appreciated the special requirements of
    character-development in a novel. Porter has failed to
    discriminate some of her characters, has overdeveloped
    others, and underdeveloped still another group. Some
    characters are inconsistent and some fail to contribute to
    the forward motion of the action. Only a more formally
    compelling work can justify such a departure from tradi-
    tional requirements.

22   MOSS, HOWARD. "A Poet of the Story," New York Times Book Re-
        view (12 September), sec. vii, pp. 1, 26.
          The Collected Stories reminds us that Porter's first
    concern is always aesthetic. She has an especial gift for
    characterization and style, but she never seeks these as
    ends in themselves any more than she seeks realism, sym-
    bolism, lyricism, or poeticism in themselves. Evil as a
    form of moral hypocrisy is her major theme, but she also
    toys with the notion that those who allow themselves to be
    made to feel guilt are guilty. Indeed, the only Eden in
    her work is in "The Old Order" sketches. "Noon Wine" is
    the most perfect of her stories.

23   NEWQUIST, ROY. "An Interview with Katherine Anne Porter,"
        McCall's, CXII (August), 88-89.
          [Interview.] Porter comments on her youth, her educa-
    tion, her university lecturing, her having no need to look
    for fictional material, her travels, her attitudes toward
    youth, pornography, the deterioration of vocabulary and
    pronunciation, and the painting of Jackson Pollock. Hope,
    courage, and intelligence are necessary virtues, she in-

1965

sists, and she disputes that she was ever "lost" as a member of the Lost Generation. Remarks about Porter's juvenilia, her reading, her motivation to write, her early
publishing ventures, her marriage, her reaction to letters, her writing of Ship of Fools, her reaction to the
novel's reception, and her advice to young writers con-
clude the interview.

24 PERRY, ROBERT L. "Porter's 'Hacienda' and the Theme of
Change," MQ, VI (Summer), 403-15.
Porter's "Hacienda" is interesting for more than its account of Eisenstein and ¡Que Viva Mexico!, and it is more
than the amalgam of themes that Johnson has seen in it
(1960.B4). The unifying motif of the story is change.
The Russians are filming a study of the revolution on a
hacienda that seems untouched by it, and most of the
characters in the story play self-consciously modern
roles. Only Carlos really understands that change is
properly a long, organic process, and, remaining true to
this knowledge, he is the only successful person in the
tale.

25 PRYCE-JONES, ALAN. "Katherine Anne Porter's Stories--Proof of
Her Talent," New York Herald Tribune (26 October), p. 27.
The Collected Stories supports Porter's reputation as a
prodigy. She is at her best when writing of areas native
to her--Texas and Mexico--and less sure of herself in lo-
cales such as New York City. "Noon Wine," "He," "The
Jilting of Granny Weatherall," "Pale Horse, Pale Rider,"
and "Holiday" would alone render her unforgettable.

26 _____. "35 Enjoyable Books in '65," New York Herald Tribune
(9 December), p. 18.
The Collected Stories is listed among the thirty-five
enjoyable books of 1965.

27 REDDEN, DOROTHY SUE. "The Legend of Katherine Anne Porter."
Ph.D. dissertation, Stanford University.
Porter's great theme is the state of alienation in
which most people live, and she develops this theme
largely through the character Miranda. In the fourteen
stories and novel that chart her development, Miranda pro-
gresses from a pre-crisis period in which her education is
a series of disillusionments, to a crisis in which she de-
cides that love is impossible and rejects all human involvement, to a post-crisis period in which she experiences the depths of bitterness and despair while attaining
limited insight into her condition.

28   SMITH, J. OATES. "Porter's 'Noon Wine': A Stifled Tragedy,"
     Renascence, XVII (Spring), 157-62.
         Mr. Thompson tries to understand himself in Porter's
     "Noon Wine," but his motivation has been lost in time, and
     he is denied the most elementary understanding of himself.
     This denial effectively prevents us from classifying "Noon
     Wine" as a tragedy.

29   THOMPSON, BARBARA. "Katherine Anne Porter: An Interview,"
     in Writers at Work, edited by George Plimpton. Second
     Series. New York: Viking, pp. 137-63.
         Reprinted from Paris Review (1963.B20).

30   WASHBURN, BEATRICE. "It's Katherine Anne Porter, But Is It
     Art?" Miami, Florida Herald (3 October), p. 7-F.
         Although it made the best seller list, Ship of Fools was
     a very dull book. Porter's Collected Stories possesses a
     "vague distinction," but her characters are not really
     flesh and blood.

1966 A   BOOKS - NONE

1966 B   SHORTER WRITINGS

1   ALDRIDGE, JOHN W. "Art and Passion in Katherine Anne Porter,"
    in Time to Murder and Create: The Contemporary Novel in
    Crisis. New York: David McKay, pp. 178-84.
        The Collected Stories makes clear that Porter's fastidi-
    ous style too often masks a weakness of imagination and
    originality. Her psychological stories (such as "Flower-
    ing Judas") are frequently uncertain in direction and are
    inferior to her semi-fictional reminiscences (such as "Old
    Mortality," "Pale Horse, Pale Rider," and "The Old
    Order"). The Collected Stories makes clear, too, that
    Porter is at her best as a regionalist, art and passion
    failing to coincide in the international stories, and that
    she is better in the short novel than in the short story.
    Reprinted in The Devil in the Fire (1972.B1) and in Kath-
    erine Anne Porter: A Critical Symposium (1969.A1).

2   ALEXANDER, JEAN. "Katherine Anne Porter's Ship in the
    Jungle," TCL, II (January), 179-88.
        Ship of Fools has generally been read as a surprisingly
    pessimistic book, but Porter's earlier work, particularly
    "Old Mortality" and "Pale Horse, Pale Rider," should have
    prepared us for it. Those two stories record a search for
    identity and actuality outside the ancestral bounds and

1966

(ALEXANDER, JEAN)
terminate in a nightmare of meaninglessness and purpose-
lessness, symbolized by the jungle. The world of Ship of
Fools takes us on from that point, exploring the nature of
man when the bestial is loosed in him.

3   ANON. Review of The Collected Stories, LJ, XCI (15 January),
448.
The Collected Stories is representative of the best
writing in the world today, and it includes perfect examples of the short story.

4   ANON. "Dedicated Author," New York Times (16 March), p. 42.
Biographical sketch and personality description.

5   ANON. "Four Authors Are Given National Book Awards," Publisher's Weekly, CLXXXIX (21 March), 47-48.
The 1965 National Book Award for Fiction has been given
to Porter for her Collected Stories. The citation by Paul
Horgan, J. F. Powers, and Glenway Wescott asserted that
Porter's unique gift was for "absolute prose with the
poet's fire and light."

6   ANON. "Winners' Press Conference," Publisher's Weekly,
CLXXXIX (28 March), 30-32.
Extracts from Porter's press conference on receiving the
National Book Award for Fiction. Porter comments on the
nature of good writing, on Ship of Fools, on the writing
of short stories, and on the pains and pleasures of
writing.

7   ANON. "Biographical Sketches of the 1966 Winners of the
Pulitzer Prizes," New York Times (3 May), p. 43.
Biographical note.

8   ANON. "Pulitzer Drama Prize Omitted; Schlesinger's 1,000 Days
Wins," New York Times (3 May), pp. 1, 42.
Porter has been awarded the Pulitzer Prize for Fiction
for her Collected Stories.

9   BECKER, LAURENCE A. "'The Jilting of Granny Weatherall': The
Discovery of Pattern," EJ, CV (December), 1164-69.
The verbal patterns in "The Jilting of Granny Weatherall" suggest a compression of two experiences in Granny's
mind--her jilting by George years before and her jilting
by God at the moment of death. Her lost child Hapsy rep-
resents those events in her life that she weathered but
never accepted.

10   BROOKS, CLEANTH. "On 'The Grave,'" YR, LV (Winter), 275-79.
      "The Grave" is about Miranda's initiation into the
      mysteries of adult life, especially into the mysterious
      connection between birth and death. Subsumed into a
      broad social and philosophical context in the story, the
      birth-death connection suggests that truth is a beautiful,
      awesome, and terrible paradox.
      Reprinted in Katherine Anne Porter: A Critical Symposium
      (1969.A1).

11   CORE, GEORGE. "The Best Residium of Truth," GaR, XX (Fall),
      278-91.
          The Collected Stories establishes Porter as our greatest
      living writer of short fiction and as a major American
      writer. She has never imitated herself; she has never
      stooped to mere journalism; and she has been faithful to
      her ideal of a fully organic style. "Holiday," with its
      paradox of humanity achieved in inhumanity, is the best of
      the uncollected stories, and readers will want to reread
      "Hacienda," "Pale Horse, Pale Rider," and "The Leaning
      Tower" for the light they cast on Ship of Fools.
      Partially reprinted in Katherine Anne Porter: A Critical
      Symposium (1969.A1).

12   CRUTTWELL, PATRICK. "Swift, Miss Porter, and 'The Dialect of
      the Tribe,'" Shenandoah, XVII (Summer), 27-38.
          Porter's remarks on language in Harper's Magazine (Sep-
      tember 1965) are Swiftian in their equation of the "di-
      rect, legitimate line of English" with the English she
      finds morally and aesthetically sound. Porter's distaste
      for urbanization, for candid references to sex, and for
      non-Anglo-Saxon leadership in culture all enter into her
      attitude toward language.

13   DONADIO, STEPHEN. "The Collected Miss Porter," PR, XXXIII
      (Spring), 278-84.
          The Collected Stories is an uneven collection, and Por-
      ter's work is dull even at its best. Porter overdoes what
      she does well: thus her fondness for tableaux in an early
      story such as "María Concepción" and her tendency to un-
      derstand her characters too simply and too quickly in a
      story such as "Hacienda." Style alone keeps her anecdotes
      going. With the possible exception of "Old Mortality,"
      Porter's Southern stories are her worst; "Flowering Judas,"
      "Pale Horse, Pale Rider," and "The Leaning Tower" are her
      best.
      Partially reprinted in A Library of Literary Criticism
      (1969.B2).

1966

14   GOLDBERG, BARBARA. "Bleakness," Canadian Forum, XLV (January),
      240.
          Porter is an excellent writer, but The Collected Stories
      is hard to take with its "five hundred pages of bickering,
      bleakness, and unhappy endings." Porter's sympathies are
      extended only to the young and the sick.

15   HAGOPIAN, JOHN V. Review of The Collected Stories and of
      Katherine Anne Porter & the Art of Rejection, SSF, IV
      (Fall), 86-87.
          The Collected Stories is a fine volume, full of "con-
      trolled, civilized, yet passionate prose," and the stories
      all reflect Porter's characteristic technique and theme.
      Nance's Art of Rejection (1964.A1) does Porter no service,
      however, inasmuch as it deals with nothing more than plot.

16   KILCOYNE, FRANCIS P. Review of The Collected Stories, CathW,
      CCII (January), 250.
          The Collected Stories provides diverse pleasures--the
      flavor of locale, the mystery of dialogue, and the artist-
      ry of craftsmanship.

17   LEDBETTER, NAN WILSON. "The Thumbprint: A Study of People
      in Katherine Anne Porter's Fiction." Ph.D. dissertation,
      University of Texas.
          Porter has always developed her characters as individu-
      als, but several representative types seem especially to
      interest her: notably, the young discoverers, the self-
      deluded, the guilt-haunted, and the searchers.

18   LIBERMAN, M. M. "Responsibility of the Novelist: The Criti-
      cal Reception of Ship of Fools," Criticism, VIII (Fall),
      377-88.
          Solotaroff's attack on Ship of Fools (1962.B69) assumes
      that writers have a duty to deny Original Sin--clearly a
      false assumption. And Booth's dissatisfaction with the
      book (1962.B17) assumes that it is a novel and judges it
      as such, when it is in fact a modern apologue, "a work
      organized as a fictional example of the truth of a formu-
      lable statement or series of such statements."
      Reprinted in slightly different form in Katherine Anne
      Porter's Fiction (1971.A2) and in Katherine Anne Porter:
      A Critical Symposium (1969.A1).

19   RABKIN, LESLIE Y. Psychopathology and Literature. San Fran-
     cisco: Chandler, p. 271.
        "He" deals poignantly with the problem of conflicting
     parental attitudes toward mental retardation.

20   ROCKWELL, JEANNE. "The Magic Cloak," MQR, V (Fall), 283-84.
        Anecdote of the author meeting Porter in Michigan.

21   SUTHERLAND, DONALD. "Ole Woman River: A Correspondence with
     Katherine Anne Porter," SR, LXXIV (Summer), 754-67.
        An exchange of letters between Sutherland and Porter,
     commenting on Porter's attitude toward Gertrude Stein and
     the status of criticism.

22   VAN ZYL, JOHN. "Surface Elegance, Grotesque Content: A Note
     on the Short Stories of Katherine Anne Porter," ESA, IX
     (September), 168-75.
        Porter's short stories combine grotesque content with a
     surface elegance of style, the style suppressing and
     transforming one's accustomed reaction to the grotesque.
     "Flowering Judas" and "Pale Horse, Pale Rider" are the
     most notable examples of this combination; Ship of Fools
     is a less successful example.

23   WALTON, GERALD. "Katherine Anne Porter's Use of Quakerism in
     Ship of Fools," UMSE, VII (1966), 15-23.
        David Scott's struggle of wills in Ship of Fools is
     traceable to his Quaker background. Significantly, he
     avoids understandable disputes, extends sympathy to both
     Glocken and the woodcarver, and wears and prefers simple
     clothing; these things suggest a residue of religious be-
     lief that explains his guilt feelings about his various
     despicable acts.

24   WARREN, ROBERT PENN. "Uncorrupted Consciousness: The Stories
     of Katherine Anne Porter," YR, LV (Winter), 280-90.
        The Collected Stories should prove to be a permanent and
     valued text in American literature. "The Leaning Tower"
     is topically outdated, but most of the stories are radi-
     cally modern, especially in their insistence that each age
     must create its own truth. "Old Mortality" contains the
     most explicit statement of that theme, but "The Old Order"
     and "The Jilting of Granny Weatherall" make the same
     thematic statement, and variants of that theme are to be
     found in "Pale Horse, Pale Rider," "Flowering Judas,"
     "Holiday," "Theft," "He," "María Concepción," and "Noon
     Wine," all dealing with a tension between inner and outer

1966

(WARREN, ROBERT PENN)
truth. Porter differs from other modern writers by her
belief in Evil, and by her respect for the individual soul.
Partially reprinted in A Library of Literary Criticism
(1969.B2).

25   WELTY, EUDORA. "The Eye of the Story," YR, LV (Winter),
265-74.
Porter's stories deal with the interior of our lives and
she is seldom interested in the physically visible. The
visible surfaces and scenic structure of "Noon Wine" are
the exception; the more interior mode of "The Jilting of
Granny Weatherall" is the rule. Indeed, Porter's imagery
does not belong to the eye, but to the memory, and time's
dispassionate eye is the most frequent viewpoint of her
stories.
Reprinted in Katherine Anne Porter: A Critical Symposium
(1969.A1). Partially reprinted in A Library of Literary
Criticism (1969.B2).

1967 A   BOOKS - NONE

1967 B   SHORTER WRITINGS

1   EMMONS, WINFRED S. Katherine Anne Porter: The Regional Stories. SWS, no. 6. Austin: Steck-Vaughn.
Porter's regional stories include "The Source," "The
Journey," "The Witness," "The Last Leaf," " The Circus,"
"The Fig Tree," "The Grave," "Old Mortality," "Noon Wine,"
"Holiday," and "He." The first seven of these are set at
the grandmother's house or farm, and, with "Old Mortality,"
they trace Miranda's development as a child and as a young
woman. "Noon Wine" is the most intensely regional of Porter's stories, while "Holiday" develops the sense of place
more than any other story, and "He" is her earliest attempt at regionalism.

2   HOFFMAN, FREDERICK J. The Art of Southern Fiction: A Study
of Some Modern Novelists. Carbondale: Southern Illinois
University Press, pp. 39-50.
Porter is concerned with transforming life into art,
particularly in the semi-autobiographical Miranda stories
and in the "Noon Wine" illumined for us by Porter's essay
"'Noon Wine': The Sources" (1956.B5). Ship of Fools is a
flawed book, but a very great one.

3   MARSDEN, MALCOLM M.   "Love as Threat in Katherine Anne Por-
     ter's Fiction," TCL, XIII (March), 29-38.
          The failure of love in Ship of Fools should have been no
     surprise, for Porter's earlier stories had already defined
     three basic modes of failure. One group of stories de-
     picts characters who are able to renew their love after a
     purgative state of hatred ("María Concepción," "Rope"); a
     second group depicts characters for whom such renewal is
     impossible ("That Tree," "Downward Path," "Old Mortality,"
     "Noon Wine"); a third group depicts characters who iso-
     late themselves emotionally ("Theft," "Flowering Judas,"
     "The Cracked Looking-Glass," "Pale Horse, Pale Rider").
     The characters in Ship of Fools fail in love according to
     these same three modes.

4   WOLFE, PETER.   "The Problems of Granny Weatherall," CLAJ,
     XI (December), 142-48.
          "The Jilting of Granny Weatherall" is about "the finali-
     ty and inescapability of human imperfection," but the
     record of Granny's practical energy is more impressive
     than the record of her spiritual despair, and the story
     is read properly as a celebration of Granny's triumph.

1968 A   BOOKS - NONE

1968 B   SHORTER WRITINGS

1   BAKER, HOWARD.   "The Upward Path: Notes on the Work of Kath-
     erine Anne Porter," SoR, IV n. s. (Winter), 1-19.
          Like Heraclitus, Porter is a "maker of darkish para-
     bles" who sees downward paths as leading to wisdom: as a
     modern who read Pound and Eliot and who spent ten forma-
     tive years living in Mexico, she could scarcely be any-
     thing else. The archaic, older world is continually Por-
     ter's frame of reference, as in "María Concepción," "Ha-
     cienda," "Flowering Judas," "Noon Wine," and Ship of
     Fools, but she is not the pessimist that Nance thinks
     her (1964.A1).
          Reprinted in Sense and Sensibility in 20th Century Writ-
     ing (1970.B2).

2   GROSS, BEVERLY.   "The Poetic Narrative: A Reading of 'Flower-
     ing Judas,'" Style, II (Spring), 129-39.
          "Flowering Judas" is "poetic" both in language and in
     form. Sound quality, rhythm, syntax, dictional patterns,
     and metaphors reinforce meaning in the story to such a
     degree that the experience recorded is forged out of the

1968

(GROSS, BEVERLY)
language, not merely conveyed through it; and the sequence
of tenses in the story conveys admirably the repression
which characterizes Laura's condition.

3   LIBERMAN, M. M.   "The Short Story as Chapter in Ship of
Fools," Criticism, X (Winter), 65-71.
Ship of Fools has been faulted as a bad novel when it is
really a kind of modern apologue in which individual
scenes employ the shape of the short story and the whole
book strives for the single effect of the short story.
The scene in which Jenny proposes to David that Freytag
join them at their table is, for instance, a self-
contained short story that functions as part of the whole
apologue in four distinct ways.
Reprinted in slightly different form in Katherine Anne
Porter's Fiction (1971.A2).

4   PORTER, KATHERINE ANNE.   "'Noon Wine': The Sources," in The
Art of Writing Fiction, edited by Ray B. West, Jr.   New
York: Crowell, pp. 67-80.
Reprinted from YR (1956.B5).

5   PORTER, KATHERINE ANNE.   "'Noon Wine': The Sources," in
Reading the Short Story, edited by Ray B. West, Jr.   New
York: Crowell, pp. 190-203.
Reprinted from YR (1956.B5).

6   SCHORER, MARK.   "Katherine Anne Porter," in The World We
Imagine. New York: Farrar, Straus, and Giroux,
pp. 264-73.
Reprinted from Pale Horse, Pale Rider (1962.B66).

7   VLIET, VIDA ANN RUTHERFORD.   "The Shape of Meaning: A Study
of the Development of Katherine Anne Porter's Fictional
Form." Ph.D. dissertation, Pennsylvania State University.
Porter's attitude in her work has shifted from an ini-
tial optimism to an ultimate nihilism; her methodological
allegiances have shifted from nostalgic impressionism and
neo-primitivism to symbolic naturalism, then to a Joycean
stream of consciousness, and finally to surrealism. Symbolic imagery is Porter's favorite technique, but her
ability to juxtapose the speech rhythms of her characters
with the tongue-in-cheek tones of an anonymous narrator
is particularly notable, as is her employment of multiple
points of view.

8   WALSH, THOMAS F.   "The 'Noon Wine' Devils," GaR, XXII
      (Spring), 90-96.
         "Noon Wine" is based on the Faust legend and is markedly
      similar in structure to Benét's "The Devil and Daniel Web-
      ster." Helton and Hatch are both devils, attacking Thomp-
      son through his pride and seeking his soul. Unlike Benét,
      and like Marlowe and Goethe, Porter is interested in the
      Faust legend for its tragic potential.

1969 A   BOOKS

1   HARTLEY, LODWICK, and GEORGE CORE, eds.   Katherine Anne Por-
      ter: A Critical Symposium. Athens: University of Geor-
      gia Press.
         Essays reprinted from Kenyon Review (1942.B12), Accent
      (1947.B4), CE (1953.B5), WHR (1954.B3), MFS (1959.B4),
      VQR (1960.B3), SWR (1960.B6), Four Quarters (1962.B38) and
      (1962.B77), University Review (1963.B8), Paris Review
      (1963.B20), Images of Truth (1963.B22), Time to Murder and
      Create (1966.B1), YR (1966.B10), Criticism (1966.B18), YR
      (1966.B25), and an essay partially reprinted from GaR
      (1966.B11).

2   WALDRIP, LOUISE, and SHIRLEY ANN BAUER. A Bibliography of the
      Works of Katherine Anne Porter and A Bibliography of the
      Criticism of the Works of Katherine Anne Porter. Metuchen,
      N. J.: Scarecrow.
         The first half of this book is a descriptive bibliogra-
      phy of all writings by Porter, including translations, in-
      troductions, and afterwords, up to and including some
      entries for 1968, and identifying the first appearance of
      all writings. The second half, based partially on Porter's
      own file of clippings, is a comprehensive listing of crit-
      ical estimates of Porter's work in books, periodicals, and
      newspapers, up to and including some entries for 1968.
      The entries are frequently accompanied by a brief quota-
      tion from the work.

1969 B   SHORTER WRITINGS

1   BARNES, DANIEL R., and MADELINE T. "The Secret Sin of Granny
      Weatherall," Renascence, XXI (Spring), 162-65.
         A "baby" motif runs through Granny Weatherall's rambling
      discourse, and it suggests that she was pregnant with
      Hapsy at the time she married John. Memory of that "sin"
      is the source of her death-bed disturbance.

1969

2 CURLEY, DOROTHY NYREN, ed. "Katherine Anne Porter," in A Library of Literary Criticism: Modern American Literature. Vol. III, 4th ed. New York: Frederick Ungar, pp. 16-22.
    Extracts reprinted from New Republic (1930.B2), Nation (1930.B5), New Republic (1939.B9), Nation (1939.B12), SatR (1939.B13), SR (1940.B4), Nation (1940.B5), SatR (1944.B12), ArQ (1946.B1), Hopkins Review (1952.B19), VQR (1960.B3), Crit (1962.B65), Commentary (1962.B69), Atlantic (1962.B76), Katherine Anne Porter (1965.A1), Pioneers and Caretakers (1965.B6), New York Review of Books (1965.B10), PR (1966.B13), YR (1966.B24) and (1966.B25).

3 GIVNER, JOAN. "A Re-Reading of Katherine Anne Porter's 'Theft,'" SSF, VI (Summer), 463-65.
    Like Ship of Fools, "Theft" recounts a series of confrontations with incarnate evil; and, like the voyagers to Bremerhaven, the protagonist of "Theft" encourages evil by failing to oppose the evil-doers.

4 GOTTFRIED, LEON. "Death's Other Kingdom: Dantesque and Theological Symbolism in 'Flowering Judas,'" PMLA, LXXXIV (January), 112-24.
    "Flowering Judas" is a portrayal of hell with no accompanying portrayal of heaven. Its characters, action, and imagery (particularly the pattern of ironic inversions) have their source in Eliot's poems and in Dante's Inferno, and in Cassian and Aquinas as well. Porter seems to have assimilated those writers indirectly.

5 HARTLEY, LODWICK. "Stephen's Lost World: The Background of Katherine Anne Porter's 'The Downward Path to Wisdom,'" SSF, VI (Fall), 574-79.
    The best gloss for "The Downward Path" is the first chapter of Philip Horton's biography of Hart Crane. Stephen corresponds to Crane in his family situation, in his love of colors, in his Oedipal inclinations, and in his search for affection among strangers.

6 LIBERMAN, M. M. "Some Observations on the Genesis of Ship of Fools: A Letter from Katherine Anne Porter," PMLA, LXXXIV (January), 136-37.
    Porter's 1931 letter to Malcolm Cowley (quoted in full) supports a reading of Ship of Fools as an apologue [cf. (1966.B18)], for Porter sees the Germans as "fictionalized figures and types" and reveals an attitude morally and aesthetically similar to Brant's even in 1931.
    The letter is reprinted in Katherine Anne Porter's Fiction (1971.A2).

7   McDONALD, GERALD D. Review of The Collected Essays, LJ, XCIV
         (15 December), 4527-28.
            Many of the offerings in The Collected Essays have not
         been collected before, and all of the offerings are marked
         by "truth, tenderness, and severity." Porter is a writer
         to be admired and trusted.

8   NANCE, WILLIAM L. "Variations on a Dream: Katherine Anne
         Porter and Truman Capote," SHR, III (Fall), 338-45.
            Both Porter and Truman Capote have contributed to the
         literature of the American Dream, but Porter sees her
         Neoplatonic paradise as engulfed in nightmare in "Pale
         Horse, Pale Rider," distilling from it a feeling of cap-
         tivity, while Capote uses a similar sort of vision to dis-
         till a feeling of liberation.

9   PRATER, WILLIAM. "'The Grave': Form and Symbol," SSF, VI
         (Spring), 336-38.
            The two-part structure of "The Grave" emphasizes that
         the "grave" of the title refers to Miranda's mind and that
         the subject of the story is Miranda's tendency to bury un-
         welcome experience.

10   REDDEN, DOROTHY S. "'Flowering Judas': Two Voices," SSF, VI
         (Winter), 194-204.
            Laura is repelled equally by life and by death in "Flow-
         ering Judas," and she finds that a kindred dualism informs
         her experience at every level. She can survive only by
         keeping the terms of the dualism in equilibrium--by
         choosing to live a deadlock between inner needs and in-
         culcated precepts. Porter seems to support Laura in both
         of her attitudes.

11   WIESENFARTH, JOSEPH. "Internal Opposition in Porter's 'Granny
         Weatherall,'" Crit, XI (no. 2), 47-55.
            Like Porter's "The Source," "The Jilting of Granny
         Weatherall" is about order and disorder. Granny tried to
         impart a mechanical order to her life in an effort to com-
         pensate for the supreme disorder of her wedding day, but
         because she never dared to love again her heart was never
         healed, and the disorder of her past and present asserts
         itself on her death-bed.

12   YANELLA, PHILIP R. "The Problems of Dislocation in 'Pale
         Horse, Pale Rider,'" SSF, VI (Fall), 637-42.
            Porter's characters are frequently dislocated by a move-
         ment from the institutions and values of the late
         nineteenth-century rural South to a modern world for which

1969

they are unprepared. "Pale Horse, Pale Rider" is Porter's
most successful crystallization of this theme, and it is
"a dismal assessment of modern selfhood."

1970 A BOOKS - NONE

1970 B SHORTER WRITINGS

1   ANON. "Notes of a Survivor," Time, XCV (4 May), 99-100.
      "Noon Wine" and "Pale Horse, Pale Rider" are the bedrock
    of Porter's reputation, for Ship of Fools lacks both the
    form and the objectivity of the earlier stories. Porter's
    literary essays are worth reading for both their content
    and their style, but the other writings in The Collected
    Essays are valuable only for their style. The dominant
    tone of The Collected Essays is that of a woman who has
    "gone it alone" and survived.

2   BAKER, HOWARD. "The Upward Path: Notes on the Work of Kath-
    erine Anne Porter," in Sense and Sensibility in 20th Cen-
    tury Writing: A Gathering in Memory of William Van O'Con-
    nor, edited by Brom Weber. Carbondale: Southern Illinois
    University Press, pp. 75-93.
      Reprinted from SoR (1968.B1).

3   CULLIGAN, GLENDY. Review of The Collected Essays, SatR, LIII
    (28 March), 29-30.
      The Collected Essays is uneven in quality. When control
    and passion function together, as in the critical pieces
    and the shorter pieces, Porter is at her best; when they
    are out of balance they produce "banal enthusiasms" and
    "defensive bitterness."

4   LIBERMAN, M. M. "Circe," SR, LVIII (October-December),
    689-93.
      Reviews of The Collected Essays and "placings" of Por-
    ter's work have been predictably tiresome and impertinent.
    Although poorly edited, The Collected Essays is a valuable
    book because it illumines the consistency of Porter's mind
    in its many roles: it shows her always challenging Error
    and always treating literature and its writers as if they
    were in themselves of the greatest importance.

5 MADDEN, DAVID. "The Charged Image in Katherine Anne Porter's
   'Flowering Judas,'" SSF, VII (Spring), 277-89.
   "Flowering Judas" is a fully charged work, in the Pound-
   ian sense of the term, conveying the intensity of experience with technical expertise. With an almost cinematic
   sense of technique, Porter arranges a dynamic interplay of
   static images into an unfolding pattern that renders per-
   fectly Laura's self-delusion and final paralysis of will.

6 NANCE, WILLIAM L. "Katherine Anne Porter and Mexico," SWR,
   LV (Spring), 143-53.
   Mexico has been many things to Porter: it has been the
   inspiration and subject of much of her work; it has been
   her personal and literary symbol of independence; it has
   provided her with "the atmosphere of the living arts";
   and, with its sensitivity to oppression and its desire for
   freedom, it has been for her a kindred spirit.

7 OSTA, WINIFRED HUBBARD. "The Journey Pattern in Four Contemporary American Novels," Ph.D. dissertation, University
   of Arizona.
   Like Cortázar's Los Premios, Fuentes' Cambio de Piel,
   and Lopes' Belona, Latitude Noite, Porter's Ship of Fools
   is based on a journey through space and time. Space and
   time have both psychological and symbolic values and functions: the slow but direct passage of the Vera influences
   the series of unhappy encounters aboard ship, and the pattern of the Heroic Quest underlies Dr. Schumann's search
   for meaning.

8 OVERMEYER, JANET. "Roving Lady Novelist at Large," Christian
   Science Monitor (7 May), p. B9.
   In The Collected Essays Porter proves she can be as witty, lucid, outspoken, and intelligent in an essay as she
   is in her stories. Some chaff is mixed with the grain in
   this volume, but it is on the whole a delightful book.

9 PARTRIDGE, COLIN. "'My Familiar Country': An Image of Mexico
   in the Work of Katherine Anne Porter," SSF, VII (Fall),
   597-614.
   Porter's experiences in Mexico were very formative upon
   her, and her articles and stories about Mexico trace as a
   set the same progression from mere "adventure" (frequently involving betrayal) to more profound "experience"
   (frequently involving a reversal of values) that is often
   the structure of a Porter story. With varying degrees of
   structural success, "María Concepción," "The Martyr,"

1970

(PARTRIDGE, COLIN)
"Virgin Violeta," "Flowering Judas," and "Hacienda" all
trace that progression in their structures.

10   PINKERTON, JAN. "Katherine Anne Porter's Portrayal of Black
      Resentment," University Review, XXXVI (Summer), 315-17.
         The sketches collected under the title "The Old Order"
      impart glimpses of black resentment. Unable to challenge
      the social order directly, Jimbilly can tell his guilt-
      producing stories only to children, and Nannie can rebuke
      her white family only by retiring. Both know the score
      can never be settled, but they will take what satisfaction
      they can.

11   SAMUELS, CHARLES THOMAS. "Placing Miss Porter," New Republic,
      CLXII (7 March), 25-26.
         The Collected Essays contains some valuable pieces not
      collected before, "St. Augustine and the Bullfight," "A
      Wreath for the Gamekeeper," and "A Goat for Azazel" in
      particular, but little of the rest is worth reprinting and
      no editorial apparatus adds interest to it. Because Por-
      ter is distinctive in neither style nor vision, her work
      catches fire only when its material is truly rich--when it
      pushes her beyond "an irony that is always lucid but often
      without resonance." "The Jilting of Granny Weatherall,"
      "Magic," "Noon Wine," and "Old Mortality" are based on
      such material, but too much of her work is not.

12   SOLOTAROFF, THEODORE. "Ship of Fools: Anatomy of a Best
      Seller," in The Red Hot Vacuum. New York: Atheneum,
      pp. 103-21.
         Reprinted from Commentary (1962.B69).

13   SULLIVAN, WALTER. "Katherine Anne Porter: The Glories and
      Errors of Her Ways," SLJ, III (Fall), 111-21.
         Porter is a great writer, but The Collected Essays is a
      painful book: Porter's egotism, her condescension to
      other writers, and her insistence on judging everything
      according to her own, narrow views are all too evident.
      Porter might have understood her weaknesses and her
      strengths somewhat better: indeed, she seems incapable of
      dealing with the complexities of themes she has employed
      in Ship of Fools, "The Leaning Tower," and even "Old Mor-
      tality."
      Reprinted in Death by Melancholy: Essays on Modern South-
      ern Fiction (1972.B11).

14 WIESENFARTH, JOSEPH. Review of The Collected Essays, Commonweal, XCII (7 August), 396-98.
Porter is a truth teller with a merciless eye, and the
majority of items in The Collected Essays celebrate those
unafraid of "dangerous humanity and harsh truth." The
volume is a necessary complement to her stories.

15 WOLFF, GEOFFREY. "Miss Porter," Newsweek, LXXV (6 April), 91.
Some of the pieces in The Collected Essays should not
have reached print the first time, but the pieces on Cotton Mather, Gertrude Stein, and D. H. Lawrence are master-
ful. The essays make clear that Art is Porter's god and
that Craft is her delight.

16 YODER, ED. Review of The Collected Essays, Harper's, CCXL
(March), 112.
The Collected Essays contain impressively varied offer-
ings, the best of which are the critical pieces with their
"tough-minded humanism." Porter will have nothing to do
with edification: our "first lady of letters" is secular
and sensible, concerned with one's duty to language,
people and places.

1971 A BOOKS

1 KRISHNAMURTHI, M. G. Katherine Anne Porter: A Study.
Mysore: Rao and Raghavan.
Porter's fiction reflects her sustained attempt to understand the stresses upon modern man and the causes of
his failures. Her major themes are the confusions that
children experience in attempting to understand the adult
world, the reality of the past, the difficulty of acknowl-
edging reality, the rejection of the family, and the pur-
suit of new experience.

2 LIBERMAN, M. M. Katherine Anne Porter's Fiction. Detroit:
Wayne State University Press.
Some of the critics who have disparaged Porter's work
have been guilty of fundamental misunderstandings and narrow critical approaches: they have required that Ship
of Fools conform to the standards of a novel when it is
really an apologue; they have viewed "Old Mortality" as
barely-disguised autobiography when it is highly classical
in its formal resolution of the conflict between the sub-
jective writer and the objective artist; they have thought
of "Noon Wine" as a short novel when it is crucial to
think of it as a novella; they have failed to see the

1971

(LIBERMAN, M. M.)
  relationship between "María Concepción" and Porter's attitude toward Lawrence; and they have read "Flowering Judas"
  and "The Leaning Tower" in too narrowly symbolic a manner.
  Parts of this book are reprinted in slightly different
  form from Criticism (1966.B18) and (1968.B3) and in Midwest Educational Review (1972.B9).

1971 B SHORTER WRITINGS

  1   BROOKS, CLEANTH. "The Southern Temper," in A Shaping Joy:
      Studies in the Writer's Craft. New York: Harcourt,
      Brace, Jovanovich, pp. 205-08, 218-19.
        Porter allows her feminist sympathies to emerge in "Old
      Mortality," presenting Miranda's rebellion with dramatic
      sympathy, while Miranda's final state of hopefulness and
      ignorance is very much in the "Southern temper." "Pale
      Horse, Pale Rider" is wonderfully concrete about the frus-
      tration of Southern idealism.

  2   HOWELL, ELMO. "Katherine Anne Porter As a Southern Writer,"
      SCR, IV (December), 5-15.
        The Southernness of Porter's work is only incidental,
      for she generally fails to relate a Southern background to
      the larger themes of her stories. Indeed, her stories are
      most Southern when they have no theme and when their con-
      crete rendering of a Southern world is allowed to domi-
      nate. "Old Mortality" is a vivid example of her failure
      with theme, and "The Old Order" vignettes are an example
      of her success without theme. Porter's evident mistrust
      of a regional approach is due, no doubt, to the interna-
      tional spirit of her time.

  3   KIERNAN, ROBERT F. "The Story Collections of Katherine Anne
      Porter: Sequence as Context." Ph.D. dissertation, New
      York University.
        Porter's story collections should be thought of as story
      sequences, for they are characterized in each of their
      versions by thematic and rhetorical unities that override
      the segmentation of the individual stories. The three
      versions of Flowering Judas are characterized by dialecti-
      cal structures, Pale Horse, Pale Rider, by a generalizing
      structure, and the two versions of The Leaning Tower,
      by combinations of dialectical and generalizing struc-
      tures. The structure of Ship of Fools is analogous to
      that of a story sequence inasmuch as its individual
      scenes tend to be self-contained and related to one
      another as units, in the manner of the sequences.

4 McCORMICK, JOHN. The Middle Distance: A Comparative History
     of American Imaginative Literature 1919–1932. New York:
     Free Press, pp. 90–91.
          Porter is "an amusingly hostile witness" to the literary
     experiments of the 1920s.

5 WIESENFARTH, JOSEPH. "The Structure of Katherine Anne Porter's
     'Theft,'" Cithara, X (May), 65–71.
          "Theft" dramatizes "the disorder which lurks below an
     order that does not develop from a personal commitment to
     love." It is structured on two epiphanies, one of loss
     and the other of guilt, responsibility being the link be-
     tween them. Images of heat, fire, and dryness are sym-
     bolic of the lovelessness for which the protagonist is
     responsible, and each of her encounters with other persons
     dramatizes her responsibility.

1972 A BOOKS – NONE

1972 B SHORTER WRITINGS

1 ALDRIDGE, JOHN W. "Art and Passion in Katherine Anne Porter,"
     in The Devil in the Fire. New York: Harper's Magazine
     Press, pp. 128–33.
          Reprinted from Time to Murder and Create (1966.B1).

2 FARRINGTON, THOMAS ARTHUR. "The Control of Imagery in Kath-
     erine Anne Porter's Fiction." Ph.D. dissertation, Uni-
     versity of Illinois at Urbana–Champaign.
          Porter writes both symbolic and realistic fiction, the
     former emphasizing the spiritual and the unconscious, and
     the latter emphasizing the empirical and the rational.
     Her use of images is an important control upon her
     meaning.

3 FEATHERSTONE, JOSEPH. "Katherine Anne Porter's Stories," in
     The Critic as Artist, edited by Gilbert A. Harrison. New
     York: Liveright, pp. 111–19.
          Reprinted from New Republic (1965.B11).

4 GAUNT, MARCIA ELIZABETH. "Imagination and Reality in the Fic-
     tion of Katherine Anne Porter and John Cheever: Implica-
     tions for Curriculum." Ph.D. dissertation, Purdue
     University.
          Porter reconciles imagination and reality in her ironical
     viewpoint, but she sees the world of experience as domi-
     nant. Inasmuch as literary experiences should integrate
     affective and cognitive responses, Porter's work is appro-
     priate in the classroom.

1972

5   GIVNER, JOAN.   "Katherine Anne Porter and the Art of Carica-
        ture," Genre V (1972), 51-60.
            In her essays and prefaces, Porter seems to think of
        caricature not as a vicious attack but as an honest and
        clear-headed vision of real malevolence, and her use of
        caricature as a technique in her own fiction is reserved
        for the absolutely wicked, as in "Theft," "Flowering
        Judas," "The Leaning Tower," and Ship of Fools. Appro-
        priately, a person's ability to draw caricatures is always
        a mark of courage and moral insight in her fiction.

6   HERNANDEZ, FRANCES.   "Katherine Anne Porter and Julio Cortá-
        zar: The Craft of Fiction," in Proceedings of the Compar-
        ative Literature Symposium, Vol. 5: Modern American Fic-
        tion, Insights and Foreign Lights, edited by Wolodymyr T.
        Zyla and Wendell M. Aycock. Lubbock: Texas Technical
        University Press, pp. 55-66.
            The careers and achievements of Porter and Julio Cortá-
        zar are markedly similar. Both have been translators and
        both have been rebels in their personal lives and in their
        work; both have been obsessed with perfecting their tech-
        niques while remaining free of literary influence, and
        both possess delicately attuned ears and ruthless blue
        pencils; both use symbols deftly and both are fascinated
        by a dying man's perceptions; finally, both are "born"
        short story writers and have written novels that are them-
        selves very similar.

7   HOWELL, ELMO.   "Katherine Anne Porter and the Southern Myth:
        A Note on 'Noon Wine,'" LaS, XI (Fall), 252-59.
            Although Porter has always championed the regional in
        fiction, she herself makes little use of it. "Noon Wine"
        is her most comprehensive regional effort, but the story
        is flawed (and typically so) by the introduction of a
        moral question that belies its regional aspects and ren-
        ders them superfluous. Porter may admire the regionalists,
        but she belongs to another generation and to another
        school of writers.

8   HUBBELL, JAY B.   Who Are the Major American Writers? Durham:
        Duke University Press, pp. 228, 279, 283, 297, 299.
            Porter is placed in a hierarchy of American writers by
        various polls taken among authors, critics, and editors.

9   LIBERMAN, M. M.   "The Publication of Porter's 'He' and the
        Question of the Use of Literature." Midwest Educational
        Review, IV (Spring), 1-7.

(LIBERMAN, M. M.)
The curious publication of "He" in the Marxist New Masses suggests that the editors did not see it as a story at all but rather as a documentary about poor whites. Partially reprinted from Katherine Anne Porter's Fiction (1971.A2)

10   MAJOR, MABEL, and T. M. PEARCE. Southwest Heritage. 3rd ed., rev. Albuquerque: University of New Mexico Press, pp. 132, 242-43.
Porter is one of America's most distinguished writers of short fiction. Ship of Fools should be read as a "domestic" novel with a dozen plots.

11   SULLIVAN, WALTER. "Katherine Anne Porter: The Glories and Errors of Her Ways," in Death by Melancholy: Essays on Modern Southern Fiction. Baton Rouge: Louisiana State University Press, pp. 52-65.
Reprinted from SLJ (1970.B13).

1973 A   BOOKS

1   HARDY, JOHN EDWARD. Katherine Anne Porter. Modern Literature Monographs. New York: Frederick Ungar.
Porter's stories deal thematically with four main topics --with the family as a "hideous institution," with childless couples who are generally even more miserable than parents, with the influence of black servants upon white employers, and with a self-preoccupation that cuts persons off from effective communication with others. Ship of Fools is successful as a "tragic satire, basically allegorical in structure, in which many different stories of realistic romance are deliberately aborted." (A biographical essay prefaces the book.)

1973 B   SHORTER WRITINGS

1   ANON. "Katherine Anne Porter," Publisher's Weekly, CCIII (12 February), 36-37.
Porter is the "first lady of American letters," still working enthusiastically at her craft and still a fascinating conversationalist.

2   BALDESHWILER, EILEEN. "Structural Patterns in Katherine Anne Porter's Fiction," SDR, XI (Summer), 45-53.
Porter employs three basic forms in her work: traditional "syllogistic" forms, "fictions of memory" forms,

1973

(BALDESHWILER, EILEEN)
and the "new" forms associated with the post-Chekhovian
story. "Noon Wine" and "The Downward Path" are examples
of the first, "The Fig Tree" and "The Grave" of the second, and "Flowering Judas" and "The Jilting of Granny
Weatherall" of the third. Porter has had successes and
failures in all three modes.

3   KAZIN, ALFRED. Bright Book of Life: American Storytellers
     from Hemingway to Mailer. Boston: Little, Brown,
     pp. 165-73.
        Porter has always aspired to an ideal of narrative "per-
     fection," moral and intellectual as well as formal, and
     critics of the Forties and Fifties generally gave her
     credit for attaining it. Ship of Fools compromised Por-
     ter's ideals, however. It was mechanical in form, glibly
     prophetic about the past, and personal in viewpoint when
     it should have been epical. Its failure illustrates the
     imbalance of Porter's defensive sensibility.

4   MILES, LEE ROBERT. "Unused Possibilities: A Study of Kath-
     erine Anne Porter." Ph.D. dissertation, University of
     California, Los Angeles.
        Porter's fiction has several recurrent themes: the im-
     manence of evil, the rarity of love, the need for ration-
     ality, and the importance of childhood in the molding of
     personality.

5   VOSS, ARTHUR. "Symbolism and Sensibility," in The American
     Short Story: A Critical Survey. Norman: University of
     Oklahoma, pp. 288-301.
        Porter is the best of the short story writers who came
     into prominence in the 1930s; she should be ranked with
     Joyce, Mansfield, Anderson, and Hemingway in her mastery
     of the form. "Flowering Judas" is the best of her Mexican
     stories and one of the best of all twentieth-century sto-
     ries, while "Pale Horse, Pale Rider" is one of her most
     subtle, most complex, and most artistic stories. In
     general, Porter's stories display a remarkable range of
     subject and style.

6   WIESENFARTH, JOSEPH. "Negatives of Hope: A Reading of Kath-
     erine Anne Porter," Renascence, XXV (Winter), 85-94.
        Porter's stories dramatize the belief expressed in her
     essays that human life is a struggle from confusion to
     confusion. Sexual frustration is part of the dilemma,
     and external forms of order offer no relief. The only
     possibility for spiritual rebirth, she insists, inheres

(WIESENFARTH, JOSEPH)
in facing the truth, for knowledge of oneself and of the
human condition leads to the necessity of love. Porter's
sustained effort to tell us the truth about ourselves is
witness to her hope for man.

1974 A   BOOKS - NONE

1974 B   SHORTER WRITINGS

1   GUNN, DREWEY WAYNE. "'Second Country': Katherine Anne Por-
     ter," in American and British Writers in Mexico, 1556-1973.
     Austin: University of Texas, pp. 102-22.
        Porter has probably used Mexican material more promi-
     nently than any other writer of her period. Her auto-
     biographical remarks, her fiction, and her non-fiction all
     bear testimony to the enormous influence that Mexico has
     had upon her. Curiously, Porter's early fiction is not
     political at all; "Flowering Judas," "That Tree," "Haci-
     enda," and Ship of Fools are significantly political, re-
     flecting a disappointment with the revolution, but Porter's
     love for the true Mexico continues to underlie all of the
     ugliness she reveals.

Introduction

Although Carson McCullers' literary reputation fluctuated considerably in the early years of her career, she was recognized as an important voice in fiction very quickly. Her first novel, for instance, The Heart Is a Lonely Hunter, was published in 1940 to only a small number of reviews, but the majority of reviewers were enthusiastic about its success and about her promise. "It is astonishing that a twenty-two year old girl could produce a first novel so fraught with power and understanding," wrote a reviewer for The Catholic World, "so adroitly selective and so technically competent as this present book." Ben Ray Redman, writing in The Saturday Review, insisted that the novel was extraordinary by any standard of measurement, and Rose Feld, writing in the New York Times, was reminded of the paintings of Van Gogh and the novels of Faulkner. Some reviewers argued that McCullers' themes were too obsessive and that her interests were too derivative, but Clifton Fadiman sounded the keynote of early McCullers criticism when he noted that the obsessive quality of her work distinguished it from the ordinary run of novels and presaged a brilliant career.

The publication of Reflections in a Golden Eye in 1941, however, seemed to many reviewers to fail the promise of The Heart Is a Lonely Hunter. Although a few reviewers were enthusiastic, most felt that McCullers had written pretentiously about a sociological and emotional world beyond her experience. Fadiman and Feld continued to defend her talent, but both were disappointed. Fadiman suggested that she avoid grotesque subjects completely, and Feld accused her of imitating Faulkner's morbidity. Other reviewers were still more harsh: Hubert Creekmore opined that her ideas came from Krafft-Ebing, while Basil Davenport found her characters "unnatural," and Robert Littell thought the whole book rather nasty. As these remarks suggest, the reviewers seem to have been alienated by McCullers' subject matter: if The Heart Is a Lonely Hunter had dealt with grotesques, McCullers had sugar-coated the pill with her obvious feeling for her grotesques and by publicizing her claim that the novel was "an ironic parable of Fascism"; the grotesques of Reflections in a Golden Eye, on the other hand, were awkwardly realized, and they held commissions in the United States Army on the eve of Pearl Harbor.

INTRODUCTION

Some reviewers objected even to the themes of The Member of the Wedding (1946), but the majority of reviewers were charmed by McCullers' ability to evoke once again the world of haunted adolescence that she had dealt with briefly in The Heart Is a Lonely Hunter. Although they realized that The Member of the Wedding was plotless, the reviewers thought in general that the characterizations gave adequate substance to the book and that it was distinguished for its honesty, its seriousness, and its delicacy. Indeed, Philip Scruggs, writing in the Virginia Quarterly Review, saw McCullers as finally having accepted a responsibility proportionate to her exceptional gifts, and many reviewers found the story rich in implication. For Isaac Rosenfeld it was a parable of the Southern writer's situation; for George Dangerfield it dramatized McCullers' unconscious mind; and for Marguerite Young it questioned the metaphysical status of the world.

The plotlessness of The Member of the Wedding was carried over into McCullers' 1950 adaptation of the novel for the stage, and a number of reviewers felt that the play was too shapeless and too unevenly paced to be successful. The majority of reviewers, however, felt that the characters and mood were wonderfully achieved, and they argued that The Member of the Wedding was theatrically successful sui generis. Indeed, Robert Coleman suggested that The Member of the Wedding was literally a rendition of mood rather than a drama, and Margaret Marshall insisted that it was "an authentic experience" if not a play. A conviction that The Member of the Wedding succeeded more than it deserved stands behind even the most enthusiastic reviews, however: no one credited McCullers with a genuine feeling for the theatre or suggested that she had a future as a dramatist, and the acting of Ethel Waters, Julie Harris, and Brandon de Wilde, coupled with the direction of Harold Clurman, was generally credited with making her difficult script viable.

With the 1951 publication of her omnibus volume, The Ballad of the Sad Café, McCullers called for a summing-up of her work, as several critics noted. The time must have seemed premature for such a volume, but the time was also propitious, for the reviewers, critics, and surveyists who attempted to fix her place in American letters heaped laurels upon her and ceded her a more honored place in the hierarchy of American writers than she might reasonably have hoped for on the basis of the mixed reviews she had always received. Time magazine was moved to declare McCullers one of the top dozen American writers; Gore Vidal insisted that she, Paul Bowles, and Tennessee Williams were simply the most interesting American writers on the scene; V. S. Pritchett called her the best American novelist in a generation. Almost overnight she ceased to be a young writer of promise and became an established author of significant achievement. The title story of the omnibus volume was very much admired and might have had something to do with this shift of reputation, yet "The Ballad of the Sad Café" received less attention than it probably should have, for time has established it as the most poised, the most mature, and the most durable of McCullers' fictions.

Introduction

McCullers attempted to write again for the stage with The Square Root of Wonderful in 1957, but her lack of theatrical knowledge was not transcended in this play as it was in The Member of the Wedding. The play was roundly panned by the New York theatre critics for its inane characterizations, its stilted dialogue, and its structural confusion. It closed quickly, and it has generally been forgotten.

McCullers' last major publication has the reputation for being as great a disaster as The Square Root of Wonderful, but, in fact, Clock Without Hands (1961) was the only one of McCullers' publications that was widely reviewed, and it received a substantially equal number of good and bad reviews with a smattering of mixed reviews. British reviewers were particularly enthusiastic about the novel, and such eminent critics as Granville Hicks and Edna O'Brien argued the book's worth in America. The more forceful reviews were negative, however, and they were negative with a vengeance: Robert Bowen labeled the novel "a comic book for intellectual delinquents"; Henrietta Buckmaster classified it as a minstrel show with a tragic theme; and Dorothy Parker placed it in "yesterday's tower of ivory." Doris Grumbach insisted in America that the novel had no distinction except the name of its author, and time has seemed generally to confirm her opinion, for the novel passed quickly into obscurity and it is today the only McCullers work which has been allowed to go out of print. Academic study of the novel has been largely incidental to broad surveys of her work and tends to dismiss the novel as unfocussed and sentimental.

In 1971, four years after McCullers' death, Margarita G. Smith edited a collection of her sister's published but uncollected poems, short stories, and essays under the title The Mortgaged Heart. Smith's claim for the volume was somewhat misleading, for "Wunderkind" had been collected in The Ballad of the Sad Café and McCullers' outline for "The Mute" (an early title for The Heart Is a Lonely Hunter) was readily available as an appendix to Evans' Carson McCullers: Her Life and Work. The volume was reviewed courteously, but with little enthusiasm. Most reviewers felt that the inclusions were apprentice work that McCullers would probably have wished uncollected, and that their value to a study of McCullers' development was diluted by the occasional essays written as hack work for women's magazines. Students of McCullers' work have made little use of the volume to date.

Academic essays on McCullers' work have been appearing regularly at the rate of two or three a year since the publication of her omnibus volume in 1951, and a substantial body of criticism now exists. Explicators of individual works have been especially attracted to "The Ballad of the Sad Café," and in particular to its narrator and its ballad form. The Heart Is a Lonely Hunter has attracted almost as many explicators to a consideration of its structure, its imagery, and its allegorical meaning. The majority of essayists, however, have preferred to deal with McCullers' work as a whole, and the best essays on her work are probably among those which view her work broadly. Frank Baldanza's "Plato in Dixie" and Klaus Lubbers' "The Necessary Order" are particularly astute and influential essays, the first for its classification of McCullers as a philosophical Platonist, and the second for its reading of The Heart Is a Lonely Hunter, and Tennessee Williams' alignment of McCullers with the Southern Gothicists has had an extraordinary influence in Europe and is often quoted. Barbara Folk's "The Sad Sweet Music of Carson McCullers" has been seminal in drawing attention to McCullers' imagery, and Dayton Kohler's suggestion that McCullers is a mythic writer has been equally seminal. The best treatment of McCullers' evolution is probably Dale Edmonds' pamphlet in the Southern Writers Series, but Oliver Evans and Richard Cook have both published book-length studies of some significance in this area and which are valuable, too, for their readings of individual works. The best treatment of McCullers' attitude toward love is probably Ihab Hassan's "The Alchemy of Love and Aesthetics of Pain," and the best biographical treatment is Virginia Spencer Carr's The Lonely Hunter.

If a substantial amount of material has been published about McCullers, its substance has varied little. The loneliness of McCullers' characters and her tragic view of love are commonplaces argued again and again in the critical literature, and her tendency to use music symbolically and freaks representatively has been noted with wearying repetitiveness. European critics have been particularly guilty of propounding clichés about McCullers' work as if no one had said them before, but critics writing in English have been guilty of the same fault. Significantly, I think, there are no disagreements of a really substantive nature among McCullers' critics, and there have been no important reevaluations: individuals may disagree about which novel is her best, but the approximate degree of success of the individual novels has always been agreed upon, and polarized interpretations and heated exchanges are conspicuously absent from the body of criticism.

*   *   *

In preparing this research guide I have listed all books and pamphlets about McCullers' writing, and all periodical reviews and essays, interviews, unpublished dissertations, and chapters or significant passages in books which bear upon her reputation, as well as reviews from the major newspapers. I have cited single references to prizes and awards where they seemed to reflect McCullers' reputation, but I have not cited reviews or essays on Albee's dramatic version of "The Ballad of the Sad Café" or on the various film treatments of the novels, unless they treat McCullers as a writer. In my abstracts of books, reviews, and essays, I emphasize critical judgments, and in my abstracts of interviews, bibliographies, and biographical notes I emphasize scope, except in the case of very brief items. Where it has been impossible to lay hands on an item, I have marked it with an asterisk and noted a source for the cita-

Introduction

tion. In order to make clear the difference between the omnibus entitled The Ballad of the Sad Café and the short story entitled "The Ballad of the Sad Café," I have standardized the use of italics and quotation marks, even when the sources do not follow standard usage; the difference between the narrative and dramatic versions of The Member of the Wedding is always clear in context. Further to avoid confusion, I have referred to the novels by their American titles even in the abstracts of foreign language reviews. My index lists all treatments of McCullers' work by title and by author, and all significant treatments of a work under the name of that work as well. Subject headings have been used in the index where appropriate. Reprints are not indexed under the titles of McCullers' works but are cross-indexed within the bibliography itself.

No bibliography of this kind is ever complete, but within the limits I have set, this guide is as comprehensive as I can make it through 1973. I have included items for 1974 and 1975 of which I am aware, but the entries for those years are undoubtedly incomplete.

I would like to express my appreciation to Professor Mary Ann O'Donnell of Manhattan College for technical advice in the preparation of this book, and to Ms. Maíre Duchon, Acquisitions Librarian of the Cardinal Hayes Library, Manhattan College for her assistance in obtaining some obscure materials.

Abbreviations

AR	Antioch Review
BA	Books Abroad
BB	Bulletin of Bibliography
BuR	Bucknell Review
CathW	Catholic World
CE	College English
CLAJ	College Language Association Journal
CMC	Crosscurrents/Modern Critiques
Crit	Critique
DR	Dalhousie Review
EJ	English Journal
Expl	Explicator
GaR	Georgia Review
HudR	Hudson Review
JA	Jahrbuch für Amerikastudien
L&P	Literature and Psychology
LJ	Library Journal
MFS	Modern Fiction Studies
MHRA	Modern Humanities Research Association
MissQ	Mississippi Quarterly
NVT	Nieuw Vlaams Tijdschrift
NY	New Yorker
SAB	South Atlantic Bulletin
SAQ	South Atlantic Quarterly
SatR	Saturday Review
SHR	Southern Humanities Review
SLJ	Southern Literary Journal
SoWS	Southern Writers Series
SR	Sewanee Review
SSF	Studies in Short Fiction
SWR	Southwest Review
SWS	Southwest Writers Series
TamR	Tamarack Review
TCL	Twentieth Century Literature
TLS	Times Literary Supplement
TUSAS	Twayne's United States Authors Series
UMPAW	University of Minnesota Pamphlets on American Writers

ABBREVIATIONS

```
VlG     De Vlaamse Gids
VQR     Virginia Quarterly Review
WSCL    Wisconsin Studies in Contemporary Literature
YR      Yale Review
```

Writings About Carson McCullers, 1940 - 1975

1940 A BOOKS - NONE

1940 B SHORTER WRITINGS

1   ANON. Review of The Heart Is a Lonely Hunter, Time, XXXV
        (10 June), 90.
            The Heart Is a Lonely Hunter recalls Dostoevski in its
        confrontation of Christ-figures with a suffering world,
        but it is wholly undistinguished on the verbal level.

2   ANON. Review of The Heart Is a Lonely Hunter, CathW, CLII
        (November), 252.
            The Heart Is a Lonely Hunter is an astonishing book,
        "fraught with power and understanding," adroitly selec-
        tive, and technically competent. Its theme is the loneli-
        ness suffered by the human heart in pursuing its desire,
        and John Singer is one of the noteworthy characters in
        contemporary fiction.

3   BLOCK, MAXINE, ed. "Carson McCullers," in Current Biography.
        New York: Wilson, pp. 535-36.
            Biographical sketch, autobiographical statement, and de-
        scription of The Heart Is a Lonely Hunter.

4   FADIMAN, CLIFTON. "Pretty Good for Twenty-Two," NY, XVI
        (8 June), 77-78.
            The Heart Is a Lonely Hunter has "an extraordinary ob-
        sessive quality," eerie, nightmarish, and yet believable.
        McCullers is an original writer with a style distinctive-
        ly her own, and her future is promising.

5   FELD, ROSE. "A Remarkable First Novel of Lonely Lives," New
        York Times Book Review (16 June), p. 6.
            The Heart Is a Lonely Hunter has remarkable power,
        sweep, and certainty for a first novel. McCullers clearly
        has knowledge beyond her years. Her art suggests a Van
        Gogh painting peopled with Faulkner figures.
            Partially reprinted in A Library of Literary Criticism
        (1969.B2).

1940

6   LITTELL, ROBERT. Review of The Heart Is a Lonely Hunter, YR,
    XXX n.s. (Autumn), viii.
        The Heart Is a Lonely Hunter is a strange, sad book that
    Chekhov would have liked. McCullers needs to see life
    more completely and to work on a bigger scale, but, if she
    can manage to do so without harmful influence, she may
    well emerge as an important writer.

7   McDONALD, EDWARD D. "The Mirroring Stream of Fiction," VQR,
    XVI (Autumn), 612-13.
        The Heart Is a Lonely Hunter is a miracle of compassion,
    pity, and irony. Form and matter are perfectly blended in
    the novel.

8   MacDOUGALL, SALLY. "Author, 22, Urges Aid to Refugees," New
    York World Telegram (1 July), p. 12.
        [Interview.] Touches on McCullers' New York apartment,
    the sensation caused by her first novel, her sympathy for
    refugees, her next novel, her literary tastes, and her
    schooling.

9   PATTERSON, ISABEL M. "Turns With a Bookworm," New York Herald
    Tribune Book Review (23 June), p. 11.
        McCullers quoted on The Heart Is a Lonely Hunter: it is
    a parable about fascism and its theme is man's revolt
    against his inner isolation and urge to express himself.

10 PRUETTE, LORINE. "She Understands Lonely Hearts," New York
    Herald Tribune Books (9 June), sec. ix, p. 4.
        The Heart Is a Lonely Hunter is a mature, unsentimental
    novel; but, because Singer is an enigmatic figure, sug-
    gesting several different commentaries upon the novel but
    no one commentary with any clarity, its parts seem larger
    than its whole.
        Partially reprinted in A Library of Literary Criticism
    (1969.B2).

11 PUTZEL, MAX. Review of The Heart Is a Lonely Hunter, Accent,
    I (Autumn), 61-62.
        The Heart Is a Lonely Hunter never lives up to the
    promise of its lovely title; rather, it conforms entirely
    to the outworn formula about starving, brutalized America.
    McCullers needs a positive view to leaven her writing.

12 REDMAN, BEN RAY. "Of Human Loneliness," SatR, XXII (8 June),
    6.
        The Heart Is a Lonely Hunter is an extraordinary novel
    by any standard, but especially so written by a twenty-

(REDMAN, BEN RAY)

two-year-old. A tale of loneliness, it has universal significance and almost mystical overtones. Surprising insights punctuate it, and the author's narrative skill and
originality speed it on its way.
Partially reprinted in A Library of Literary Criticism
(1969.B2).

13 SOLOMON, LOUIS B. "Someone to Talk To," Nation, CLI
(13 July), 36.
The Heart Is a Lonely Hunter strikes its one, plaintive
theme rather too persistently, but its characters are
beautifully created, and its author is admirably
straightforward.

14 WRIGHT, RICHARD. "Inner Landscape," New Republic, CIII
(5 August), 195.
The Heart Is a Lonely Hunter is both a "projected
movie" and "an attitude externalized in naturalistic detail" more than it is a novel. Its interest lies in its
angle of vision, for its picture of loneliness is the most
desolate yet to emerge from the South, and McCullers is
surely the first white Southerner to deal with Negroes
easily and with justice. Indeed, McCuller's despair is
more natural and authentic than Faulkner's, her characters
are more lost than Anderson's, and her prose is more carefully neutral than Hemingway's.
Partially reprinted in A Library of Literary Criticism
(1969.B2).

1941 A BOOKS - NONE

1941 B SHORTER WRITINGS

1 ALSTERLUND, B. "Carson McCullers," Wilson Library Bulletin,
XV (June), 808.
Biographical sketch, dealing with McCullers' childhood,
juvenilia, New York experiences, studies, marriage, and
writings.

2 ANON. "Masterpiece at 24," Time, XXXVII (17 February), 96.
Having returned from the "freakish household of esthetes
in Brooklyn Heights" (where she lived with W. H. Auden,
Louis MacNeice, Benjamin Britten, and Pavel Tchelitchew)
to her native Columbus, Georgia, McCullers has been able
to complete a second novel, and it is a masterpiece. Reflections in a Golden Eye is told with simplicity, with

1941

(ANON.)
>   insight, and with a gift for phrases, as if Faulkner had
>   acquired a Tolstoian lucidity.

3   ANON. Review of Reflections in a Golden Eye, Nation, CLII
>   (1 March), 247.
>   Reflections in a Golden Eye is a remarkable, haunting
>   novelette that recalls Lawrence's "Sun" and "The Prussian
>   Officer" while maintaining its originality.

4   CARGILL, OSCAR. Intellectual America: Ideas on the March.
>   New York: Macmillan, pp. 396-97.
>   The Heart Is a Lonely Hunter proves that a novelist can
>   be both tough and feminine.

5   CREEKMORE, HUBERT. Review of Reflections in a Golden Eye,
>   Accent, II (Autumn), 61.
>   McCullers is a dreary writer. She substitutes "words
>   for characters" and "innuendo for blood," and she distills
>   her ideas from Krafft-Ebing. Indeed, Reflections in a
>   Golden Eye has the atmosphere of "children snickering in a
>   privy."

6   DAVENPORT, BASIL. Review of Reflections in a Golden Eye,
>   SatR, XXIII (22 February), 12.
>   Reflections in a Golden Eye is a disappointment after
>   The Heart Is a Lonely Hunter. McCullers can clearly
>   write, but her sick and unnatural characters are inade-
>   quately understood and insufficiently employed. The book
>   should end in tragedy, but it trails off into futility.

7   FADIMAN, CLIFTON. Review of Reflections in a Golden Eye, NY,
>   XVII (15 February), 78.
>   McCullers based The Heart Is a Lonely Hunter on her own
>   experiences, but Reflections in a Golden Eye seems to be
>   based on her reading (particularly of D. H. Lawrence) and
>   its effect is wholly unconvincing. McCullers has talent,
>   but she should not strain so obviously to create gro-
>   tesque people and situations.

8   FELD, ROSE. Review of Reflections in a Golden Eye, New York
>   Herald Tribune Books (16 February), sec. ix, p. 8.
>   Reflections in a Golden Eye is an impressively mature
>   exploration of an emotional underworld, and it is more
>   confidently structured than McCullers' first book. McCul-
>   lers seems deliberatedly to be emulating Faulkner's mor-
>   bidity, however, and one hopes she will abandon her reli-
>   ance on the grotesque and the abnormal in future work.

9   FERGUSON, OTIS. "Fiction: Odd and Ordinary," <u>New Republic</u>,
        CIV (3 March), 317.
           <u>Reflections in a Golden Eye</u> is a brilliantly executed
        tour de force, hard, exact, and graceful. It observes all
        of the classic unities, excludes all that is not absolutely
        necessary, and increases its intensity continually. The
        antagonists are calculatedly strange, and reader involve-
        ment is kept to a minimum.

10   LITTELL, ROBERT. Review of <u>Reflections in a Golden Eye</u>, <u>YR</u>,
        XXX n.s. (Spring), xii.
           <u>Reflections in a Golden Eye</u> is a disappointment after
        <u>The Heart Is a Lonely Hunter</u>, and McCullers' admirers will
        want to forget it quickly. McCullers has obvious talent,
        but the novel's inversions, mutilations, and nastiness are
        decidedly unpleasant.

11   MARSH, FRED T. "At an Army Post," <u>New York Times Book Review</u>
        (2 March), p. 6.
           <u>Reflections in a Golden Eye</u> is vastly inferior to <u>The</u>
        <u>Heart Is a Lonely Hunter</u>. McCullers' talent is clear, but
        it has an "enfant-terrible" quality in this book that sug-
        gests the book was written either too hastily or before
        the more mature <u>The Heart Is a Lonely Hunter</u>.
        Partially reprinted in <u>A Library of Literary Criticism</u>
        (1969.B2).

12   WEEKS, EDWARD. "First Person Singular," <u>Atlantic</u>, CLVII
        (April), unpaged.
           McCullers has considerable talent, but <u>Reflections in a</u>
        <u>Golden Eye</u> makes clear her need for both development and
        experience. She tends to label her characters rather than
        allow them to reveal themselves, and she clearly knows too
        little about army life.

1942 A BOOKS - NONE

1942 B SHORTER WRITINGS

1   ANON. Review of <u>Reflections in a Golden Eye</u>, <u>TLS</u> (30 May).
        p. 269.
           McCullers' style in <u>Reflections in a Golden Eye</u> promises
        a significance greater than what is there, for this "col-
        lection of arbitrary psychological violences" has little
        point.

1942

2   KUNITZ, STANLEY J., and HOWARD HAYCRAFT, eds. "Carson McCul-
      lers," in Twentieth-Century Authors. New York: Wilson,
      pp. 868-69.
        Brief autobiographical statement by McCullers and a
      short description of her first two novels.

1943 A BOOKS - NONE

1943 B SHORTER WRITINGS

1   ANON. "Creative Artists Win $1,000 Prizes," New York Times
      (14 April), p. 46.
        McCullers has been awarded a grant of one thousand dol-
      lars by the American Adacemy of Arts and Letters to enable
      her to continue her work.

2   ANON. "In the Deep South," TLS (27 March), p. 153.
        The Heart Is a Lonely Hunter is a better book than Re-
      flections in a Golden Eye but it lacks both power and dis-
      tinction. McCullers shows promise as a writer, but at
      this point in her career she is too derivative in her man-
      ner, and she relies on the merely strange to produce an
      effect of profundity.

1946 A BOOKS - NONE

1946 B SHORTER WRITINGS

1   ANON. "The End of F. Jasmine Addams," Time, XLVII (1 April),
      98.
        McCullers' earlier novels dealt with the morbid rela-
      tionships between adults, but The Member of the Wedding
      captures the moment when childhood turns into adolescence.
      It is a serious, touching book, devoid of plot and yet
      never static.

2   ANON. Review of The Member of the Wedding, United States
      Quarterly Book List, II (September), 180-81.
        The Member of the Wedding is a brilliant and discerning
      novella about human loneliness. Although meagerly de-
      scribed, even the minor characters are fully realized.

3   BOYLE, KAY. "I Wish I Had Written 'The Ballad of the Sad
      Café,'" in I Wish I'd Written That: Selections Chosen by
      Favorite American Authors, edited by Eugene J. Woods.
      New York: McGraw Hill, pp. 300-01.

(BOYLE, KAY)
"The Ballad of the Sad Café" is admirable for its bold-
ness, objectivity, and balanced proportions. It transcends all limitations of time and place, and its language
communicates its truth with precision.

4   DANGERFIELD, GEORGE. "An Adolescent's Four Days," SatR, XXIX
     (30 March), 15.
        McCullers is a unique writer, and The Member of the Wed-
     ding is a very unusual book, firmly shaped and yet written
     in a suggestive mode. In one sense, this book about lone-
     liness is a masquerade, a self-dramatization of McCullers'
     unconscious mind, but it is in no sense autobiographical.
     Partially reprinted in A Library of Literary Criticism
     (1969.B2).

5   DOWNING, FRANCIS. Review of The Member of the Wedding, Com-
     monweal, XLIV (24 May), 148.
        McCullers' writing is dangerously intensive, and she may
     exhaust herself quickly, but The Member of the Wedding is
     a fine book, urging thought upon us and germinating recol-
     lections and beliefs. The writing is beautifully adapted
     to its purpose.
     Partially reprinted in A Library of Literary Criticism
     (1969.B2).

6   FRANK, JOSEPH. Review of The Member of the Wedding, SR, LIV
     (Summer), 536-37.
        McCullers is obsessed with the revolting and the per-
     verse in The Member of the Wedding. The theme is too weak
     to support this obsession, and it remains unfocused in the
     novel.

7   GRAY, JAMES. On Second Thought. Minneapolis: University of
     Minnesota Press, p. 254.
        The Heart Is a Lonely Hunter and Reflections in a Golden
     Eye are the works of a conscientious neurotic and are
     largely unintelligible. The Member of the Wedding, how-
     ever, if an equally disturbing book, is honest and
     unmannered.

8   KAPP, ISA. "One Summer: Three Lives," New York Times Book
     Review (24 March), p. 5.
        The Member of the Wedding is a winning and disarming
     book. It is both reasonable and paradoxical, its lan-
     guage is both fresh and quaint, and its emotional turbu-
     lence is delicately conveyed.

1946

9   MATCH, RICHARD. "No Man's Land of Childhood," <u>New York Herald</u>
       <u>Tribune Weekly Book Review</u> (24 March), sec. vii, p. 5.
         The Member of the Wedding is a tender, subtle tragicom-
       edy about the transition from childhood to adolescence.
       It has the depth and originality of McCullers' earlier
       novels, but it lacks their breadth.

10   NORTH, STERLING. "A Difficult Girl at a Difficult Age," <u>Chi</u>-
       <u>cago Sun Book Week</u> (24 March), p. 2.
         The Member of the Wedding is not quite a success.
       Frankie Addams is more an individual than the type she
       seems intended to be, and she is not entirely believable.
       The characterizations in the novel are appealing, however,
       and the novel raises some important questions about child-
       hood and the roots of juvenile delinquency.

11   RICHARD, JEAN-PIERRE. Review of <u>Reflections in a Golden Eye</u>,
       <u>Fontaine</u>, X (no. 53), 135-36.
         Reflections in a Golden Eye is a perfectly achieved work
       in its own style, a style somewhere between Faulkner's
       lyricism and Caldwell's black humor. It is a story of in-
       finitely stupid people, and its genre straddles tragedy,
       the detective story, and the psychological drama.

12   ROSENFELD, ISAAC. Review of <u>The Member of the Wedding</u>, <u>New</u>
       <u>Republic</u>, CXIV (29 April), 633-34.
         McCullers employs a folk idiom in The Member of the Wed-
       ding, but her wedding-alienation theme is not at all in
       the folk mode. This dichotomy is typical of Southern fic-
       tion and prevents it from being a truly folk art. Indeed,
       the novel is really a parable on the life of the writer in
       the South and of the alienation that he feels.

13   SCRUGGS, PHILIP LIGHTFOOT. "A Southern Miscellany," <u>VQR</u>, XXII
       (Summer), 451.
         The Member of the Wedding is a finely conceived and
       finely written novel, probing minds very difficult to
       write about, and succeeding wholly. McCullers has accept-
       ed the responsibility of her exceptional gifts.

14   TRILLING, DIANA. "Fiction in Review," <u>Nation</u>, CLXII (6 April),
       406-07.
         The Member of the Wedding is a remarkable evocation of
       early adolescence, but McCullers stands in a wrong rela-
       tionship to her story, identifying so closely with her
       heroine that she cannot interpose mature judgments into
       the tale. Elizabeth Bowen's way of treating an adolescent

(TRILLING, DIANA)
    state of mind in Death of the Heart is more impressive and
    more literate.

15   WILSON, EDMUND. "Two Books That Leave You Blank: Carson
        McCullers, Siegfried Sassoon," NY, XXII (30 March), 87.
        McCullers has both sensitivity and talent, but she seems
        unable to find a dramatically effective subject. Reflec-
        tions in a Golden Eye is dramatic, but unreal, and The
        Member of the Wedding is undramatic, formless, and point-
        less. The kitchen scenes are admirably atmospheric, how-
        ever, and the characters are both droll and natural.

1947 A   BOOKS - NONE

1947 B   SHORTER WRITINGS

  1.   ANON. Review of The Member of the Wedding, TLS (15 March),
        p. 113.
        McCullers repeats her characteristic failure in The Mem-
        ber of the Wedding, creating the impression that her story
        means more than it can say in words. Her wearisome ex-
        ploration of adolescent profundities and her pretty whim-
        sicality tend to falsify the character of Frankie, and
        even the humor of the story seems overly contrived.

  2   YOUNG, MARGUERITE. "Metaphysical Fiction," Kenyon Review, IX
        (Winter), 151-55.
        The Member of the Wedding is not so much a study of tur-
        bulent adolescence as a symbolic examination of the meta-
        physical status of the world—whether there is a music of
        the spheres or whether all is chaos. The book is many-
        leveled, and everything in it is functional.

1949 A   BOOKS - NONE

1949 B   SHORTER WRITINGS

  1   BLANZAT, JEAN. "Frankie Addams de Carson McCullers," Le Figa-
        ro Littéraire, CXC (10 December), 7.
        McCullers is an international novelist with a classic
        sense of form, but her intuition of a chaotic world full
        of obscurely dangerous forces is very much in the American
        mode, recalling the work of Faulkner, Steinbeck, and Cald-
        well. All of her novels, including the recent The Member
        of the Wedding, oppose a banal reality to a complex inner

1949

(BLANZAT, JEAN)
life, and the result is loneliness. Frankie Addams is a
desperately lonely person, caught between childhood and
adolescence and afflicted with a Puritanical American conscience which cannot reconcile love and sensual pleasure.

1950 A   BOOKS - NONE

1950 B   SHORTER WRITINGS

1   ANON. "New Play in Manhattan," _Time_, LV (16 January), 45.
        The Member of the Wedding is more a picture of persons
     than a play, but McCullers' writing excuses her lack of
     playwriting, and the production helps a great deal.

2   ANON. Review of _The Member of the Wedding_, _Newsweek_, XXXV
     (16 January), 74.
        Despite its sketchiness and hasty resolution, _The Member
     of the Wedding_ is written with wisdom and feeling, and its
     characters are wholly absorbing. The failure of the play
     to hide its bookish origin is unimportant.

3   ANON. "Play Tells How a Lonely Girl Yearns to Belong with
     People," _Life_, XXVIII (23 January), 64-65.
        Although _The Member of the Wedding_ has literary distinc-
     tion, it is diffuse by conventional theatrical standards;
     it is really "a kind of poetic vaudeville show" about a
     lonely adolescent's needs.

4   ANON. Review of _The Member of the Wedding_, _Theatre Arts_,
     XXXIV (March), 13.
        The Member of the Wedding is "rain from heaven to a dry
     theatre season."

5   ANON. Review of _The Member of the Wedding_, _Bulletin critique
     du livre français_, V (April), 221.
        McCullers' _The Member of the Wedding_ places her in the
     first rank of young American writers. She combines fan-
     tasy, humor, and acute psychological analysis in this
     study of a child moving into adolescence, and her style is
     both fresh and charming.

6   ANON. "The Laurels," _Time_, LV (17 April), 80.
        McCullers was advised at one time to abandon the script
     for _The Member of the Wedding_. Last week it won the Drama
     Critics Circle Award as the best play of the New York
     theatrical season.

7   ATKINSON, BROOKS. Review of The Member of the Wedding, New
      York Times (6 January), p. 26.
      McCullers' portraits in The Member of the Wedding are
      wonderfully perceptive and masterfully developed. The
      play lacks conventional dramatic form, but it is art none-
      theless.
      Reprinted in New York Theatre Critics' Reviews (1951.B9).

8   BARNES, HOWARD. Review of The Member of the Wedding, New York
      Herald Tribune (6 January), p. 12.
      McCullers' dramatization of The Member of the Wedding is
      theatrically weak: the play moves too slowly for two acts
      and then bursts into hysterics and melodrama in the third
      act. In addition, Berenice's reminiscences are too long,
      John Henry's death is unnecessary, and the resolution of
      the play is haphazard. The acting is the production's
      chief virtue.
      Reprinted in New York Theatre Critics' Reviews (1951.B9).

9   BREIT, HARVEY. "Behind the Wedding," New York Times
      (1 January), sec. iv, p. 3.
      [Interview.] Account of an interview with McCullers,
      touching on "identity" as the theme of The Member of the
      Wedding, the mysterious source of such themes, Tennessee
      Williams' influence on the play, McCullers' difficulty in
      translating the narrative version into dramatic terms, and
      McCullers' admiration for the cast of the play.

10 BROWN, JOHN MASON. "Plot Me No Plots," SatR, XXXIII
      (28 January), 27-29.
      McCullers substitutes character and mood for plot in
      The Member of the Wedding. If the play is not wholly suc-
      cessful, however, the absence of plot is not to blame so
      much as the play's lack of inward progression and its
      failure to develop its characters.

11 CALLAWAY, JOE A. " ... Deplorable Dependence on Broadway,"
      Player's Magazine, XXVI (March), 126.
      The Member of the Wedding is appropriate material for
      an art theatre, but it is a very difficult play to pro-
      duce, inasmuch as it depends on expert characterization
      and acting rather than on plot development.

12 CHAPMAN, JOHN. "Member of the Wedding and Its Cast Earn
      Cheers at the Empire," New York Daily News (6 January)
      p. 55.
      The Member of the Wedding is not an ideal piece of play-
      making, for the first two acts move too slowly and the

1950

(CHAPMAN, JOHN)
third act moves too quickly but the script is creative,
sensitive, and intelligent, and the play is wholly
absorbing.
Reprinted in New York Theatre Critics' Reviews (1951.B9).

13   CLURMAN, HAROLD.   "From a Member," New Republic, CXXII
(30 January), 28-29.
Action is crucial to the viability of any play, and The
Member of the Wedding succeeded as a play because Frankie's
action of "getting out of herself" was grasped as the
underlying structure of the play by the actors.

14   COLEMAN, ROBERT.   "Member of the Wedding Is a Stirring Hit,"
New York Daily Mirror (6 January), p. 86.
The Member of the Wedding is a mood rather than a play,
but it is spellbinding and clearly a hit.
Reprinted in New York Theatre Critics' Reviews (1951.B9).

15   GARLAND, ROBERT.   "Something Special But Not Quite a Play,"
New York Journal American (6 January), p. 18.
The Member of the Wedding is a rare treat in the theatre,
but as a playwright McCullers remains a novelist.   The
cast works hard to transform the novel into a play, but
McCullers stopped trying halfway through the evening.
Reprinted in New York Theatre Critics' Reviews (1951.B9).

16   GIBBS, WALCOTT.   Review of The Member of the Wedding, NY, XXV
(14 January), 46-49.
The Member of the Wedding is touching, strangely witty,
and very close to poetry at the same time that it is somewhat uneven and shapeless.   The racial subplot confuses the
the play and introduces a note of melodrama inappropriate
to the general mood.

17   HAINES, HELEN E.   Living With Books: The Art of Book Selec-
tion.   2nd ed.   New York: Columbia University Press,
p. 518.
The Member of the Wedding has the sensitivity, candor,
and charm that characterize recent fiction about child
psychology and adolescence.

18   HAWKINS, WILLIAM.   "Waters, Harris Roles Spark Wedding," New
York World-Telegram and The Sun (6 January), p. 32.
Everything about The Member of the Wedding is success-
ful--the script, the acting, the directing.   The play is
touching without indulging in sentimentality.
Reprinted in New York Theatre Critics' Reviews (1951.B9).

19 MARSHALL, MARGARET. Review of The Member of the Wedding, Nation, CLXX (14 January), 44.
   If The Member of the Wedding is not a major play and not a play at all in the technical sense, it is "an authentic experience," "deeply felt," and "articulated in authentic characters and speech." Like Shaw's Caesar and Cleopatra, it is truly creative theatre.

20 MOREHOUSE, WARD. "Carson McCullers Cuts Her Own Hair," New York World-Telegram and The Sun (31 March), p. 36.
   [Interview.] Touches on McCullers' personal habits, the writing of The Member of the Wedding, Member's cast, and her personal interests.

21 NATHAN, GEORGE JEAN. The Theatre Book of the Year 1949-50. New York: Knopf, pp. 164-66.
   In turning The Member of the Wedding into a play, McCullers has actually eliminated the dramatic qualities of the original. Critics have been unwarrantedly kind to the play, as is their habit when a playwright attempts to deal with untheatrical material.

22 PHELAN, KAPPO. Review of The Member of the Wedding, Commonweal, LI (27 January), 437-38.
   The Member of the Wedding is an irresistible, delightful play. The script is psychologically sensitive and manages to avoid the clichés of the Southern Grotesque. McCullers lacks a dramatic imagination, however, and the actors and directors are responsible for glossing successfully the numerous weak points in her script.

23 WATTS, RICHARD, JR. "A Striking New American Play," New York Post (6 January), p. 45.
   The Member of the Wedding is a sensitive, unusual, and touching drama of striking individuality. If McCullers is not completely successful in her use of the dramatic form, she has managed to bring a rare delicacy to the commercial stage.
   Reprinted in New York Theatre Critics' Reviews (1951.B9).

24 WILLIAMS, TENNESSEE. "Introduction," to Reflections in a Golden Eye by Carson McCullers. New York: Bantam, vii-xvii.
   Reflections in a Golden Eye should not be attacked for its morbidity. It is "one of the purest and most powerful of those works which are conceived in that Sense of the Absurd [sic] which is the desperate root of nearly all significant modern art." It is inferior to The Member of the

1950

(WILLIAMS, TENNESSEE)
Wedding and "The Ballad of the Sad Café," but it is greater than The Heart Is a Lonely Hunter in its mastery of
design and its establishment of its own reality.

25 WYATT, EUPHEMIA VAN RENSSELAER. Review of The Member of the
Wedding, CathW, CLXX (March), 467-68.
The Member of the Wedding is an analysis of loneliness.
It opens a child's heart for us with heart-rending pa-
thos, and it is drama of the purest quality.

1951 A BOOKS - NONE

1951 B SHORTER WRITINGS

1 ANON. Review of The Member of the Wedding, LJ, LXXVI
(15 May), 867.
McCullers' novel is·excellently adapted in its dramatic
version and is highly recommended.

2 ANON. Review of The Ballad of the Sad Café, Wisconsin Library
Bulletin, XLVII (June), 166.
McCullers' later work fails to maintain the depth and
poignancy of The Heart Is a Lonely Hunter, but a preoccupation with our misunderstanding of one another is constant in her work.

3 ANON. "The Shy and the Lonely," Time, LVII (4 June), 106.
McCullers' omnibus volume establishes her as one of the
top dozen American writers. Love and loneliness are her
standard themes, and her writing belongs to the American
tradition of "mooning." She can be diffuse and weak in
her writing, but at her best (as in "The Ballad of the
Sad Café") she has both insight and warmth.

4 ANON. Review of The Ballad of the Sad Café, NY, XXVII
(9 June), 114-15.
McCullers' innocents are too articulate and too sensitive to be completely believable, and the atmosphere of
betrayal in which they live is often "merely sticky," but
to note these things is to complain pettishly about very
artful work.

5 ANON. "Carson McCullers," New York Herald Tribune Book Review
(17 June), p. 2.
[Interview.] Touches on McCullers' early career and
training, her theatrical intentions, her present work, and
her favorite authors.

6   BOWEN, ELIZABETH. "A Matter of Inspiration," SatR, XXXIV
     (13 October), 64.
          McCullers is cited as one of those American writers
     whose "intensity of imagination" has something to teach
     British writers.

7   CHAPIN, RUTH. "A Writer of Compassion," Christian Science
     Monitor (15 July), p. 7.
          McCullers has "mapped the heights and depths of human
     affections--capricious, absurd, even magnificent," but
     she has no values beyond the human itself. Her work has
     generally grown more positive and she has clearly mastered
     her craft.

8   CLANCY, WILLIAM P. Review of The Ballad of the Sad Café, Com-
     monweal, LIV (15 June), 243.
          McCullers' collected novels and stories justify Spen-
     der's notion that the recurrent theme of American litera-
     ture is the transformation of the primal energy of crea-
     tive art into "the inebriate...the feeling ox...
     the lost child." Indeed, McCullers' work is not properly
     Gothic, but metaphysical in spirit.
          Partially reprinted in A Library of Literary Criticism
     (1969.B2).

9   COFFIN, RACHEL W., ed. New York Theatre Critics' Reviews:
     1950. Vol. XI. New York: Critics' Theatre Reviews,
     pp. 397-400.
          Reviews reprinted from New York Times (1950.B7), New
     York Herald Tribune (1950.B8), New York Daily News
     (1950.B12), New York Daily Mirror (1950.B14), New York
     Journal American (1950.B15), New York World-Telegram and
     The Sun (1950.B18), and New York Post (1950.B23).

10   CREEKMORE, HUBERT. "The Lonely Search for Love," New York
     Times Book Review (8 July), p. 5.
          McCullers' omnibus volume makes clear that she has con-
     tinually narrowed her field of vision and that nothing she
     has written is quite so good as her first novel. "The
     Ballad of the Sad Café" is too attenuated, but its tone
     is ingratiating, and it suggests that McCullers may be
     working toward an integration of the humanity of The
     Heart Is a Lonely Hunter with her later fondness for
     eccentrics.

1951

11 ENGLE, PAUL. "An Original Gift; Unique and Incredible," Chi-
    cago Sunday Tribune (10 June), sec. iv, p. 5.
        The Ballad of the Sad Café makes clear that McCullers
    was a fine writer long before The Member of the Wedding
    became a popular play. Her art transforms the grotesque
    and extraordinary into accurate comments upon the human
    situation.

12 HUGHES, RILEY. Review of The Ballad of the Sad Café, CathW,
    CLXXIII (August), 391.
        McCullers' omnibus volume does not reflect development
    on the author's part so much as the continual reworking of
    a few themes, especially the theme of loneliness. McCul-
    lers is a sensitive sociologist, although she is incurably
    attracted to the grotesque, and her high reputation is
    merited.

13 HUTCHENS, JOHN K. "Carson McCullers," New York Herald Tribune
    Books (17 June), sec. vi, p. 2.
        Biographical sketch and random quotations from McCullers
    about her work and literary tastes.

14 JOOST, NICHOLAS. "'Was All for Naught?': Robert Penn Warren
    and New Directions in the Novel," in Fifty Years of the
    American Novel: A Christian Appraisal, edited by Harold C.
    Gardiner, S.J. New York: Scribners, pp. 284-86.
        McCullers' fiction is unlike the Southern Gothicism
    which merely titillates, for even a weak novel like Re-
    flections in a Golden Eye contains profound depths of
    meaning. McCullers' theme is the loneliness of the indi-
    vidual--a loneliness which love can mitigate only slightly
    and only intermittently.

15 KOHLER, DAYTON. "Carson McCullers: Variations on a Theme,"
    CE, XIII (October), 1-8.
        McCullers is a subjective novelist who has taught her-
    self to write objectively: all of her work has a dream-
    like quality at the same time that it is precisely and
    evocatively detailed, and it combines the simple and the
    elusive, the realistic and the symbolic, the individual
    and the general. Loneliness and longing is the single
    theme of her fiction, and she handles it in a mythic way
    rather than in any systematic or mechanical way.
    Printed simultaneously in EJ, XL (October), 415-22, and
    partially reprinted in A Library of Literary Criticism
    (1969.B2).

16 POORE, CHARLES. Review of The Ballad of the Sad Café, New
    York Times (24 May), p. 33.
        McCullers always speaks for the undefeated and unde-
    featable human spirit, and in the writings collected in
    The Ballad of the Sad Café she does so with considerable
    artistry. The new title story is brilliant, and McCullers
    should consider turning it into a play.

17 REDMAN, BEN RAY. Review of The Ballad of the Sad Café, SatR,
    XXXIV (25 June), 30.
        McCullers' novels and stories are even better on second
    reading than they are on first. It is too early to say
    whether or not her work is of lasting value, but she has a
    rare ability to deal with sentiment, and, like Defoe, she
    enables us to believe temporarily in the improbable.

18 ROSENBERGER, COLEMAN. "A Carson McCullers Omnibus," New York
    Herald Tribune (10 June), sec. vi, p. 1.
        McCullers' collected works make clear that her theme is
    man's tragic failure of communication. She uses freaks to
    suggest that failure, and their goal is always communica-
    tion.

19 STRAUMANN, HEINRICH. American Literature in the Twentieth
    Century. London: Hutchinson House, pp. 89-91.
        McCullers has affinities with Faulkner, but, unlike him,
    she does not confuse her issues. She sustains an even
    stronger sense of atmosphere than Faulkner, and her sense
    of vision is like Wolfe's. The Heart Is a Lonely Hunter,
    Reflections in a Golden Eye, and The Member of the Wedding
    are all about lonely visionaries.

20 WARFEL, HARRY R. American Novelists of Today. New York:
    American Book, p. 292.
        Biographical sketch and brief description of The Heart
    Is a Lonely Hunter, Reflections in a Golden Eye, and The
    Member of the Wedding.

21 WATERS, ETHEL. His Eye Is on the Sparrow. New York: Double-
    day, pp. 272-76.
        The Member of the Wedding is a peculiar play, without
    climax or movement; the character Berenice has to hold the
    play together.

1952

1952 A BOOKS - NONE

1952 B SHORTER WRITINGS

1   ANON. "14 Win Admission to Arts Institute," New York Times
     (8 February), p. 18.
          With the belief that McCullers' works will win a perma-
     nent place in American culture, the National Institute of
     Arts and Letters has elected McCullers to membership.

2   EVANS, OLIVER. "The Theme of Spiritual Isolation in Carson
     McCullers," in New World Writing: First Mentor Selection.
     New York: New American Library of World Literature,
     pp. 333-48.
          McCullers' essential theme is the loneliness of the in-
     dividual in a world full of lonely individuals, but she
     insists, too, that love offers no genuine relief from that
     world because it is always flawed. The Member of the Wed-
     ding is a more overt statement of this secondary theme
     than either The Heart Is a Lonely Hunter or Reflections in
     a Golden Eye, but "The Ballad of the Sad Café" is the most
     impressive and most elaborate statement, subsuming all the
     rest. Indeed, the evolution of the theme to its culmina-
     tion in "The Ballad of the Sad Café" is the essential pat-
     tern of McCullers' career.
     Partially reprinted in A Library of Literary Criticism
     (1969.B2), and reprinted in slightly revised form in
     South: Modern Southern Literature in Its Cultural Setting
     (1961.B18).

3   GASSNER, JOHN. Best American Plays, Third Series: 1945-51.
     New York: Crown, p. 174.
          Biographical sketch and account of the writing of The
     Member of the Wedding.

4   PRITCHETT, V. S. "Books in General," New Statesman and Na-
     tion, XLIV (2 August), 137-38.
          McCullers is the best American novelist in a generation.
     Classicism informs her regionalism, and her studies of the
     human heart reflect a bold imagination. She is always
     discovering new facets of her characters, and she analyzes
     them authoritatively. The Member of the Wedding has its
     defects, but no story of a similar kind has a comparable
     degree of insight.

5   STEGNER, WALLACE. The Writer in America. Japan: Hokuseido,
       pp. 46-47.
         With Williams and Capote, McCullers belongs to a group
       of writers who are emotionally sterile, but she rises
       above them and is a writer of extraordinary merit. Her
       precocity shows no signs of exhausting itself.

1953 A BOOKS - NONE

1953 B SHORTER WRITINGS

   1   ANON. "Human Isolation," TLS (17 July), p. 460.
          McCullers seeks a fabulous rather than a literal truth
        in her fiction, and she transforms ordinary loneliness
        into something rich and strange. She employs freaks in
        "The Ballad of the Sad Café" and The Member of the Wedding
        to suggest that even the abnormal experience an urgent
        need to love. Fulfilled love is an illusion, but illusion
        is an important enrichment of life, as The Heart Is a
        Lonely Hunter makes clear. McCullers' triumph consists in
        using her preoccupation with freaks and loneliness to make
        fictions which touch and illumine the real world.

   2   CLURMAN, HAROLD. "Some Preliminary Notes for The Member of
         the Wedding," in Directing the Play, edited by Toby Cole
         and Helen Chinnoy. New York: Bobbs-Merrill, pp. 311-20.
           A director's notes for The Member of the Wedding, com-
         menting on the main action of the play ("to get connect-
         ed") and the main actions and characteristics of the lead-
         ing characters (Frankie--"to get out of herself"; Bere-
         nice--"to do her work normally"; John Henry--"to learn to
         connect").

   3   NATHAN, GEORGE JEAN. The Theatre in the Fifties. New York:
         Knopf, p. 10.
           The Member of the Wedding appeals to audiences that like
         a good cry; it proves that the lachrymose genre is not
         exhausted.

   4   VAN DRUTEN, JOHN. Playwright at Work. New York: Harper,
         pp. 35-36, 174-75, 181-83.
           In transforming The Member of the Wedding into a play,
         McCullers was very successful in creating mood and theme,
         even if she developed no plot and almost no story. In-
         deed, because she wanted to study loneliness from the in-
         side and thought only of her subject, McCullers omitted
         many crucial scenes in the action, thus distancing us

1953

(VAN DRUTEN, JOHN)
.from the action. John Henry's unmotivated death is a
brilliant dismissal of plot.

5   VIDAL, GORE ["Libra"]. "Ladders to Heaven: Novelists and
Critics," in New World Writing, #4. Philadelphia: Lip-
pincott, pp. 303-16.
McCullers, Paul Bowles, and Tennessee Williams are at
this moment the most interesting writers in America, each
exploring the inside of man and telling the truth about
what he sees. McCullers is able to show the potential
within the most banal human relationships and to use words
like "love" and "compassion" with meaning.
Reprinted in slightly revised form in Rocking the Boat
(1962.B16) and in On Contemporary Literature (1964.B9).

1954 A   BOOKS - NONE

1954 B   SHORTER WRITINGS

1   BROWN, JOHN. Panorama de la littérature contemporaine aux
États-Unis. Paris: Librairie Gallimard, pp. 225-27.
Biographical note and descriptive list of McCullers'
fiction.

2   COWLEY, MALCOLM. The Literary Situation. New York: Viking,
p. 94.
The Member of the Wedding might be thought a typical
rite de passage novel of the new Southern fiction, but it
is not at all typical in its intensity of feeling and
rightness of language.

3   GASSNER, JOHN. The Theatre in Our Times. New York: Crown,
pp. 78, 353, 514.
The Member of the Wedding is persuasive and revealing
at the same time that it is nothing but an adroit portrait
of dawning adolescence. It replaces dramatic action with
a series of vignettes.
Partially reprinted in On Contemporary Literature
(1964.B9).

1955 A   BOOKS - NONE

1955 B   SHORTER WRITINGS

1   CHRISTIE, ERLING. "Carson McCullers og Hjertenes Fangenskap,"
     Vinduet (Oslo), IX (no. 1), 55-62.
          McCullers is a much-admired American writer with a par-
     ticular talent for making her vision of life seem authen-
     tic. Indeed, she is almost a mystic. She writes of "the
     bondage of the human heart," and isolation, loneliness,
     and an incipient homosexuality dominate the lives of her
     characters. Musical imagery is frequent in her writing.

2   FIEDLER, LESLIE A. An End to Innocence: Essays on Culture
     and Politics. Boston: Beacon, pp. 149, 202-03.
          McCullers is the most important writer of the new homo-
     sexual sensibility, and The Heart Is a Lonely Hunter is a
     "heartbreakingly wonderful" book. The Member of the Wed-
     ding depicts a female homosexual romance between Frankie
     and Berenice.

3   KAZIN, ALFRED. "We Who Sit in Darkness," in The Inmost Leaf:
     A Selection of Essays. New York: Harcourt Brace,
     pp. 127-35.
          By failing to absorb the audience in its action, The
     Member of the Wedding has the effect of freeing Ethel
     Waters (Berenice) from the play and allowing her a per-
     sonal triumph.

4   KUNITZ, STANLEY, ed. "Carson McCullers," in Twentieth Century
     Authors: First Supplement. New York: Wilson, pp. 610-11.
          McCullers is one of the most distinguished of younger
     American writers. She depicts a narrow, lonely world with
     sure artistry, and The Member of the Wedding is her most
     successful novel.

5   RICHARDS, ROBERT FULTON, ed. "McCullers, Carson," in Concise
     Dictionary of American Literature. New York: Philosophi-
     cal Library, p. 135.
     Brief identification of McCullers and her work.

6   SCHUCHART, MAX. "Visie en Verbeelding bij Carson McCullers,"
     NVT (Antwerp), IX (no. 6), 650-63.
          McCullers' novels and short stories are not realistic
     so much as lyrical, psychological, and grotesque. Her
     theme is always loneliness, and her characters are always
     individuals, locked into their selfhood and failing in
     every attempt to develop satisfying, harmonious relations
     with others.

1955

7   SIEVERS, W. DAVID.   Freud on Broadway: A History of Psycho-
     analysis and the American Drama.   New York: Cooper
     Square, pp. 431-33.
         The Member of the Wedding is a superb portrait of ado-
     lescence, and one of the more significant psychological
     plays of modern America.

1956 A   BOOKS - NONE

1956 B   SHORTER WRITINGS

1   ALDRIDGE, JOHN.   In Search of Heresy: American Literature in
     an Age of Conformity.   New York: McGraw-Hill, pp. 144-46.
         Unlike Salinger's characters, McCullers' characters are
     always placed in a concrete world.

2   GASSNER, JOHN.   Form and Idea in Modern Theatre.   New York:
     Dryden, p. 85.
         The dramatic structure of The Member of the Wedding is
     assuredly very fluid, but it has also a classical
     stability.

1957 A   BOOKS - NONE

1957 B   SHORTER WRITINGS

1   ANON.   Review of The Square Root of Wonderful, Time, LXX
     (11 November), 93-94.
         The Square Root of Wonderful is a hopelessly disordered
     play with its clashing themes, tones, and tempos.   McCul-
     lers' individuality and special feeling for life are ab-
     sent from this play.

2   ASTON, FRANK.   "Square Root Is Like Magic," New York World
     Telegram (31 October), p. 32.
         The Square Root of Wonderful is "a sturdy entertain-
     ment," realistic, well-built, and ironic.
     Reprinted in New York Theatre Critics' Reviews (1958.B4).

3   ATKINSON, BROOKS.   Review of The Square Root of Wonderful,
     New York Times (31 October), p. 40.
         The Square Root of Wonderful lacks McCullers' usual gen-
     ius and other-worldliness.   The play is frail and listless,
     and it seems commonplace after The Member of the Wedding.
     Reprinted in New York Theatre Critics' Reviews (1958.B4).

4   CARPENTER, FREDERICK I. "The Adolescent in American Fiction,"
     EJ, XLVI (September), 313-19.
        McCullers deals with the problems of adolescence with
     greater complexity and greater realism than Salinger, al-
     though she does so, too, with less art.

5   CHAPMAN, JOHN. "The Square Root of Scatters Neuroses Along
     the Psychopath," New York Daily News (31 October), p. 65.
        The Square Root of Wonderful is a trauma in three acts
     and gives one the uncomfortable sensation of being a re-
     luctant psychiatrist. Unlike O'Neill, McCullers cannot
     handle an assortment of neurotics simultaneously; she
     would do better to concentrate on one neurotic at a time,
     as she did in The Member of the Wedding.
        Reprinted in New York Theatre Critics' Reviews (1958.B4).

6   CLURMAN, HAROLD. Review of The Square Root of Wonderful, Na-
     tion, CLXXXV (23 November), 394.
        McCullers' writing in The Square Root of Wonderful is
     beautifully, lyrically awry, and her characters are won-
     derfully intuitive. Inept stage direction, however, has
     turned the play into a dismal failure.

7   COLEMAN, ROBERT. "Square Root Less Than Wonderful," New York
     Daily Mirror (31 October), p. 83.
        The Square Root of Wonderful has its amusing and human
     moments, but on the whole it is an odd and unsuccessful
     mixture of the romantic and the brutal.
        Reprinted in New York Theatre Critics' Reviews (1958.B4).

8   DRIVER, TOM F. Review of The Square Root of Wonderful,
     Christian Century, LXXIV (27 November), 1425.
        The Square Root of Wonderful is adequate when comic,
     but disastrous when serious. McCullers should limit her-
     self to depicting the world of children and not attempt to
     plumb adults.

9   DURHAM, FRANK. "God and No God in The Heart Is a Lonely Hunt-
     er," SAQ, LVI (Autumn), 494-99.
        An ironic religious allegory reinforces the theme of
     loneliness in The Heart Is a Lonely Hunter, emphasizing
     the alienation of men from one another and from God. Jake
     Blount, Dr. Copeland, Biff Brannon, and Mick Kelly find
     their god-image in Singer, who, in turn, finds his god-
     image in Antonapoulas.

1957

10   GIBBS, WALCOTT. Review of The Square Root of Wonderful, NY,
         XXXIII (9 November), 103–05.
         The Square Root of Wonderful is compounded of trite
      characters, an inane situation, and cinema-style dialogue;
      thus, it collapses helplessly into absurdity.

11   HART, JANE. "Carson McCullers, Pilgrim of Loneliness," GaR,
         XI (Spring), 53–58.
         McCullers transcends the Gothic school of Southern writ-
      ers in that her abnormal figures are functional, repre-
      senting the loneliest of all men. Indeed, the theme of
      loneliness is central to McCullers' work, dominating both
      characterization and imagery, and the comparatively normal
      Mick Kelly and Frankie Addams are as afflicted with lone-
      liness as Singer and Miss Amelia. McCullers sees love as
      benefiting the beloved not at all and the lover only
      briefly.

12   HAYES, RICHARD. "Private Worlds," Commonweal, LXVII
         (13 December), 288–99.
         The Square Root of Wonderful is a thematically confused
      play, issuing from a genuine, if diffuse, sensibility.
      Its surface is unsuccessful, but its depths are profound,
      and one suspects that it does not succeed in the way that
      McCullers intended.

13   KERR, WALTER. Review of The Square Root of Wonderful, New
         York Herald Tribune (31 October), p. 22.
         The Square Root of Wonderful is a confusing and confused
      play: comedy continually punctures its seriousness, and
      McCullers seems unable to mesh the two in any meaningful
      way.
         Reprinted in New York Theatre Critics' Reviews (1958.B4).

14   LEWIS, THEOPHILUS. Review of The Square Root of Wonderful,
         America, XCVIII (31 November), 299.
         The Square Root of Wonderful is an odd play: its sec-
      ondary characters are more interesting than its principals.

15   McCLAIN, JOHN. "Diffuse Doubletalk Adds Up to Big 0," New
         York Journal American (31 October), p. 22.
         The plot of The Square Root of Wonderful is implausible,
      its characters are grotesque, and the play as a whole is
      as pretentious and precious as its title.
         Reprinted in New York Theatre Critics' Reviews (1958.B4).

*16 RANTAVAARA, IRMA. "Yksinäinen Sydän," Parnasso (Helsinki),
VII (1957), 341-45.
Cited in MHRA Annual Bibliography of English Language
and Literature, XXXIII (1957-58), p. 542.

17 TREWIN, J. C. "One of the Party," Illustrated London News,
CCXXX (16 February), 276.
Although it is a striking mood-piece, the dramatic version of The Member of the Wedding is less compelling than
the novel version. Some of the novel's greatest scenes
are clumsy on the stage.

18 WATTS, RICHARD. "The New Carson McCullers Play," New York
Post (31 October), p. 30.
McCullers has still a wonderfully fresh perception of
character, but The Square Root of Wonderful is only inter-
mittently effective. McCullers seems never to have made
up her mind about the female lead, and the play is too often out of focus.
Reprinted in New York Theatre Critics' Reviews (1958.B4).

19 WORSLEY, T. C. "Growing Up," New Statesman, LIII (16 February), 201-02.
The Member of the Wedding is a dramatic "mess" with its
stagnant two acts and furious third act. Its success
seems to be founded on a happy recollection of the novel.

1958 A   BOOKS - NONE

1958 B   SHORTER WRITINGS

1 ANON. Review of The Square Root of Wonderful, Theatre Arts,
XLII (January), 24.
The Square Root of Wonderful has some honesty and depth,
but its characters are uninspired and the style is coarse.
It is difficult to believe that The Member of the Wedding
was written by the same author.

2 BALDANZA, FRANK. "Plato in Dixie," GaR, XII (Summer), 151-67.
The stories and novels of McCullers and Truman Capote
are Platonic in spirit. McCullers seems preoccupied with
Plato's distinction between physical and spiritual love,
and, while concerning herself almost entirely with spiritual love, she seems to be convinced that it is self-
wasting. "A Tree. A Rock. A Cloud" recalls both Plato's
notion of the orderly stages of love and his allegory of
the cave. The Heart Is a Lonely Hunter recalls many

1958

(BALDANZA, FRANK)
Platonic dialogues in its blend of erotic and epistemological needs. The Member of the Wedding echoes the Symposium, and Reflections in a Golden Eye and "The Ballad of the Sad Café" both echo the Phaedrus.

3   CLURMAN, HAROLD. "Carson McCullers," in Lies Like Truth: Theatre Reviews and Essays. New York: Macmillan, pp. 62–64.
The Member of the Wedding succeeded as a play because it was a play to begin with, the action springing from Frankie Addams' desire "to become connected." All of the other characters have similar desires, some of them mature, some unconscious, some stumbling, and some violent.

4   COFFIN, RACHEL W., ed. New York Theatre Critics' Reviews: 1957. Vol. XVIII. New York: Critics Theatre Reviews, pp. 199–202.
Reviews reprinted from New York World Telegram (1957.B2), New York Times (1957.B3), New York Daily News (1957.B5), New York Daily Mirror (1957.B7), New York Herald Tribune (1957.B13), New York Journal American (1957.B15), and New York Post (1957.B18).

5   COWLEY, MALCOLM, ed. Writers at Work. First Series. New York: Viking, pp. 279, 293, 296.
William Styron and Truman Capote state their admiration of McCullers' work.

6   FREEDLEY, GEORGE. Review of The Square Root of Wonderful, LJ, LXXXIII (1 June), 1800.
Although The Square Root of Wonderful was a failure in production, it is attractively written and should be a favorite with community theatre groups.

7   McCORD, BERT. "State Department Invites 6 to Visit Russia as Part of Cultural Exchange Plan," New York Herald Tribune (17 July), p. 12.
McCullers has accepted an invitation to visit Russia in the Fall of 1958 as part of the Cultural Exchange Program.

8   MAGILL, FRANK N., ed. "McCullers, Carson," in Cyclopedia of World Authors. New York: Harper, pp. 680–82.
Survey of McCullers' life, works, reputation, and themes.

9   SCOTT, NATHAN A., JR. <u>Modern Literature and the Religious</u>
       <u>Frontier</u>. New York: Harper, pp. 94, 96, 102.
         McCullers' work is part of the new personalism in our
       literature, but it tends to focus the chaos rather than
       the harmony of existence.

10   TINKHAM, CHARLES B. "The Members of the Side Show," <u>Phylon</u>,
       XVIII (October), 383-90.
         <u>The Member of the Wedding</u> deals eloquently with the very
       real problems of loneliness and its compensations.

11   WYATT, EUPHEMIA VAN RENSSELAER. Review of <u>The Square Root of</u>
       <u>Wonderful</u>, <u>CathW</u>, CLXXXVI (January), 306.
         <u>The Square Root of Wonderful</u> lacks the tenderness and
       understanding of <u>The Member of the Wedding</u>, and it is per-
       sistently indelicate.

1959 A   BOOKS - NONE

1959 B   SHORTER WRITINGS

1   ALVAREZ, A. "Circling the Squares," <u>London Observer</u>
       (15 March), p. 23.
         The theatre leaves little room for McCullers' verbal
       music, and <u>The Square Root of Wonderful</u>, with its stock
       situation, fey characters, and cute chatter, illustrates
       that her best medium is formal prose and that her best
       genre is the <u>nouvelle</u>.

2   ANON. Review of <u>The Square Root of Wonderful</u>, <u>TLS</u>
       (27 February), p. 110.
         <u>The Square Root of Wonderful</u> is a successful piece of
       sentimental stagecraft, but it is lacking as an emotional
       experience. Its tension is dissipated by the author's
       too-evident hand.

3   BROOKS, CLEANTH, and ROBERT PENN WARREN. <u>Understanding Fic-</u>
       <u>tion</u>. 2nd ed. New York: Appleton-Century-Crofts,
       pp. 270-71.
         The special quality of "A Domestic Dilemma" consists in
       its revelation of the range of feelings in so ordinary a
       man as Martin Meadows.

4   HASSAN, IHAB. "Carson McCullers: The Alchemy of Love and
       Aesthetics of Pain," <u>MFS</u>, V (Winter), 311-26.
         Some of McCullers' critics have dismissed her fiction as
       simply Gothic, but, if McCullers is no Faulkner, her mode

1959

(HASSAN, IHAB)
of Gothicism includes all the vital elements in the Southern tradition. The Protestantism and subjectivism of the
Gothic is particularly clear in McCullers' work, but
McCullers knows their inadequacy, and the tension between
the self and the world in her novels corresponds formally
to the tension between love and pain in her vision.
Partially reprinted in A Library of Literary Criticism
(1969.B2). Reprinted in slightly revised form in Radical
Innocence (1961.B28) and in Recent American Fiction: Some
Critical Views (1963.B6). Material reworked in EJ
(1962.B9) and reprinted in Recent American Fiction: Some
Critical Views (1963.B7) and in On Contemporary Literature (1964.B9), and reworked again in Literary History of
the United States (1963.B8).

5   _____. "The Victim: Images of Evil in Recent American Fiction," CE, XXI (December), 140-46.
    Seeing a religious significance in victimhood, McCullers
takes up where Tennessee Williams leaves off. Indeed, her
notion of love is practically a Christian definition of
evil.

6   McPHERSON, HUGO. "Carson McCullers: Lonely Huntress," TamR,
XI (Spring), 28-40.
    McCullers has always seen love as the only experience
which gives meaning to life. Reflections in a Golden Eye
is her masterpiece: concerned with the question of whether
or not any human being can be denied the right to live
fully, it ends with a tragic impasse and a disturbing picture of society. The Square Root of Wonderful was a disappointment, but its failure should not detract from
McCullers' other work, for she is a pre-eminent story-
teller, with a knack for the stripped-down story and effective dialogue.

7   STEWART, STANLEY. "Carson McCullers, 1940-1956: A Selected
Checklist," BB, XXII (January-April), 182-85.
    A partial listing of writing by and about McCullers be-
tween 1940 and 1956, exclusive of foreign language writings, and based almost entirely on standard bibliographical indices. The bibliography is divided into McCullers'
book publications (together with listings of contents),
McCullers' writings in periodicals, McCullers' writings in
anthologies, McCuller's poetry, writings about McCullers,
reviews of McCullers' books, and review of McCullers'
plays. A few items are annotated with regard to bibliographical difficulties.

8   WASSERSTROM, WILLIAM. <u>Heiress of All the Ages: Sex and Sen-
     timent in the Genteel Tradition</u>. Minneapolis: University
     of Minnesota Press, p. 103.
         McCullers' women are grotesques "to whom love is a bond-
     age of the spirit which distorts the flesh, at once the
     source of hope and the exact condition of frustration."

<u>1960 A BOOKS - NONE</u>

<u>1960 B SHORTER WRITINGS</u>

1   DUSENBURY, WINIFRED L. <u>The Theme of Loneliness in Modern
     American Drama</u>. Gainesville: University of Florida
     Press, pp. 57-67.
         McCullers allows her theme of loneliness to dictate an
     unconventional dramatic form in <u>The Member of the Wedding</u>.
     A flowing, conversational style and desultory, irrelevant
     dialogue in the first two acts is appropriate to the at-
     tempt of her characters to communicate with one another,
     and the action-filled third act emphasizes the relativity
     of time and the isolation of human beings. The play suc-
     ceeds well in production.

2   FIEDLER, LESLIE A. <u>Love and Death in the American Novel</u>.
     New York: Stein and Day, pp. 126, 325, 449-51, 453.
         <u>The Heart Is a Lonely Hunter</u> is, in one sense, a Depres-
     sion novel--the last of the "proletarian novels"--but it
     is wholly convincing and quite awesome in its contempla-
     tion of the failure of love. The novel is homosexual in
     attitude, but it is neither stereotypical nor sentimental.

3   TAYLOR, HORACE. "<u>The Heart Is a Lonely Hunter</u>: A Southern
     Waste Land," in <u>Studies in American Literature</u>, edited by
     Waldo McNeir and Leo B. Levy. Baton Rouge: Louisiana
     State University Press, pp. 154-60.
         <u>The Heart Is a Lonely Hunter</u> deals poignantly with the
     spiritual isolation and loneliness of man. Each of the
     characters is a solipsist, either living a routine, empty
     existence, or asserting himself through anti-social ges-
     tures of whose psychological origin he is ignorant. The
     ultimate problem of both the individuals and society is
     an absence of religious faith.

4   VICKERY, JOHN B. "Carson McCullers: A Map of Love," <u>WSCL</u>,
     I (Winter), 13-24.
         McCullers is primarily interested in the drama within
     the soul of the lover who discovers his ultimate isolation

1960

(VICKERY, JOHN B.)
in trying to communicate with his beloved. "The Ballad of the Sad Café" illumines this drama most clearly in its study of "love as romance." The Heart Is a Lonely Hunter studies "love as understanding," while Reflections in a Golden Eye studies the disasters and horrors of thwarted sexual love, and The Member of the Wedding studies the search for love within the family. McCullers' characters recognize the inviolability of the individual only gradually, and that constitutes wisdom for them.

1961 A BOOKS - NONE

1961 B SHORTER WRITINGS

1   ANON. Review of Clock Without Hands, Bookmark, XX (July), 233.
     Clock Without Hands is a powerful and original novel dealing with conscience and the need for faith in man's dignity.

2   ANON. Review of Clock Without Hands, Booklist and Subscription Books Bulletin, LVIII (1 September), 23.
     Clock Without Hands is a strong novel, if not so compelling as McCullers' earlier work. It gives force and meaning to individual lives and relationships by discovering in them the love, loneliness, and tragedy of human existence.

3   ANON. "Carson McCullers," New York Times Book Review (17 September), p. 5.
     Brief sketch of McCullers' career.

4   ANON. "Novelist, Short Story Writer, and Playwright," New York Herald Tribune Books (17 September), sec. vi, p. 5.
     Biographical and personality sketch.

5   ANON. "Call on the Author," Newsweek, LVIII (18 September), 106.
     [Interview.] Brief account of McCullers' life in Nyack: her physical condition, her taking in boarders, her attempt to write something every day.

6   ANON. "Lonely Hunter Hearts," <u>Newsweek</u>, LVIII (18 September), 106.

> <u>Clock Without Hands</u> is loosely constructed but its characters are vividly real. McCullers' talent and humanity manage to transcend her unfortunate preoccupation with freaks.

7   ANON. "The Member of the Funeral," <u>Time</u>, LXXVIII (22 September), 118, 120.

> All Southern writers are obsessed with violation; McCullers' interest is the violation of innocence. <u>Clock Without Hands</u> has no direction or point, and the motivations of its characters are confused and inept.

8   ANON. "From Life into Death," <u>TLS</u> (20 October), p. 749.

> <u>Clock Without Hands</u> is a fine, moving book, worthy of McCullers' reputation. Its characterizations, dialogue, and claustrophobic atmosphere are all well developed, and McCullers manages to treat the racial situation without melodrama or exaggeration.

9   ANON. "Free from the Fetters of Dogma," London <u>Times Weekly Review</u> (26 October), p. 10.

> <u>Clock Without Hands</u> is essentially a novel of character and in particular a study of aggressive and tragic old age. A tireless imagination always distinguishes McCullers' work.

10   BALAKIAN, NONA. "Carson McCullers Completes New Novel Despite Adversity," <u>New York Times</u> (3 September), p. 46.

> Announcement of the publication of <u>Clock Without Hands</u>, together with brief personality and biographical sketches.

11   BALLIETT, WHITNEY. Review of <u>Clock Without Hands</u>, <u>NY</u>, XXXVII (23 September), 179.

> <u>Clock Without Hands</u> is tiresomely familiar, resolutely grotesque, and insistently symbolic. McCullers' prose "gives the peculiar impression of having been slept in."

12   BLACKSHEAR, ORRELLA. Review of <u>Clock Without Hands</u>, <u>Wisconsin Library Bulletin</u>, LVII (September), 306-07.

> <u>Clock Without Hands</u> portrays the racial situation in the South skillfully; it is certain to be one of the year's outstanding novels.

13 BOWEN, ROBERT O. Review of Clock Without Hands, CathW, CXCIV (December), 186.
    Clock Without Hands is pitiful, formulistic Gothic, far below the level of Faulkner's achievement. The style is tasteless, and the narrative is shallow. With its "pseudo-liberalistic bent, its unviable homosexuality, and its shocking vocabulary," the novel is a "comic book for the intellectual delinquent."

14 BRADBURY, MALCOLM. Review of Clock Without Hands, Punch (8 November), p. 696.
    Clock Without Hands is a substantial book that begins well. It slips into sentimentality in short order, however, and it presents a confused picture of Sherman Pew.

15 BUCKMASTER, HENRIETTA. "The Break-Through and the Pattern," Christian Science Monitor (21 September), p. C7.
    Clock Without Hands represents the dead-end of Faulknerian sentimentality. Its spiritually feckless characters are tiresome in their lack of maturity, and the novel might be described as a minstrel show with a tragic theme.

16 BUTCHER, FANNIE. "Georgia Ways, Caricatured from Life," Chicago Sunday Tribune Magazine of Books (17 September), p. 3.
    Although Clock Without Hands offers no solutions for the race problem and for the agonies of soul that it depicts, it is a skillful, compassionate novel and sometimes a comic one. McCullers is clearly a writer's writer with a deft hand for caricature and a quick eye for truth.

17 DE MOTT, BENJAMIN. "Fiction Chronicle," HudR, XIV (Winter), 625-26.
    Unlike McCullers' earlier work, Clock Without Hands seems hastily put together. There is a curious lack of sensation and of solid specification in the book, attributable, perhaps, to McCullers' trying to write both a narrative and a dramatic version of the story simultaneously.

18 EVANS, OLIVER. "The Theme of Spiritual Isolation in Carson McCullers," in South: Modern Southern Literature in Its Cultural Setting, edited by Louis D. Rubin and Robert D. Jacobs. Garden City, N. Y.: Doubleday, pp. 333-48.
    Reprinted in slightly revised form from New World Writing: First Mentor Selection (1952.B2).

19   FALK, SIGNI LENEA. Tennessee Williams. TUSAS. New York:
        Twayne, pp. 24-27.
            McCullers returns again and again to the same material,
        as if trying to explain to herself the meaning of her
        myth. She is intrigued by contrasts, by colors, by
        images, by the simple and the vaguely significant, by the
        realistic and the symbolic. Like Williams, she creates
        her own world of lost souls.

20   FULLER, JOHN. Review of Clock Without Hands, The Listener
        (London), LXVI (9 November), 783.
            Clock Without Hands is a very good novel which struggles
        to suppress the very bad roman à thèse which it might have
        been. The plan and meaning of the novel are not realized
        with complete success, but the dialogue and characteriza-
        tions are adequate compensation.

21   GODDEN, RUMER. "Death and Life in a Small Southern Town,"
        New York Herald Tribune Books (17 September), sec. vi,
        p. 5.
            Clock Without Hands upholds McCullers' prestigious repu-
        tation. It is a marvelous book, rich, powerful, and dig-
        nified. In keeping with McCullers' especial talent, it
        tells the unvarnished truth. Malone is the book's great-
        est achievement.

22   GOLD, HERBERT, and DONALD L. STEVENSON, eds. Stories of Mod-
        ern America. New York: St. Martin's, pp. 194, 203.
            The unresolved dilemma of "A Domestic Dilemma" suggests
        that the institution of marriage is itself in trouble.

23   GOSSETT, LOUISE YOUNG. "Violence in Recent Southern Fic-
        tion." Ph.D. dissertation, Duke University.
            McCullers' theme of loneliness and the violence that
        springs from loneliness is an important theme among young-
        er writers.

24   GRIFFIN, LLOYD W. Review of Clock Without Hands, LJ, LXXXVI
        (August), 2682.
            Clock Without Hands is a thoughtful and intermittently
        brilliant study of changing attitudes in the South.

25   GROSS, JOHN. Review of Clock Without Hands, New Statesman,
        LXII (27 October), 614.
            Clock Without Hands has much to recommend it, but it is
        McCullers' weakest work: the writing is slack, the sym-
        bolism is too obvious, and the climax is inept.

1961

26 GRUMBACH, DORIS. Review of Clock Without Hands, America, CV
    (23 September), 809.
        Clock Without Hands has no distinction except the name
    of its author. It is filled with clichés, it is written
    in a forced style, and it deals meretriciously with the
    race struggle.

27 HARTT, J. N. "The Return of Moral Passion," YR, LI n.s.
    (December), 300-01.
        Clock Without Hands is developed mechanically, it is
    stocked with familiar characters, and it is confused
    philosophically. One cannot even be sure that the moral
    achievements of Malone and Jester are not simply by-
    products of disease.

28 HASSAN, IHAB. "Carson McCullers: The Alchemy of Love and
    Aesthetics of Pain," in Radical Innocence: The Contempo-
    rary American Novel. Princeton, Princeton University
    Press, pp. 205-29.
        Reprinted in slightly revised form from MFS (1959.B4).

29 HICKS, GRANVILLE. "The Subtler Corruptions," SatR, XLIV
    (23 September), 14-15.
        Nothing McCullers has written is quite so fine as her
    first novel, but everything she has written is good and
    Clock Without Hands is no exception. McCullers writes
    perceptively, if somewhat contrivedly, about the race prob-
    lem, and she writes familiarly about the problems of love
    and adolescence.

30 HOGAN, WILLIAM. "The Georgia Scene by Carson McCullers," San
    Francisco Chronicle (18 September), p. 39.
        Clock Without Hands is angrier and more complex than
    McCullers' earlier fiction, and also more uneven and more
    confused. Many of the individual scenes are handled
    beautifully, but as a whole the novel is not successful.

31 HOWE, IRVING. "In the Shadow of Death," New York Times Book
    Review (17 September), p. 5.
        Clock Without Hands is more robust, realistic, and con-
    ventional than McCullers' earlier work, but it is also
    less successful: the social realism of the Malone sec-
    tions never meshes with the Clane-Pew sections; the sym-
    bolic scheme lacks conviction; and the writing is
    lethargic.

1961

32   HUGHES, CATHERINE. "A World of Outcasts," Commonweal, LXXV
     (13 October), 73–75.
         All of McCullers' novels have been disappointing, if
     successful, for her characters are always stopped short of
     their final destinies and their careers are too often
     truncated arbitrarily by death. Clock Without Hands dis-
     appoints on a more elementary level, however, for its two
     plots never really mesh and its sub-plot looms too large.
     Partially reprinted in A Library of Literary Criticism
     (1969.B2).

33   HUTCHENS, JOHN K. Review of Clock Without Hands, New York
     Herald Tribune (18 September), p. 21.
         Clock Without Hands is an uneven book, full of dazzling
     but unrelated patches, and wandering uncontrolledly be-
     tween realism and fantasy. McCullers had led her readers
     to expect finer work.

34   JACKSON, KATHERINE GAUSS. Review of Clock Without Hands,
     Harper's Magazine, CCXXIII (October), 111–12.
         Clock Without Hands is slow-moving but tightly organized.
     Its subject is response and responsibility.

35   McCARTHY, MARY. On the Contrary. New York: Farrar, Straus,
     and Cudahy, pp. 184–85.
         Her lack of manner, her "leukemia of treatment," and her
     preoccupation with pathology place McCullers in the deca-
     dent school of American writing.

36   McCONKEY, JAMES. Review of Clock Without Hands, Epoch, XI
     (Fall), 197–98.
         Clock Without Hands is resolutely affirmative about
     life, and the source of that affirmation is undoubtedly
     in McCullers' very serious illness. Nonetheless, McCul-
     lers' novels about separation and isolation are more con-
     vincingly universal than the uneven and optimistic vision
     of her latest book.

37   MARTIN, JEAN. Review of Clock Without Hands, Nation, CXCIII
     (18 November), 411–12.
         McCullers chisels her story in Clock Without Hands until
     only the most pertinent things are left, and her eschewal
     of allegory is an important step forward for her. Sur-
     prisingly, McCullers has been able to grow as a novelist
     despite the albatross of early success.

1961

38   MILLER, JORDAN Y. _American Dramatic Literature: Ten Modern_
        Plays in Historical Perspective. New York: McGraw-Hill,
        pp. 426-28.
           Because McCullers treats traumatic events casually, _The_
        Member of the Wedding is a "comedy of sensibility." The
        comic element is important to prevent undue sentimentality
        that threatens the play. (A biographical sketch is
        appended.)

*39   MIZUTA, J. "Carson McCullers' _The Heart Is a Lonely Hunter_,"
        Rikkyo Review, XXII (1961), 79-95.
           Cited in _BB_ (1964.B9).

40   MORTIMER, PENELOPE. "Southern Justice," _Time and Tide_ (Lon-
        don), XLII (19 October), 1757.
           Although _Clock Without Hands_ is not the masterpiece that
        The Member of the Wedding was, it is a very good novel,
        exciting our pity, joy, and indignation.

41   O'BRIEN, EDNA. "The Strange World of Carson McCullers," _Books_
        and Bookmen, VII (October), 9, 24.
           McCullers is our "best living woman writer." In _Clock_
        Without Hands, a sad and worthy book, she deals once again
        with the "dark and melancholy struggle towards life and
        freedom."

42   PARKER, DOROTHY. "_Clock Without Hands_ Belongs in Yesterday's
        Tower of Ivory," _Esquire_, LVI (December), 72-73.
           Clock Without Hands' stock characters and tired points
        are a disappointment. McCullers seems to have left her
        intensely private world only to enter the public world of
        ten years ago.

43   PRESCOTT, ORVILLE. "Books of the Times," _New York Times_
        (18 September), p. 27.
           Clock Without Hands has attracted a great deal of inter-
        est, but it is unsuccessful as a novel. Improbable dia-
        logue and situations abound in it, its satirical jibes are
        ineffective, and its prose style is generally flat and
        pedestrian.

44   QUIGLY, ISABEL. Review of _Clock Without Hands_, Manchester
        Guardian (20 October), p. 7.
           If McCullers is not the foremost contemporary American
        novelist, she is certainly the most attractive; _Clock_
        Without Hands is a vivid, engrossing, and engaging novel.

45 RAVEN, SIMON. "Two Kinds of Jungle," Spectator (20 October),
    p. 551.
       Clock Without Hands can be read on any level from the
    anecdotal to the tragic.

46 ROLO, CHARLES. "A Southern Drama," Atlantic, CCVIII (October),
    126-27.
       Clock Without Hands is a masterly novel that deals not
    only with McCullers' usual themes of loneliness and flawed
    love, but also, as McCullers has pointed out, with "re-
    sponse and responsibility." The characterizations of
    Judge Clane and Sherman Pew are magnificent, and the gen-
    eral craftsmanship is sure. Gothic elements and devices
    are less evident than in previous novels.

47 SULLIVAN, WALTER. Review of Clock Without Hands, GaR, XV
    (Winter), 467-69.
       Clock Without Hands is distressingly contrived: its
    characters are either wooden or straw, and their motiva-
    tion is unbelievable. The novel starts well, but it de-
    clines rapidly.

48 TISCHLER, NANCY M. Tennessee Williams: Rebellious Puritan.
    New York: Citadel, pp. 134-35, 166.
       Account of the friendship between McCullers and Tennes-
    see Williams.

49 TRACY, HONOR. "A Voice Crying in the South," New Republic,
    CXLV (13 November), 16-17.
       Clock Without Hands has many brilliant scenes, but it is
    also commonplace and euphoric on occasion, and it has se-
    rious weaknesses of structure and conception. The racial
    theme fails to inspire McCullers' usual powers of
    imagination.

50 TYNAN, KENNETH. Curtains. London: Longmans, Green, p. 70.
       By Tennessee Williams' own statement, McCullers helped
    him to overcome his imaginary sense of dying in the sum-
    mer of 1946.

51 VIDAL, GORE. "The World Outside," New York Reporter, XXV
    (28 September), 50, 52.
       McCullers is probably the greatest and most lasting of
    the Southern writers, her prose having managed to escape
    the gaseous influence of Faulkner and Wolfe. In Clock
    Without Hands she leaves her private world for the first
    time to embrace a public world that is uncongenial to
    her, and this causes a marvelous novel very nearly to fail.

1961

(VIDAL, GORE)
Reprinted in Rocking the Boat (1962.B15) and partially
reprinted in A Library of Literary Criticism (1969.B2).

52   WALKER, GERALD. "Carson McCullers: Still the Lonely Hunter,"
Cosmopolitan, CLI (November), 26-27.
Clock Without Hands is "an imaginative, tragicomic fan-
tasy about race relations in Dixie" and marks McCullers'
return to an involvement with large social issues. A new
preoccupation with sickness and health has an obvious
basis in McCullers' illness.

53   WILLIAMS, TENNESSEE. "The Author," SatR, XLIV (23 September),
14-15.
Personality sketch of McCullers, describing the friend-
ship between Williams and McCullers and emphasizing her
compassion and physical courage.

1962 A   BOOKS - NONE

1962 B   SHORTER WRITINGS

1   ANON. "McCullers, Carson." Lexikon der Weltliteratur im
20. Jahrhundert. Vol. 2, 3rd ed. Freiburg: Herder, 414.
Brief identification of McCullers and of her novels.
Enlarged, updated, and translated in Encyclopedia of
World Literature in the Twentieth Century (1967.B6).

2   ANON. Review of Clock Without Hands, VQR, XXXVIII (Winter),
viii.
Clock Without Hands is written at McCullers' usual high
level. Its humor is rich, and its pathos is controlled.

3   ANTONINI, GIACOMO. "Ossessione nella McCullers," Fiera Lette-
raria, XVII (22 April), 5.
McCullers' writings indulge freely in the bizarre and
even the horrible, but her effect is always pure and po-
etical. A kind of magic transforms the raw material, giv-
ing it a symbolic resonance unaccounted for by plot, protagonist, or style. Clock Without Hands is in this
tradition.

4   EMERSON, DONALD. "The Ambiguities of Clock Without Hands,"
WSCL, III (Fall), 15-28.
Clock Without Hands incorporates all of McCullers' best
qualities, but, failing to fuse the private and the symbolic, and failing adequately to tighten and focus the

(EMERSON, DONALD)

structure, it fails to achieve the distinction of her best work. Malone is not adequate as a symbol of the Southern conscience; Judge Clane is not adequate as the Old South; and Jester Clane is not adequate as a "man of good will." Similarly, the relationship between Jester and Sherman Pew has no real social signification. Clock Without Hands is richest in the context of McCullers' other work, for it does sharpen the contrasts with which she has always worked.

5   EVANS, OLIVER. "The Achievement of Carson McCullers," EJ, LI (May), 301-08.

Academic critics tend to be hard on McCullers's work, while fellow writers tend to be enthusiastic about it; this suggests both that McCullers tells us unflattering truths about ourselves and that she is a "writer's writer" with a very special sensibility. Her work is primarily allegorical, and she is probably our finest allegorist since Hawthorne and Melville. "The Ballad of the Sad Café" is her best work, although The Member of the Wedding is an extraordinary miracle of characterization. Reprinted in slightly revised form as part of Carson McCullers: Her Life and Work (1965.A1).

6   FOLK, BARBARA NAUER. "The Sad Sweet Music of Carson McCullers," GaR, XVI (Summer), 202-09.

Musical allusions permeate McCullers' work, serving as architectural framework (as in "The Ballad of the Sad Café"), as extended correlative (as in "The Sojourner" and The Heart Is a Lonely Hunter), and as incidental symbols (as in Reflections in a Golden Eye, The Member of the Wedding, and The Heart Is a Lonely Hunter). McCullers' use of music is always intelligent and functional.

7   FORD, NICK AARON. "Search for Identity: A Critical Survey of Significant Belles-Lettres by and about Negroes Published in 1961," Phylon, XXIII (Summer), 128-38.

Clock Without Hands is the most significant novel about race relations published this year. Moral without being rhetorical, it uses both suspense and irony to raise serious questions about the relationship between the races.

8   HARDY, JOHN EDWARD. Commentaries on Five Modern Short Stories. Frankfurt: Diesterweg, p. 11-14.

"The Sojourner" centers on the theme of love as a defense against time and mortality. At the end, Ferris

1962

(HARDY, JOHN EDWARD)
   recognizes and accepts the facts of his age, exile, and
   lost family.
   Reprinted in The Modern Talent: An Anthology of Short
   Stories (1964.B8).

9   HASSAN, IHAB. "The Character of Post-War Fiction in America,"
     EJ, LI (January), 1-8.
       McCullers' work is similar to Capote's, Malamud's, Sal-
     inger's, and Hawkes' in its compact exploration of "tight-
     er and more nervous fictional forms," and her image of
     spiritual isolation in love is one of the most important
     of our time. In her capable hands, the Gothic novel
     acquired a firm, poetic language.
     A re-working in part of material in MFS (1959.B4). Re-
     printed in Recent American Fiction: Some Critical Views
     (1963.B7) and in On Contemporary Fiction (1964.B9), and in
     reworked form in Literary History of the United States
     (1963.B8).

10   HERZBERG, MAX J. "McCullers, Carson," in The Reader's Ency-
     clopedia of American Literature. New York: Crowell,
     pp. 672-73.
       Sketch of McCullers' career and works.

11   KAZIN, ALFRED. "The Alone Generation," in Contemporaries.
     Boston: Little, Brown, 207-16.
       McCullers' novels ask us only to understand, as so many
     modern novels tiresomely do. Society is wholly stagnant
     in The Heart Is a Lonely Hunter, and the loneliness of
     Frankie Addams is the undramatic heart of The Member of
     the Wedding. One sometimes longs for more energetic
     fiction.

12   MALIN, IRVING. New American Gothic. CMC. Carbondale:
     Southern Illinois University Press, pp. 21-26, 54-59,
     111-17, 133-39.
       McCullers' fiction is part of the "New American Gothic"
     in its concern, both in plot and in symbol, with narcis-
     sistic characters, with family situations frightening to
     one of the members, with journeys that represent attempts
     to escape, and with reflections that render the self a
     stranger.

13   MICHA, RENÉ. "Carson MacCullers[sic]ou la cabane de l'enfance,"
     Crit, XIV (August-September), 696-707.
        McCullers is a short story writer in the tradition of
     Hawthorne, Crane, and Melville rather than a novelist; her
     short work is her best, and The Member of the Wedding is
     really an elongated short story. Her reputation is not
     as high in France as it should be, despite the efforts of
     John Brown and others, for she merits classification with
     Farrell, Dos Passos, Faulkner, and Hemingway. Her great
     themes are autobiographical: childhood, love, and music.

14   O'CONNOR, WILLIAM VAN. The Grotesque: An American Genre and
     Other Essays. CMC. Carbondale: Southern Illinois Uni-
     versity Press, pp. 13, 21.
        The psychological motivations of McCullers' characters
     are almost always abnormal or perverse, but she asks us
     to understand them as "normal," if pathetic and shocking
     in a country that believes man is naturally innocent.

15   VIDAL, GORE. "Carson McCullers' Clock Without Hands," in
     Rocking the Boat. Boston: Little, Brown, pp. 178-83.
        Reprinted from Reporter (1961.B51).

16   _____. "Ladders to Heaven: Novelists and Critics of the
     1940's," in Rocking the Boat. Boston: Little, Brown,
     pp. 125-46.
        Reprinted in slightly revised form from New World Writ-
     ing (1953.B5) and reprinted in On Contemporary Literature
     (1964.B9).

17   WEALES, GERALD. American Drama Since World War II. New York:
     Harcourt, Brace, and World, pp. 154-81.
        Member of the Wedding is an unusually successful adapta-
     tion. The first two acts are effectively limited to the
     kitchen and might parody a symposium, but the third act is
     different in form and moves quickly and erratically. The
     most significant differences between the narrative and
     dramatic versions of the story involve Honey and the al-
     lusions to sex. Unlike The Member of the Wedding, The
     Square Root of Wonderful is a disastrous play.

1963

1963 B   SHORTER WRITINGS

1   ALBEE, EDWARD. "Carson McCullers--The Case of the Curious
        Magician," Harper's Bazaar, XCVI (January), 98.
          McCullers is a very talented and very wise writer who
        knows both the illusions and the realities of both art and
        life.

2   BRADBURY, JOHN M. Renaissance in the South: A Critical His-
        tory of the Literature, 1920-1960. Chapel Hill: Univer-
        sity of North Carolina Press, pp. 110-12.
          All of McCullers' work is concerned with "lonely hunt-
        ers." The Heart Is a Lonely Hunter and The Member of the
        Wedding view them realistically and sympathetically, while
        Reflections in a Golden Eye and "The Ballad of the Sad
        Café" view them symbolically and parabolically. Eros is
        always defective in her work.

3   DODD, WAYNE D. "The Development of Theme Through Symbol in
        the Novels of Carson McCullers," GaR, XVII (Summer),
        206-13.
          McCullers uses music, Godhead, children, and art works
        symbolically in order to develop her statements about iso-
        lation. The various attachments in her novels always re-
        sult from a need to preserve an individuality threatened
        by an aggressive lover.

4   EISINGER, CHESTER E. "Carson McCullers and the Failure of
        Dialogue," in Fiction of the Forties. Chicago: Univer-
        sity of Chicago Press, pp. 243-58.
          All of McCullers' works deal in a simple, primitivistic
        way with the problem of moral isolation, and the total
        failure of dialogue in her stories is its symptom. Char-
        acters such as Mick Kelly, Biff Brannon, Captain Pendelton
        and Frankie Addams are isolated not only from one another
        but also from parts of themselves; they are tortured by
        the antagonism of male and female principles within
        themselves.

5   HARTE, BARBARA, and CAROLINE RILEY. "Carson McCullers," in
        Contemporary Authors: A Bio-Bibliographical Guide to Cur-
        rent Authors and Their Work. Vol. V/VI. Detroit: Gale
        Research, pp. 754-56.
          Survey of McCullers' life, writings, and critical
        reputation.

1963

6 HASSAN, IHAB. "Carson McCullers: The Alchemy of Love and Aesthetics of Pain," in Recent American Fiction: Some Critical Views, edited by Joseph Waldmeir. Boston: Houghton Mifflin, pp. 215-30.
  Reprinted in slightly revised form from MFS (1959.B4).

7 ____. "The Character of Post-War Fiction in America," in Recent American Fiction: Some Critical Views, edited by Joseph J. Waldmeir. Boston: Houghton Mifflin, pp. 27-35.
  Reprinted from EJ (1962.B9).

8 ____. "Since 1945," in Literary History of the United States, edited by Robert Spiller, et al. 3rd ed. New York: Macmillan, pp. 1414, 1420, 1421, 1423, 1437.
  Material reworked from EJ (1962.B9).

9 HYMAN, STANLEY EDGAR. The Promised End: Essays and Reviews 1942-1962. Cleveland: World, pp. 345, 350.
  McCullers sees happiness as a sort of infantile regression in The Member of the Wedding. "Pre-existentialism" is absent from her work.

10 LUBBERS, KLAUS. "The Necessary Order: A Study of Theme and Structure in Carson McCullers' Fiction," JA, VIII (no. 8), 187-204.
  McCullers' novels move gradually from an interest in the freakish, the defeated, and the chaotic to an interest in the normal, the accepted, and the orderly. In The Heart Is a Lonely Hunter, order is imposed by an aesthetic principle of organization only; in Reflections in a Golden Eye, the theme of isolated love is only tentatively developed and is not really concluded; The Member of the Wedding develops a balanced world; "The Ballad of the Sad Café" uses narrative detachment to modify its morbidity; and Clock Without Hands depicts an orderly world.

11 SCHAEFER, TED. "The Man in the Gray Flannery McCullers-alls," SatR, XLVI (23 February), 6.
  A parody of several of McCullers' themes and characters.

12 SCHAEFFER, KRISTIANE. "Jeder starb, Keiner starb: Über Uhr ohne Zeiger' von McCullers," Monatshefte für Deutschen Unterricht, XV (February), 65-66, 68-69. Unlocatable.
  Cited in BB (1964.B9).

1963

13 SCHORER, MARK. "McCullers and Capote: Basic Patterns," in
The Creative Present: Notes on Contemporary American Fiction, edited by Nona Balakian and Charles Simmons. Garden
City, New York: Doubleday, pp. 83-107.
McCullers tries to achieve the "objective externality of
myth" by focusing on the subjectivity which is its oppo-
site. Except for Clock Without Hands, all of her work has
the same theme of love and loneliness and the same lyric
expansiveness which transcends social realities and ap-
proximates myth. Reflections in a Golden Eye is her least
successful work, and "The Ballad of the Sad Café" is her
most successful.
Reprinted in The World We Imagine (1968.B9).

1964 A BOOKS - NONE

1964 B SHORTER WRITINGS

1 ALLEN, WALTER. The Modern Novel in Britain and the United
States. New York: Dutton, pp. 132-37.
McCullers is the most remarkable Southern novelist after
Faulkner. The Heart Is a Lonely Hunter is the best intro-
duction to her work. It is a parable about human isola-
tion, told gravely and sadly in an artfully plain style.
Reflections in a Golden Eye is a lesser book, without an
adequate grounding in humanity. The Member of the Wedding
is a warmer and more human novel, but "The Ballad of the
Sad Café" is the most haunting of her work. Clock Without
Hands is McCullers' most traditional novel.

2 ANON. Review of Sweet as a Pickle, Clean as a Pig, LJ, LXXXIX
(15 December), 5009.
McCullers' poetry in Sweet as a Pickle, Clean as a Pig
is contrived and unappealing. The book is not recommended.

3 BEJA, MORRIS. "It Must Be Important: Negroes in Contemporary
American Fiction," AR, XXIV (Fall), 327.
McCullers treats the familiar theme of the Negro's
search for identity with both irony and pity in Clock
Without Hands. Sherman Pew is an adolescent Joe
Christmas.

4 EVANS, OLIVER. "The Case of Carson McCullers," GaR, XVIII
(Spring), 40-45.
Many critics have found McCullers' work distasteful,
while novelists, poets, and playwrights have almost invariably praised it. If McCullers is not widely appreci-

(EVANS, OLIVER)
ated, it is because readers do not like her ideas about love, because they do not appreciate that her characters are symbolically freakish rather than sensationally so, and because she has not clearly subordinated the realistic level of her work to the symbolic.
Reprinted in slightly revised form as part of Carson McCullers: Her Life and Work (1965.A1).

5 _____ . "The Pad in Brooklyn Heights," Nation, CXCIX (13 July), 15-16.
An account of the establishment at 7 Middagh St. in Brooklyn where McCullers lived with Louis MacNeice, Christopher Isherwood, Richard Wright, Paul Bowles, W. H. Auden, Benjamin Britten, Gypsy Rose Lee, and others.
Reprinted in slightly revised form as part of Carson McCullers: Her Life and Work (1965.A1).

6 FELHEIM, MARVIN. "Eudora Welty and Carson McCullers," in Contemporary American Novelists, edited by Harry T. Moore. CMC. Carbondale: Southern Illinois University Press, pp. 41-53.
Unlike Eudora Welty, McCullers seems never to have realized her potential as a novelist. Her central theme is the loneliness of love, and she is fond of grotesque characters and the necessity for violence. Her exact, economical, dramatic, and curiously dead-pan openings are characteristic of her style, and her favorite symbols are music and time. Her novels move typically from order to disorder; only in one of her novels are the tragic details resolved.
Partially reprinted in A Library of Literary Criticism (1969.B2).

7 GIBSON, WALKER. Review of Sweet as a Pickle, Clean as a Pig, New York Times Book Review, (1 November), sec. vii, part ii, p. 57.
Sweet as a Pickle, Clean as a Pig "may seem slight and disappointing from so distinguished a pen."

8 HARDY, JOHN EDWARD. The Modern Talent: An Anthology of Short Stories. New York: Holt, Rinehart, and Winston, pp. 436-39, 497.
Reprinted from Commentaries on Five Modern Short Stories (1962.B8).

1964

9 KOSTELANETZ, RICHARD, ed. On Contemporary Literature. New
   York: Avon, pp. 29-35, 36-47, 48-63.
       Essays reprinted from EJ (1962.B9) and Rocking the Boat
   (1962.B16) and a partial reprint from The Theatre in Our
   Times (1954.B3).

10 PEDEN, WILLIAM. The American Short Story. Boston: Houghton
   Mifflin, pp. 89, 90, 126-27, 190, 197.
       "The Ballad of the Sad Café" illumines McCullers' inter-
   est in the grotesque, the loveless, and the lonely. Like
   Truman Capote and I. B. Singer, she contrasts the real and
   the ideal.

11 PHILLIPS, ROBERT S. "Carson McCullers: 1956-1964, A Selected
   Checklist," BB, XXIV (September-December), 113-16.
       A bibliography of new and previously unlisted writings
   by and about McCullers between 1956 and 1964 and updating
   Stewart's 1959 checklist (1959.B7). The bibliography is
   divided into McCullers' new writings, McCullers' record-
   ings, studies and critical comments on McCullers' work,
   book reviews omitted in the Stewart bibliography, reviews
   of Clock Without Hands, reviews of the stage version of
   "The Ballad of the Sad Café," parodies of McCullers, and
   biographical sketches.

12 _____. "Dinesen's 'Monkey' and McCullers' 'Ballad': A Study
   in Literary Affinity," SSF, I (Spring), 184-90.
       Dinesen's "The Monkey" has many affinities with McCul-
   lers' "The Ballad of the Sad Café" and seems to have been
   an influence upon it. The worlds, characters, themes, and
   denouements of the two works are markedly similar, and
   both stories evoke a world of ancient fairy tale and myth.

13 _____. "The Gothic Architecture of The Member of the Wedding,"
   Renascence, XVI (Winter), 59-72.
       The new Gothic novels are concerned with spiritual iso-
   lation, with the failure of love, with mental tortures,
   and with violent deaths. McCullers' five novels are all
   written in the Gothic mode, and Member of the Wedding il-
   lustrates the mode well, inasmuch as Frankie Addams is the
   typically frail Gothic heroine in a moribund settting, afflicted with dark dreams and death scenes, and touched by
   fear of Catholicism and the supernatural.

14 SMITH, SIMEON MOZART, JR. "Carson McCullers: A Critical
   Introduction." Ph.D. dissertation, University of Pennsylvania.

(SMITH, SIMEON MOZART, JR.)
McCullers tries to portray the universal experience of overcoming solitude; the value of her fiction inheres both in the honesty with which she accomplishes this and in the technical brilliance which she brings to its execution.

15 WITHAM, W. TASKER. The Adolescent in the American Novel: 1920-1960. New York: Ungar, pp. 16, 19, 25, 42, 59, 60, 61, 80, 98, 145-46, 169, 197, 265, 268, 270, 275.
McCullers was one of the first to write frankly about the sexual problems of teenage girls. Her heroines are critical of their environments and typically rebel against them.

1965 A BOOKS

1 EVANS, OLIVER. Carson McCullers: Her Life and Work. London: Peter Owen.
Evans traces the development of McCullers' life and work, stressing the biographical elements that influence the work and which provided McCullers with forms, characters, situations, and symbols. All of the major work is analyzed in detail, and critical reactions are summarized. McCullers' outline of "The Mute" is appended. Parts reprinted in slightly revised form from EJ (1962.B5), GaR, (1964.B4), Nation (1964.B5), and GaR (1965.B7). Reprinted in America as The Ballad of Carson McCullers (1966.A1).

1965 B SHORTER WRITINGS

1 ANON. "McCullers, Carson." Oxford Companion to American Literature, edited by James D. Hart. 4th ed. New York: Oxford, p. 506.
Listing and brief description of McCullers' work.

2 ANON. Review of Sweet as a Pickle, Clean as a Pig, TLS (9 December), p. 1141.
Sweet as a Pickle, Clean as a Pig is distinguished primarily by its author's name, but a few poems are pleasing.

3 ANON. "McCullers Honored," New York Times (18 December), p. 27.
McCullers has been awarded the "Prize of the Younger Generation" by the German newspaper Die Welt for The Heart Is a Lonely Hunter.

1965

4   AUCHINCLOSS, LOUIS. Pioneers and Caretakers: A Study of Nine
    American Women Novelists. Minneapolis: University of
    Minnesota Press, pp. 161-69.
        In The Heart Is a Lonely Hunter McCullers embraced all
    of the themes she was to deal with in her career--partic-
    ularly the themes of loneliness, freakishness, and flawed
    love. Reflections in a Golden-Eye is a more controlled
    book than Heart, but The Member of the Wedding and "The
    Ballad of the Sad Café" are the peak of her achievement
    and superior in plotting to all other novellas written in
    America. Clock Without Hands is something of a throwback
    to McCullers' first book and has not the brilliant writing
    of the later volumes.
        Partially reprinted in A Library of Literary Criticism
    (1969.B2).

5   BRUSTEIN, ROBERT. "The Playwright as Impersonator," in Sea-
    sons of Discontent: Dramatic Opinions 1959-1965. New
    York: Simon and Schuster, pp. 155-58.
        McCullers' "The Ballad of the Sad Café" is partially re-
    deemed by its "suggestive" style and its "penumbral" at-
    mosphere, but Albee's adaptation for the stage is wholly
    without merit.

6   DOMMERGUES, PIERRE. "L'ambiguité de l'innocence," Les langues
    modernes, LIX (March-April), 182-85.
        A school of American writers (McCullers, Capote, Wil-
    liams, and Styron) tends to view innocence tragically.
    Innocence is the only protection their characters have
    against reality, but their loneliness causes them to probe
    reality in search of another, and experience waits to
    crush them. Indeed, McCullers' stories center on a con-
    flict between man's desperate need for another and the
    solitary nature of his love. In "The Ballad of the Sad
    Café," The Heart Is a Lonely Hunter, Reflections in a
    Golden Eye, and The Member of the Wedding, her characters
    are doomed by an "implacable geometry of the heart" to
    love those who do not love them.

7   EVANS, OLIVER. "The Case of the Silent Singer: A Reevaluation
    of The Heart Is a Lonely Hunter," GaR, XIX (Summer),
    188-203.
        The Heart Is a Lonely Hunter is basically an allegorical
    depiction of individuals striving to achieve communion.
    Love, not speech, is their only avenue of achievement.
    The book is invested with elaborate symmetry and hierarchy,
    and its meaning embraces masses of people as well as indi-
    viduals.

(EVANS, OLIVER)
Reprinted in slightly revised form as part of <u>Carson McCullers: Her Life and Work</u> (1965.A1).

8   GOSSETT, LOUISE Y. "Dispossessed Love: Carson McCullers," in <u>Violence in Recent Southern Fiction</u>. Durham: Duke University Press, pp. 159-77.
Loneliness causes people to become violent in McCullers' work, and an act of violence forms the climax in each of her novels. McCullers sees violence not as a resolution but as an expression of tension; it is psychologically damaging to adults (as in "The Ballad of the Sad Café") but maturing for adolescents (as in <u>The Member of the Wedding</u>). <u>Reflections in a Golden Eye</u> depicts the violence of perverted love and is clinical in its interest, whereas violence has social causes in <u>The Heart Is a Lonely Hunter</u> and has interest as social criticism. Curiously, conflict between the races is not violent in McCullers' work.

9   MONTGOMERY, MARION. "The Sense of Violation: Notes Toward a Definition of 'Southern' Fiction," <u>GaR</u>, XIX (Fall), 278-87.
The characters of the truly Southern writers have a strong sense of violation and its consequences and a recognition that we violate each other and must pay for our violation. Because McCullers' characters are locked into an unenlightened solitude and lack these insights, McCullers is really a more Northern writer than a Southern.

10 MOORE, JACK B. "Carson McCullers: The Heart Is a Timeless Hunter," <u>TCL</u>, XI (July), 76-81.
McCullers is a mythic novelist as well as a reporter of the contemporary scene. Mick's journey, trial, and final initiation in <u>The Heart Is a Lonely Hunter</u> correspond with notable fidelity to the initiation pattern Campbell analyzed in <u>The Hero with a Thousand Faces</u>.

<u>1966 A   BOOKS</u>

1   EVANS, OLIVER. <u>The Ballad of Carson McCullers</u>. New York: Coward-McCann. American reprint of <u>Carson McCullers: Her Life and Work</u> (1965.A1).
Partially reprinted in <u>A Library of Literary Criticism</u> (1969.B2).

1966

1966 B SHORTER WRITINGS

1   AGEE, WILLIAM HUGH. "The Initiation Theme in Selected Modern
      American Novels of Adolescence." Ph.D. dissertation,
      Florida State University.
         Both The Heart Is a Lonely Hunter and The Member of the
      Wedding are structured on initiation scenarios. The iso-
      lation of the characters and the confusion of their sexual
      identities are fundamental in the scenarios.

*2 BRAEM, H. M. "Jetzt liegen die gesammelten Werke von Carson
      McCullers," Die Zeit (21 June), p. 27.
         Cited in BB (1970.B8).

3   MITCHELL, JULIAN. Review of Carson McCullers: Her Life and
      Work, London Magazine, V (January), 82-85.
         Although McCullers' novels have a realistic surface,
      they are really allegories about man's failure to love
      properly and should be judged by the standards of abstract
      art. (Ostensibly a review of Evan's book, this article is
      primarily about McCullers.)

4   PHILLIPS, ROBERT S. "Painful Love: Carson McCullers' Para-
      ble," SWR, LI (Winter), 80-86.
         "The Ballad of the Sad Café" is not so much a Gothic
      story as a parable in which the normal male and female
      roles have been inverted, Amelia playing the role of a
      man and Lymon playing the role of a woman. It is McCul-
      lers' least realistic book and her most didactic.
      Partially reprinted in A Library of Literary Criticism
      (1969.B2).

5   SACHS, VIOLA. "Contemporary American Fiction and Some Nine-
      teenth Century Patterns," Kwartalnik Neofilologiczny,
      XIII (no. 1), 3-29.
         The Heart Is a Lonely Hunter underscores the hopeless-
      ness of man's search for understanding and love, and thus
      underscores the extreme individuality which is a tradi-
      tional theme in American literature.

6   SULLIVAN, MARGARET SUE. "Carson McCullers: 1927-1947: The
      Conversion of Experience." Ph.D. dissertation, Duke
      University.
         Much of what McCullers writes about can be traced to
      her early life in Columbus, Georgia. Her relationship to
      the city itself, to her family, and to her piano teacher
      are of especial importance.

7   TOEBOSCH, WIM. "Regionalistische Literatuur," V1G, L
        (12 December), 676-77.
        Like Faulkner, Updike, and Cheever, McCullers writes
        critically about life in the American suburbs.

1967 A   BOOKS - NONE

1967 B   SHORTER WRITINGS

1   ANON. "Carson McCullers." London Times (30 September), p. 12.
        Obituary and biographical sketch. McCullers was one of
        the most talented Gothic novelists in the United States.

2   ANON. "Carson McCullers Dies at 50," New York Times
        (30 September), p. 1.
        Notice of McCullers' death, together with an estimate of
        her critical reputation and a sketch of her life.

3   ANON. "A Lonely Hunter," New York Times (30 September), p. 32.
        [Editorial.] McCullers dignified the individual--espe-
        cially the loser--in all of her fiction, and she trans-
        cended the regional settings of her work with her love and
        grace. Today, her work is finally gaining the universal
        recognition that it deserves.

4   ANON. Obituary Notice, Time, XC (6 October), 112.
        McCullers was "the vibrant voice of love and loneliness
        in the Southern novel."

5   BIGSBY, C. W. E. "Edward Albee's Georgia Ballad." TCL, XIII
        (January), 229-36.
        McCullers' world is unattractive and her characters are
        grotesque, but her work affirms the dignity of human life.
        This combination of qualities attracted Edward Albee to
        the task of dramatizing "The Ballad of the Sad Café," but
        he failed to render the heart of McCullers' achievement.

6   FLEISCHMANN, WOLFGANG BERNARD, ed. "McCullers, Carson," in
        Encyclopedia of World Literature in the Twentieth Century.
        Vol. 2. New York: Ungar, pp. 402-03.
        An enlarged, updated, and translated reprinting from
        Lexikon der Weltliteratur im 20. Jahrhundert (1962.B1).

7   FREMONT-SMITH, ELIOT. "The Heart Stands Out," New York Times
    (30 September), p. 40.
        The Heart Is a Lonely Hunter transcends all of the cate-
    gories in which we tend to place it, and it remains McCul-
    lers' best book. McCullers had a single vision, but she
    was a master at rendering moods.

8   GRIFFITH, ALBERT J. "Carson McCullers' Myth of the Sad Café,"
    GaR, XXI (Spring), 46-56.
        Largely through the narrator's mediation, the characters
    and events in "The Ballad of the Sad Café" have the re-
    moteness, the mystery, and the suggestiveness of myth.
    Since McCullers' subject is not in itself rational, this
    mythic level is very appropriate.

9   HOFFMAN, FREDERICK J. The Art of Southern Fiction: A Study
    of Some Modern Novelists. CMC. Carbondale: Southern
    Illinois University Press, pp. 65-75.
        McCullers is not so careful a writer as Eudora Welty,
    but she has made a substantial contribution to American
    fiction. She has a single theme: the loss of love and
    need to identify with others. The Heart Is a Lonely Hunt-
    er develops the theme with youthful genius, Reflections in
    a Golden Eye develops it with inadequate artistry, and
    "The Ballad of the Sad Café" develops it with powerful
    simplicity. The Member of the Wedding moves the problem
    of the trapped ego to a new setting and deals with it
    "cutely" rather than tragically.

10 McGILL, RALPH. "Carson McCullers: 1917-1967," SatR
    (21 October), 31.
        Obituary notice. One of our best Southern writers,
    McCullers was an appealing woman as well. (A series of
    anecdotes traces her biography.)

11 MADDEN DAVID. "The Paradox of the Need for Privacy and the
    Need for Understanding in Carson McCuller's The Heart Is
    a Lonely Hunter," L&P, XVII (no. 2/3), 128-40.
        A series of ironic situations in The Heart Is a Lonely
    Hunter suggests that the needs for privacy and understand-
    ing are generally frustrated and mutually frustrating.
    The characters exist in analogous psychic and material
    worlds, they react similarly, and they are all possessed
    by fixed ideas; yet they do not really desire communion
    with each other, for they know they are doomed to
    solitude.

12   RECHNITZ, ROBERT MAX. "Perception, Identity, and the Gro-
        tesque: A Study of Three Southern Writers." Ph.D. dis-
        sertation, University of Colorado.
            For O'Connor, McCullers, and Welty, the grotesque is
        that which.is perceived as a threat to one's identity.
        Most of McCullers' characters realize that their percep-
        tions of the grotesque characterize themselves more than
        the world, but little comes of this insight.
        Partially reprinted in GaR (1968.B5).

13   REED, REX. "Frankie Addams at 50," New York Times (16 April),
        sec. ii, p. 15.
            [Interview.] Touches on McCullers' health, her plans to
        visit Ireland, her affection for youths, her literary in-
        fluences, her plans for a new book, the filming of Reflec-
        tions in a Golden Eye, and the plans for a musical version
        of The Member of the Wedding.
        Reprinted in Do You Sleep in the Nude? (1968.B6).

1968 A   BOOKS - NONE

1968 B   SHORTER WRITINGS

1   DRAKE, ROBERT. "The Lonely Heart of Carson McCullers,"
        Christian Century, LXXXV (10 January), 50-51.
            McCullers does not really belong among the great twenti-
        eth-century writers: her fiction often lacks form and
        thematic control, her spiritual and structural centers
        often fail to coincide, and her sense and sensibility are
        often at war. McCullers would have done better to have
        trusted her heart more and her head less.

2   DWYER, REBECCA. "McCullers in Baltimore," Drama Critique, XI
        (Winter), 47-48.
            In its Baltimore production, The Member of the Wedding
        lost its universality, meaning, and clarity in the very
        attempt to foster those qualities.

3   GOZZI, FRANCESCO. "La Narrativa di Carson McCullers," Studi
        Americani (Rome), XIV (1968), 339-76.
            All of McCullers' characters have obsessions akin to
        those of Sherwood Anderson's grotesques. These obsessions
        isolate them from others, from nature, and from themselves
        and comprise a type of spiritual death. In The Heart Is a
        Lonely Hunter the only alternative to such isolation is
        death; in Reflections in a Golden Eye the "accident" of
        unique personality renders every union problematic and

155

(GOZZI, FRANCESCO)
fatally imperfect; in The Member of the Wedding Frankie's
fantasies harden fatally into a brutal and useless delu-
sion. "The Ballad of the Sad Café" is wholly fatalistic
(as the ballad genre requires), but in Clock Without Hands
the irrevocable condemnation to solitude is absent.
McCullers never abandons her "love-equals-solitude-equals-
pain" formula, but she does move gradually from ironic nihilism to an exaltation of eros.

4　HENDRICK, GEORGE. "'Almost Everyone Wants to be the Lover':
The Fiction of Carson McCullers," BA, XLII (Summer),
389-91.
Some of McCullers' novels are among the most important
art of our time.

5　RECHNITZ, ROBERT M. "The Failure of Love: The Grotesque in
Two Novels by Carson McCullers," GaR, XXII (Winter),
454-63.
Fearful of confronting themselves in a love relation-
ship, McCullers' characters construct limited, safe worlds
for themselves which quickly become grotesque.
Partially reprinted from "Perception, Identity, and the
Grotesque: A Study of Three Southern Writers" (1967.B12).

6　REED, REX. Do You Sleep in the Nude? New York: New American
Library, pp. 38-43.
Reprinted from New York Times (1967.B13).

7　RÍOS RUIZ, MANUEL. "Carson McCullers, La Novelista del Fata-
lismo," Cuadernos Hispanoamericanos, LXXVI (December),
763-71.
McCullers' vigorous prose was the result of arduous
work, but it is simple, natural, and poetic in its intensity and it suggests well the anguish of contemporary
life. Like Faulkner, the Beat novelists, and the writers
of the Lost Generation, and in keeping with the folklore
and songs of her native land, McCullers is obsessed with
the difference between appearance and reality in North
American society. She sees society in chaos, life as
brutally individualistic, and love as all but impossible.
Her great theme is spiritual isolation. Although "The
Ballad of the Sad Café," The Member of the Wedding, and
Clock Without Hands are different in technique and content, they reflect alike McCullers' image of man and make
that image credible.

8   ROBINSON, W. R. "The Life of Carson McCullers' Imagination,"
     SHR, II (Summer), 291.-302.
         McCullers' imagination was preoccupied with the cleavage
     between heart and head. In her early stories a dominant
     intellect judges man's inner life dispassionately and the
     imagination flowers only in the grotesque. In The Member
     of the Wedding, however, the imagination survives the op-
     pression of the intellect, and in The Square Root of Won-
     derful and Clock Without Hands the cleavage between heart
     and intellect ceases to segregate while it continues to
     separate. McCullers' basic plots never change, but the
     imagination becomes an increasingly more viable aspect of
     life as her work matures.

9   SCHORER, MARK. "McCullers and Capote: Basic Patterns," in
     The World We Imagine. New York: Farrar, Straus, and
     Giroux, pp. 274-96.
         Reprinted from The Creative Present: Notes on Contem-
     porary American Fiction (1963.B13).

10   SHERRILL, ROWLAND A. "McCullers' The Heart Is a Lonely Hunt-
     er: The Missing Ego and the Problem of the Norm," Ken-
     tucky Review, II (1968), 5-17.
         The characters in The Heart Is a Lonely Hunter are gro-
     tesques only in Anderson's sense of the term--characters
     who are dominated by a single truth. Their tragedy is
     that their truths are inadequate and the reason why they
     cling so foolishly to their truths is that the world of-
     fers them no general norms for conduct. Singer and Anto-
     napoulos suggest the Super-ego and the Id of a single per-
     sonality, and the absence of a mediating Ego reinforces
     the absence of an organic center in the characters' lives.

1969 A BOOKS - NONE

1969 B SHORTER WRITINGS

1   CARR, VIRGINIA SPENCER. "Carson McCullers and the Search for
     Meaning." Ph.D. dissertation, Florida State University.
         McCullers' fiction has been based largely on her life
     and thought.

2   CURLEY, DOROTHY NYREN, Ed. A Library of Literary Criticism:
     Modern American Literature. Vol. 2, 4th ed. New York:
     Ungar, pp. 246-52.
         Extracts reprinted from New York Times Book Review
     (1940.B5), New York Herald Tribune Books (1940.B10),

1969

(CURLEY, DOROTHY NYREN)
SatR, (1940.B12), New Republic (1940.B14), New York Times
Book Review (1941.B11), SatR (1946.B4), Commonweal
(1946.B5) and (1951.B8), CE (1951.B15), New World Writing
(1952.B2), MFS (1959.B4), Commonweal (1961.B32), Reporter
(1961.B51), Contemporary American Novelists (1964.B6),
Pioneers and Caretakers (1965.B4), The Ballad of Carson
McCullers (1966.A1), and SWR (1966.B4).

3   EDMONDS, DALE. Carson McCullers. SWS. Austin: Steck-Vaughn.
The material in The Heart Is a Lonely Hunter is over-
abundant and the control is inadequate, although the excellences of the novel are many; its central themes are
the isolation of man and the difficulty of human love.
Reflections in a Golden Eye is a work of greater control
and considerable power; a metaphysical morality play
characterized by a firm, sardonic style, it is infinitely
contemptuous of the possibility of love. "The Ballad of
the Sad Café," on the other hand, is timeless, haunting,
and resonant; it is McCullers' most stylized work and suggests for the first time that the attainment of mutual
love is a possibility. The Member of the Wedding is
McCullers' most realistic work; it asks questions about
the nature of love without implying negative answers.
Clock Without Hands, however, is a dated collection of
shibboleths and stock characters and is very much a total
failure. (A biographical account precedes the discussion
of McCullers' works.)

4   GRAVER, LAURENCE. Carson McCullers. UMPAW, no. 84. St. Paul:
University of Minnesota Press.
McCullers is more a lyricist than a philosopher; she is
at her best in creating moods and characters, and at her
worst in commenting upon whole cultures. The Heart Is a
Lonely Hunter is impressive and arresting for a first
novel, if marred by lapses both in its realistic tone and
in its fable structure, while the more pretentious Reflections in a Golden Eye is badly conceived and without real
insight. "The Ballad of the Sad Café" is the best of
McCullers' "grotesque" works, but the more realistic tone
and more accessible psychology of The Member of the Wedding make it her finest work. Clock Without Hands fails
both in its psychology and in its cultural analysis. (A
short biography prefaces this pamphlet.)

5   HARTE, BARBARA, and CAROLINE RILEY, eds. "McCullers, Carson,"
    in 200 Contemporary Authors. Detroit: Gale Research,
    pp. 183-85.
        A bio-bibliography, touching as well on McCullers'
    themes and symbols and on the critical attitudes toward
    her work.

6   JAWORSKI, PHILIPPE. "La double quête de l'identité et de la
    réalité chez Carson McCullers," La nouvelle revue fran-
    çaise, XVII (July), 93-101.
        American critics have dwelt on the theme of loneliness
    in McCullers' work, but it needs to be observed that
    McCullers sees loneliness as a state of searching for con-
    tact with other consciousnesses. The tragedy with which
    her characters live is the failure of love to be recipro-
    cated; indeed, all of her couples fail to achieve emotion-
    al rapport except in an idealized past and a hypothetical
    future.

7   KNOWLES, A. S., JR. "Six Bronze Petals and Two Red: Carson
    McCullers in the Forties," in The Forties: Fiction, Po-
    etry, Drama, edited by Warren French. Deland, Florida:
    Everett/Edwards, pp. 87-98.
        If World War II has only a shadowy presence in McCullers'
    novels, she catches the sentimental, reforming spirit of
    the times very well, and her portraits of the Negro com-
    munity are prophetic. On the basis of these qualities,
    her reputation was fostered artificially in the 40s by a
    coterie of her fellow writers; she is really a minor writ-
    er with a fine, but limited, sensibility.

*8 VALER, MARIA. Introduction to "In Vara aceea verde ...."
    Bucurest: Editura pentru literatură universală,
    pp. v-xvi.
        Cited in MHRA Annual Bibliography of English Language
    and Literature, 1969, p. 594.

9   WATKINS, FLOYD C. (comp.) "Carson McCullers (1917-1967)," in
    Bibliographical Guide to the Study of Southern Literature,
    edited by Louis D. Rubin, Jr. Baton Rouge: Louisiana
    State University Press, pp. 243-44.
        A listing of 28 journal articles about McCullers'
    novels.

1970

1970 B SHORTER WRITINGS

1   CARNEY, CHRISTINA F. "A Study of Themes and Techniques in
       Carson McCullers' Prose Fiction." Ph.D. dissertation,
       Columbia University.
          The control and the poeticism of McCullers' novels are
       both founded upon a continual imbalance between realistic
       and fantastic qualities of form and content.

2   COALE, SAMUEL CHASE. "The Role of the South in the Fiction of
       William Faulkner, Carson McCullers, Flannery O'Connor, and
       William Styron." Ph.D. dissertation, Brown University.
          McCullers' South consists of milltowns and wastelands;
       she sees it tragically and sings an introspective hymn to
       its losses.

3   HAMILTON, ALICE. "Loneliness and Alienation: The Life and
       Work of Carson McCullers," DR, L (Summer), 215-29.
          Neo-Platonically, McCullers seems to think that the
       world is freakish because it is incomplete. People find
       their happiness either instinctively and intuitively, or
       by a search for and expression of inner freedom. Both
       dreams and love are essential to the life of their souls.

4   MATHIS, RAY. "Reflections in a Golden Eye: Myth Making in
       American Christianity," Religion in Life, XXXIX (Winter),
       545-58.
          Reflections in a Golden Eye suggests that contemporary
       Americans have religious needs and expressions which often
       parody Christianity. On both the realistic and allegori-
       cal levels, the novel is a series of jokes about the
       "Christian" middle-class, its secularism, its tendency to
       myth-making, and its religiosity. Ironically, Lenora is
       at once the least religious of the characters and the sym-
       bol of goodness. Her mythologization in the minds of
       characters who have been freed from the myths of the past
       is indicative of McCullers' attitude toward the Christian
       forms of religion.

5   MILLICHAP, JOSEPH ROBERT. "A Critical Reevaluation of Carson
       McCullers' Fiction." Ph.D. dissertation, Notre Dame
       University.
          In The Heart Is a Lonely Hunter the problems of the in-
       dividual and of society are perfectly and realistically
       integrated. Reflections in a Golden Eye fails to achieve
       the same degree of realism and is a work of smaller scope,
       while Member of the Wedding fails to see both the indi-

(MILLICHAP, JOSEPH ROBERT)
vidual and society as broadly and as accurately. "The Ballad of the Sad Café" succeeds in these terms almost as well as The Heart Is a Lonely Hunter, although with very different materials, while Clock Without Hands is shallow and stereotypical. McCullers belongs to the first generation of the Southern Renaissance rather than to the second. Partially reprinted in TCL (1971.B6) and in GaR (1973.B7).

6   MOORE, JANICE TOWNLEY. "McCullers' 'The Ballad of the Sad Café,'" Expl, XXIX (November), no. 27.
The language of "The Ballad of the Sad Café" associates Lymon with fowls in general and with a hawk in particular. This association connects him meaningfully with the death-symbolizing hawk that flies over the town.

*7   RADU, AURELIA. "Implicaţiile initierii sau metamorfozele singuratăţii în universul eroilor lui Carson McCullers," Analele Universitatii, Bucuresti, Literatură Universală Comparată, XIX (no. ii), 141–48.
Cited in 1972 MLA International Bibliography, p. 164.

8   STANLEY, WILLIAM T. "Carson McCullers: 1965–69, A Selected Checklist," BB, XXVII (October–December), 91–93.
A bibliography of new and previously unlisted writings by and about McCullers between 1965 and 1969, updating Phillips' 1964 checklist (1964.B11). The bibliography is divided into McCullers' new writings, bibliographical listings of McCullers' work, criticism of McCullers' work, obituary notices, reviews of Evans' The Ballad of Carson McCullers, and reviews of the film version of The Heart Is a Lonely Hunter.

9   WARDLE, IRVING. "McCullers Drama Has Unhappy Bow on London Stage," New York Times (12 March), p. 47.
The London production of The Square Root of Wonderful is a painful experience. The writing is very bad, and McCullers did not know her stage craftsmanship.

1971 A   BOOKS - NONE

1971 B   SHORTER WRITINGS

1   ADAMS, PHOEBE. Review of The Mortgaged Heart, Atlantic Monthly, CCXXVIII (November), 153.
The stories in The Mortgaged Heart are notably precocious in their handling of familiar, adolescent themes.

1971

2 CLEMONS, WALTER. "The Mortgaged Heart," New York Times Book
   Review (7 November), sec. vii, p. 7.
   None of the pieces in The Mortgaged Heart show McCullers
   at anything like her best. The Heart Is a Lonely Hunter
   remains her most impressive work, although it seems less
   good now than it did, and Reflections in a Golden Eye, her
   second-best work, seems somewhat better now than it did.
   In general, McCullers' work tended to decline, her "A-
   loves-B-who-loves-C" formula degenerating into sentimen-
   talization; the decline was probably inevitable and had
   little to do with her illness.

3 GULLASON, THOMAS A. Review of The Mortgaged Heart, SatR, LIV
   (13 November), 57.
   The items in The Mortgaged Heart are not significant in
   themselves, but they help us to see McCullers' progress
   from personal reminiscences to large, universal themes,
   and they help us to appreciate how quickly McCullers'
   talent matured.

4 HOWES, VICTOR. "Alone in a Crowd," Christian Science Monitor
   (11 November), p. B7.
   The pieces in The Mortgaged Heart are not in the Gothic
   mode; they deal, rather, with themes of childhood and
   adolescence, and evoke nostalgically the world of the
   1930s. Many of the pieces are only sketches and some are
   fugitive pieces, but there is much that is fine in them.

5 KINNEY, JEANNE. Review of The Mortgaged Heart, Best Sellers,
   XXXI (15 November), 371.
   Except for the essays on writers and writing, the pieces
   in The Mortgaged Heart are interesting only in providing
   an autobiographical and literary background to McCullers'
   work. McCullers herself might well have wished many of
   the pieces unpublished.

6 MILLICHAP, JOSEPH R. "The Realistic Structure of The Heart Is
   a Lonely Hunter," TCL, XVII (January), 11-17.
   The Heart Is a Lonely Hunter is more properly understood
   as psychological and social realism than as Gothic romance. Analysis of the novel's structure suggests that
   character, plot, style, setting, and symbol all serve to
   present "the failure of communication, the isolation, and
   the violence prevalent in modern society."
   Partially reprinted from "A Critical Reevaluation of Carson McCullers' Fiction" (1970.B5).

7   RIVIÈRE, YVETTE. "L'Aliénation dans les romans de Carson
    McCullers," Recherches Anglaises et Américaines, IV
    (1971), 79-86.
        McCullers depicts all men as alienated, as trapped by
    their biology, their history, and their milieu, but she is
    not generally schematic or scientific in her observations.
    Nevertheless, one can discern a "scale of alienation" in
    her works which is founded on economic status and race:
    unemployed blacks are the most seriously alienated charac-
    ters in her novels and are on the bottom of her scale,
    while well-to-do whites are the least seriously alienated
    and are on the top of her scale.

8   RODGERS, ANN TUCKER. "The Search for Relationships in Carson
    McCullers." Ph.D. dissertation, St. Louis University.
        McCullers analyzes the isolation and alienation of her
    characters as well as depicting it. Those characters who
    fail to develop satisfactory relationships with others are
    out of touch with the natural order and are oriented
    toward the abstract, the verbal, and the symbolic.

9   VALENSISE, RACHELE. "Tre Scrittrici del Sud: Flannery O'Con-
    nor, Caroline Gordon, Carson McCullers," Studi Americani
    (Rome), XVII (1971), 251-89.
        Like Flannery O'Connor and Caroline Gordon, McCullers is
    interested in the difficulty of communication. She sees
    men as affectively impotent, as committed to a false vi-
    sion of reality, and as doomed to love those who cannot
    love them in return. Solitude is man's most common state,
    and, while love promises to save man from solitude, it is
    feared and rejected precisely because it destroys man's
    "inner room." Religion also promises a type of salvation,
    especially in the Christ-like Singer of The Heart Is a
    Lonely Hunter, but this too is a delusion both sought and
    rejected by characters who do not really want to be saved
    from their loneliness.

1972 A BOOKS - NONE

1972 B SHORTER WRITINGS

1   AVANT, JOHN ALFRED. Review of The Mortgaged Heart, LJ, XCVII
    (1 January), 73.
        Most of the stories in The Mortgaged Heart are appren-
    tice work and fail to hold one's interest. A series of
    observations on writing and life entitled "The Flowering
    Dream" partially redeems the volume.

1972

2   BALAKIAN, NONA. "Love--Perverse and Perfect," New York Times
    (3 January), p. 25.
        A close reading of McCullers' work reveals the poetic
    apprehension that is the other side of her interest in the
    grotesque. The Mortgaged Heart will help to illumine this
    for students of McCullers' work. Naturalism was not gen-
    erally beneficial to McCullers' writing, but it gave edge
    to her theme of spiritual isolation.

3   BLUEFARB, SAM. The Escape Motif in the American Novel: Mark
    Twain to Richard Wright. Columbus: Ohio State University
    Press, pp. 114-32.
        Jake Blount in The Heart Is a Lonely Hunter is an habit-
    ual escaper whose escapes bring him no spiritual regenera-
    tion, a would-be savior rejected by those he would save.
    He believes in the American dream, but, not realizing that
    the dream has passed him by, he can only oppose the status
    quo.

4   CARLTON, ANN RUTH. "Patterns in Carson McCullers' Portrayal
    of Adolescence." Ph.D. dissertation, Ball State Univer-
    sity.
        McCullers' description of adolescence always centers on
    a fear of unusual physical development and a fear of iso-
    lation, and her adolescents usually escape into fantasy
    worlds. Seasonal, musical, and temporal symbols convey
    her themes.

5   EDMONDS, DALE. "'Correspondence': A 'Forgotten' Carson
    McCullers Short Story," SSF, IX (Winter), 89-92.
        "Correspondence" reveals McCullers' gift for light com-
    edy as her other short fiction does not. It is built
    upon McCullers' usual theme of an awkward adolescent girl
    yearning to become part of a "we," but its humor marks the
    transition from the unsuccessfully-developed Mick Kelly to
    the successfully-developed Frankie Addams. "Correspond-
    ence" is also McCullers' first successful rendering of an
    adolescent idiom.

6   FINGER, LARRY LIVINGSTON. "Elements of the Grotesque in Se-
    lected Works of Welty, Capote, McCullers, and O'Connor."
    Ph.D. dissertation, George Peabody College for Teachers.
        McCullers generally uses the grotesque in order to de-
    velop her theme of spiritual isolation, but in Reflections
    in a Golden Eye she uses it to illustrate human incom-
    pleteness, and in "The Ballad of the Sad Café" she uses it
    to illustrate her theory of love.

7   GAILLARD, DAWSON F. "The Presence of the Narrator in Carson
      McCullers' 'The Ballad of the Sad Café,'" MissQ, XXV
      (Fall), 419-27.
        The narrator of "The Ballad of the Sad Café" is a sym-
      pathetic and sensitive member of the community, a human
      spirit who bears the burden of time and mutability. His
      presence elevates the story to the level of myth.

8   GRINNELL, JAMES W. "Delving 'A Domestic Dilemma,'" SSF, IX
      (Summer), 270-71.
        Martin's diagnosis of his wife's alcoholism in "A Do-
      mestic Dilemma" is shallow and unconvincing. The chief
      causes of her addiction are Martin's insensitivity and
      concern for public opinion.

9   HUNT, TANN H. "Humor in the Novels of Carson McCullers."
      Ph.D. dissertation, Florida State University.
        McCullers used humor with increasing skill for character
      revelation (especially in Clock Without Hands), for fore-
      shadowing (especially in The Heart Is a Lonely Hunter and
      The Member of the Wedding), for plot movement (in the
      later novels) and for satirical commentary (in the later
      novels).

10 MADDEN, DAVID. "Transfixed Among the Self-Inflicted Ruins:
      Carson McCullers' The Mortgaged Heart," SLJ, V (Fall),
      137-62.
        The Mortgaged Heart contains a great deal of mediocre
      writing that will be of interest only to dedicated enthu-
      siasts and scholars. A thematic or stylistic organization
      of the material would have served the real value of the
      book somewhat better than its chronological organization,
      for the pieces illumine well McCullers' interest in point
      of view, in music, in aliens, in autobiography, and in
      religion. McCullers was a more conscious craftsman than
      is generally thought, and at her best she is a masterful
      orchestrator with a "radiant" style. The Heart Is a Lone-
      ly Hunter is among the ten greatest American novels.

11 PRESLEY, DELMA EUGENE. "Carson McCullers' Descent to Earth,"
      Descant, XVII, 54-60.
        McCullers is generally accused of heavy-handed moraliz-
      ing and of an effete skepticism in Clock Without Hands,
      but she had actually abandoned her skepticism for a belief
      in reconciliatory power in her last book and simply failed
      to find a technique for expressing it. The mechanical
      characterization and stress on the abnormal which were so

1972

(PRESLEY, DELMA EUGENE)
successful in the early fiction were inappropriate techniques for her later vision.

12 _____. "The Moral Function of Distortion in Southern Grotesque," SAB, XXXVII (May), 37-46.
The moral function of the grotesque is to counterpoint
an image of man's incompleteness with an understanding of
what man ought to be, and it often develops the latter by
implication. Thus, the "grotesque" distortion in McCullers' work should be understood as focusing an absence of
the love which her characters need desperately to find.

13 SKOTNICKI, IRENE. "Die Darstellung der Entfremdung in den
Romanen von Carson McCullers," Zeitschrift für Anglistik
und Amerikanistik (East Berlin), XX (January), 24-45.
McCullers' novels are about man's alienated state and
his consequent need to have his being affirmed by some
individual or group that accepts and values him. Although
McCullers' characters do not abandon their hopes for such
affirmation, they are powerless to foster it, and none of
them manage to achieve it. This theme has a notable basis
in McCullers' own experience of life, but it has also a
firm basis in Marx's analysis of a capitalistic society.

14 THOMAS, LEROY. "An Analysis of the Theme of Alienation in the
Fictional Works of Five Contemporary Southern Writers."
Ph.D. dissertation, Oklahoma State University.
Naturalistic forces have such strong power over man in
McCullers' works that man is effectively prevented from
attaining happiness.

15 TOYNBEE, PHILIP. "Full of the Deep South," London Observer
(4 June), p. 33.
Like Byron, Fitzgerald, and Thomas, McCullers tended to
turn herself into a myth. The Heart Is a Lonely Hunter is
her masterpiece. She lacked balance as a writer, but she
had an extraordinary ability to disturb her readers. One
is glad to have the stories published in The Mortgaged
Heart, but the occasional essays are "awful beyond
belief."

1973 A   BOOKS - NONE

Carson McCullers: A Reference Guide

1973 B SHORTER WRITINGS

1   BAUERLY, DONNA M. "Patterns of Imagery in Carson McCullers'
     Major Fiction." Ph.D. dissertation, Marquette University.
       McCullers' imagery is preoccupied at one extreme with
     fragmentation, isolation, and incompleteness, and at the
     other extreme with wholeness, unity, and completeness.
     The tension between these extremes illumines McCullers'
     view of man and his struggle between Eros and Agape.

2   BUCHEN, IRVING H. "Carson McCullers: A Case of Convergence,"
     BuR, XXI (Spring), 15-28.
       McCullers is best approached through a conjunction of
     literary criticism and psychology. Indeed, her fiction
     invites such a reading by its flagrant use of abnormal
     types and her deliberately minimal psychology. Such an
     approach to McCullers' fiction illumines the fear of in-
     cest as a key factor in her vision and illustrates proto-
     typically the proper relationship between psychology and
     criticism in dealing with a literary text.

3   JOHNSON, THOMAS SLAYTON. "The Horror in the Mansion: Gothic
     Fiction in the Works of Truman Capote and Carson McCul-
     lers." Ph.D. dissertation, University of Texas at Austin.
       Both Capote and McCullers choose the Gothic mode part
     way through their careers in an attempt to clarify the
     themes of their previous work and to free themselves from
     structural concerns.

4   JOYCE, EDWARD THOMAS. "Race and Sex: Opposition and Identity
     in the Fiction of Carson McCullers." Ph.D. dissertation,
     State University of New York at Stony Brook.
       McCullers sees each person as causing his own isolation
     and as failing to be objective about his situation. Thus,
     characters who seem opposed by race and sex in McCullers'
     fiction are actually one in their failure to achieve
     identity.

5   KAZIN, ALFRED. Bright Book of Life: American Storytellers
     from Hemingway to Mailer. Boston: Little, Brown,
     pp. 50-54.
       McCullers was essentially a myth-maker. She wrote of
     the dislocation of love, of the unreasonable hope for a
     perfect, transforming love, and of the demon of self-
     damnation. The Member of the Wedding is self-imitative
     and merely cute, but "The Ballad of the Sad Café" is per-
     fectly controlled art, and The Heart Is a Lonely Hunter
     is wonderfully alive.

1973

6   McNALLY, JOHN. "The Introspective Narrator in 'The Ballad of
        the Sad Café,'" SAB, XXXVIII (November), 40-44.
            "The Ballad of the Sad Café" employs a fictive narrator,
        emphasized as such by the tense-shifts, the intrusions,
        the digressions, and the "twelve-mortal-men" epilogue.
        In the process of telling his tale, the narrator discovers
        new meaning in his own existence and a way of overcoming
        his own boredom.

7   MILLICHAP, JOSEPH R. "Carson McCullers' Literary Ballad,"
        GaR, XXVII (Fall), 329-39.
            Critics have erred in trying to understand "The Ballad
        of the Sad Café" and, indeed, all of McCullers' work ac-
        cording to the narrator's theory of love in "Sad Café."
        The setting, timelessness, and unidentified narrator of
        the story suggest that it is more properly read within the
        tradition of the ballad.
            Partially reprinted from "A Critical Reevaluation of Car-
        son McCullers' Fiction" (1970.B5).

8   POPP, KLAUS-JÜRGEN. "Carson McCullers," in Amerikanische
        Literatur der Gegenwart, edited by Martin Christadler.
        Stuttgart: Alfred Kröner, pp. 1-21.
            McCullers can be approached in many ways, and critics
        such as Ihab Hassan, Klaus Lubbers, and Marguerite Young
        have suggested many of them. She has been seen as both a
        regionalist and a universal writer, as a feminist and as
        a Gothicist. Her work has been approached thematically,
        structurally, and symbolically, and it has been called
        humorous, morbid, and Freudian. She has been linked to
        Dostoevsky, Flaubert, Melville, Hawthorne, Kafka, Plato,
        Coleridge, Kierkegaard, Salinger, and Dickinson at the
        same time that she transcends all sources, comparisons,
        and parallels.

1975 A BOOKS

1   CARR, VIRGINIA SPENCER. The Lonely Hunter: A Biography of
        Carson McCullers. New York: Doubleday.
            An exhaustive biography, incorporating the judgments and
        observations of McCullers' family, friends, lovers, casual
        acquaintances, and enemies. The creative and destructive
        aspects of McCullers' personality and talent are empha-
        sized in chapters dealing with McCullers' Georgia girl-
        hood, her New York City apprenticeship, her marriage to
        Reeves McCullers, her success with The Heart Is a Lonely
        Hunter, her life at 7 Middagh Street in Brooklyn Heights,

1975

(CARR, VIRGINIA SPENCER)
her summers at Yaddo, her remarriage to Reeves McCullers,
her life in Nyack and Paris, her writing of The Member of
the Wedding, and her last illness and death. Genealogies
and a chronology are appended.

2   COOK, RICHARD M. Carson McCullers. Modern Literature Monographs. New York: Ungar.
The Heart Is a Lonely Hunter sees loneliness in a public
manner, as central to many types of persons and aspects of
behavior. It captures a sense of time and place better
than any other of her novels. Reflections in a Golden Eye
is a more austere book with a tighter plot and more grotesque characters, but it does not involve us so much as
Heart, lacking its warmth, humor, and psychological depth.
The Member of the Wedding studies loneliness in an inward
manner by examining its effects on a single individual, by
noting its pathos, its humor, and its impermanence, and by
detailing the self's changing identity in time. "The
Ballad of the Sad Café" celebrates the power of love and
eulogizes its passing after a moment of grace. It sees
love as a magical and unpredictable phenomenon and coun-
terpoints the tragic and the humorous in order to convey
this. Clock Without Hands is a loosely organized series
of portraits which explores the changing identities of
four persons. It is McCullers' most ambitious novel but
it is unsuccessful in its characterizations, its structure, and its definition of theme. (A biographical chapter prefaces this book.)

1975 B   SHORTER WRITINGS

1   MADDOCKS, MELVIN. "Little Precious," Time, CVI (21 July),
63-64.
McCullers faced great obstacles in her life, notably an
overambitious mother, a melodramatic bisexuality, and
several serious diseases. These things exhausted her
creative energies quickly and rendered her too intense
and flamboyant a writer for today's taste. Carr's biography (1975.A1) is ungainly but never boring.

Katherine Anne Porter Index

Curley, Daniel, 1963.B5, B.6
Curley, Dorothy Nyren, 1969.B2
Current-Garcia, Eugene, 1964.B5
Cyr, Anne, 1962.B21

Daniels, Sally, 1962.B22
"Dark Voyagers: A Study of
    Katherine Anne Porter's Ship
    of Fools," 1963.B8
Dawson, Margaret Cheney, 1930.B3
Days Before, The
--Reviews
    1952.B1-B4, B6, B8-B9, B11,
    B13-B18; 1953.B1-B2, B6-B8,
    B11
--Major Essays
    1953.B5; 1957.A1; 1964.A1
"Day's Work, A," 1964.A1;
    1965.A1
Deasy, Br. Paul Francis, 1963.B7
"Death's Other Kingdom: Dantesque
    and Theological Symbolism in
    'Flowering Judas,'" 1969.B4
"Dedicated Author," 1966.B4
"Deft Touch," 1952.B17
"Delicate Art of Katherine Anne
    Porter, The," 1939.B18
Denham, Alice, 1965.B9
"Devil's Mix From a Blender, A,"
    1962.B41
De Vries, Peter, 1962.B23
Dickson, Thomas, 1935.B11
"Difficult Contemporary Short
    Stories," 1954.B2
Dolbier, Maurice, 1962.B24
Donadio, Stephen, 1966.B13
Donoghue, Denis, 1965.B10
Downing, Francis, 1944.B10
"Downward Path to Wisdom, The,"
    1957.A1; 1964.A1; 1965.A1;
    1969.B5; 1971.A1
Drake, Robert, 1962.B25
"Dubliners and the Stories of
    Katherine Anne Porter,"
    1960.B5
Duchene, Anne, 1962.B26
Dunlap, Lennis, 1962.B32

Emmons, Winfred S., 1967.B1
English, Charles, 1962.B27
"Exquisite Story Teller, An,"
    1935.B15
"Eye of the Storm, The," 1966.B25

Fadiman, Clifton, 1939.B6
Farrington, Thomas Arthur,
    1972.B2
Featherstone, Joseph, 1965.B11
Fefferman, Stan, 1962.B28
"Fiction," 1939.B11
Fiction and Criticism of Kather-
    ine Anne Porter, The, 1957.A1
"Fiction in Review," 1944.B18
"Fictions Mystical and Epical,"
    1945.B7
"Fictions of Memory, The,"
    1960.B6
Fiedler, Leslie, 1953.B4
"Fig Tree, The," 1964.A1;
    1965.A1; 1971.A1; 1973.A1
"Figure in the Rose-Red Gown,
    The," 1962.B73
"Finally Comes the Novel,"
    1962.B74
Finkelstein, Sidney, 1962.B29
Finn, James, 1962.B30
"First-Class Passenger, A,"
    1962.B72
"First Novel," 1961.B1
"First Reader, The," 1944.B11
Flood, Ethelbert, 1961.B4
"Flowering Judas," 1947.B4;
    1950.B2; 1954.B2; 1961.B4;
    1963.B4, B23; 1964.A1, B2;
    1965.A1; 1968.B2; 1969.B4,
    B10; 1970.B5; 1971.A1-A2;
    1973.A1
Flowering Judas and Other
    Stories
--Reviews of 1930 edition
    1930.B1-B5; 1931.B2; 1933.B4
--Reviews of 1935 edition
    1935.B1, B3-B6, B8-B9, B11-B17;
    1936.B1; 1946.B2
--Major Essays
    1971.B3

"'Flowering Judas': Two Voices," 1969.B10

Ford, Ford Madox, 1933.B4

"For Katherine Anne Porter, Ship of Fools Was a Lively Twenty-Two Year Voyage," 1962.B45

"Foundering of Ship of Fools, I, The," 1962.B22

"Foundering of Ship of Fools, II, The," 1962.B75

"Four Authors Are Given National Book Awards," 1966.B5

"Four Forgotten Books Win $2,500 Prizes," 1937.B1

Frankel, Haskel, 1965.B12

Fremantle, Anne, 1952.B6

"French Song Book," 1933.B3

"Full Length Portrait," 1941.B2

Gannett, Lewis, 1934.B5; 1937.B3; 1939.B7; 1942.B4

Gardiner, Harold C., 1962.B31

Gardner, John, 1962.B32

Garnett, Emily, 1942.B5

"Gaudeamus Omnes!," 1962.B50

Gaunt, Marcia Elizabeth, 1972.B4

"Getting and Spending: Porter's 'Theft,'" 1960.B4

Girson, Richelle, 1962.B33

Givner, Joan, 1969.B3; 1972.B5

Gold, Herbert, 1961.B5

Goldberg, Barbara, 1966.B14

Goldsborough, Diana, 1962.B34

Gottfried, Leon, 1969.B4

"Grave, The," 1958.B1; 1960.B7; 1963.B6; 1964.A1, B7; 1965.A1, B7, B18; 1966.B10; 1969.B9; 1971.A1; 1973.A1

"Grave' as Lyrical Short Story, 'The," 1964.B7

"Grave,' Form and Symbol, 'The," 1969.B9

"Grave' Revisited, 'The," 1965.B7

Graves, Allen Wallace, 1954.B2

Greene, George, 1961.B6

Greene, Maxine, 1962.B35

Gross, Beverly, 1968.B2

Gullason, Thomas A., 1965.B13

Gunn, Drewey Wayne, 1974.B1

"Hacienda," 1934.B3, B4, B5, B6, B7; 1935.B2, B7, B10, B18; 1957.A1; 1962.B39; 1964.A1; 1965.A1, B5; 1971.A1; 1973.A1

Hafley, James, 1962.B36

Hagopian, John V., 1962.B37; 1966.B15

Hall, James B., 1956.B2

Hansen, Harry, 1944.B11

"Happy Harvest, A," 1952.B4

Hardy, John Edward, 1973.A1

Hart, Elizabeth, 1934.B6

"Hart Crane Aboard the Ship of Fools," 1963.B9

Hartley, Lodwick, 1940.B4; 1953.B5; 1963.B8; 1969.A1, B5

Hartung, Philip T., 1939.B8

"He," 1954.B2; 1963.B7; 1964.A1; 1965.A1, 1966.B19; 1971.A2; 1972.B9; 1973.A1

Heilman, Robert B., 1950.B2; 1952.B7; 1962.B38

Hendrick, George, 1962.B39; 1963.B9; 1965.A1

Herbst, Josephine, 1936.B2; 1948.B1

Hernandez, Frances, 1972.B6

Hertz, Robert Neil, 1964.B6; 1965.B14

Hicks, Granville, 1962.B40; 1965.B15

Higgins, Cecile, 1935.B12

Hill, William B., 1965.B16

Hobson, Laura Z., 1952.B8

Hoffman, Frederick J., 1956.B3; 1967.B2

Hogan, William, 1962.B41, B42

"Holiday," 1962.B37; 1965.A1; 1971.A1, A2

Holmes, Theodore, 1963.B10

"Honest Story Teller, An," 1935.B1

Horgan, Paul, 1966.B5

Howell, Elmo, 1971.B2; 1972.B7

Hubbell, Jay B., 1972.B8

Hutchens, John K., 1962.B43

Hyman, Stanley, 1962.B44

"Illusion and Allusion: Reflections in 'The Cracked Looking-Glass,'" 1962.B77

"Imagination and Reality in the Fiction of Katherine Anne Porter and John Cheever," 1972.B4

"Internal Opposition in Porter's 'Granny Weatherall,'" 1969.B11

"Interview with Katherine Anne Porter, An," 1965.B23

"Introduction" to Fiesta in November, 1942.B4

"Introduction" to "Katherine Anne Porter: A Critical Bibliography," 1953.B12

"Introduction" to The Itching Parrot, 1942.B1, B3, B5–B8, B10–B11, B13

"Ironic Tragedy, An," 1937.B6

"Irony with a Center: Katherine Anne Porter." See "Katherine Anne Porter (Irony with a Center)."

Isherwood, Christopher, 1939.B9

"It's Katherine Anne Porter, But Is It Art?," 1965.B30

"I've Had a Good Run for My Money," 1962.B24

Jackson, Katherine Gauss, 1952.B9

Jacobs, Robert D., 1961.B10

Janeway, Elizabeth, 1962.B45

"Jilting of Granny Weatherall, The," 1962.B20, B37; 1964.A1; 1965.A1; 1966.B9; 1967.B4; 1969.B1, B11; 1973.A1

"Jilting of Granny Weatherall': The Discovery of Pattern, 'The," 1966.B9

Johnson, James William, 1959.B1; 1960.B3

Johnson, Shirley E., 1961.B7

Jones, Howard Mumford, 1942.B6; 1944.B12

Jones, Llewelyn, 1931.B1

Joselyn, Sister M., 1963.B11; 1964.B7, B8

Josephson, Matthew, 1962.B46

"Journey, The," (originally entitled "The Old Order"), 1957.A1; 1964.A1; 1965.A1

"Journey Pattern in Four Contemporary American Novels, The," 1970.B7

Kaplan, Charles, 1959.B2

Kasten, Maurice, 1962.B47

"Katherine Anne Porter," 1939.B6; 1940.B4; 1954.B1; 1962.B66; 1965.B6; 1973.B1

Katherine Anne Porter, 1963.B23; 1965.A1; 1973.A1

"Katherine Anne Porter: A Critical Bibliography," 1953.B9

Katherine Anne Porter: A Critical Symposium, 1969.A1

"Katherine Anne Porter: A Fiercely Burning Particle," 1961.B11

"Katherine Anne Porter: An Interview," 1963.B20

"Katherine Anne Porter and 'Historic Memory,'" 1952.B19

"Katherine Anne Porter and Julio Cortázar: The Craft of Fiction," 1972.B6

"Katherine Anne Porter and Mexico," 1970.B6

"Katherine Anne Porter and the Art of Caricature," 1972.B5

Katherine Anne Porter & the Art of Rejection, 1964.A1

"Katherine Anne Porter and the Southern Myth: A Note on 'Noon Wine,'" 1972.B7

"Katherine Anne Porter as a Southern Writer," 1971.B2

Katherine Anne Porter: A Study, 1971.A1

"Katherine Anne Porter at Work," 1940.B7

"Katherine Anne Porter Cited for Writings," 1962.B9

"Katherine Anne Porter Comes to Kansas," 1963.B17

"Katherine Anne Porter: Feeling, Form, and Truth," 1962.B37

INDEX

Tate, Allen, 1930.B5
Taubman, Robert, 1962.B72
"That Tree," 1964.A1; 1965.A1
"That True and Human World,"
    1946.B3
"Theft," 1956.B2; 1960.B2, B4,
    B7; 1964.A1; 1965.A1;
    1969.B3; 1971.B5; 1973.A1
"'Theft': Porter's Politics of
    Modern Love," 1960.B7
"Theme of Destructive Innocence
    in the Modern Novel, The,"
    1960.B8
"35 Enjoyable Books in '65,"
    1965.B26
Thompson, Barbara, 1963.B20
Thompson, John, 1962.B73
Thompson, Ralph, 1937.B5;
    1939.B17
"Thumbprint: A Study of People
    in Katherine Anne Porter's
    Fiction, The," 1966.B17
"Tradewinds," 1952.B8
"Tradition of Storytelling, A,"
    1965.B15
"Tragic Parables," 1965.B13
"Treasure in 'The Grave,'"
    1963.B6
Trilling, Diana, 1944.B18
Trilling, Lionel, 1942.B10
Troy, William, 1935.B14
"True Witness: Katherine Anne
    Porter," 1959.B2
"Twenty-Five Years After,"
    1951.B1
"Twenty Years Agrowing,"
    1962.B26

"Uncorrupted Consciousness: The
    Stories of Katherine Anne
    Porter," 1966.B24
"Under the Human Crust,"
    1962.B51
"Unused Possibilities: A Study
    of Katherine Anne Porter,"
    1973.B4
"Upward Path: Notes on the Work
    of Katherine Anne Porter,
    The," 1968.B1

van Gelder, Robert, 1940.B7;
    1946.B4
Van Zyl, John, 1966.B22
"Variations on a Dream: Katherine
    Anne Porter and Truman
    Capote," 1969.B8
"Variations on a Theme in Four
    Stories of Katherine Anne
    Porter," 1958.B1
"Virgin Violeta," 1965.A1
"Vivid Awareness, A," 1935.B13
Vliet, Vida Ann Rutherford,
    1968.B7
Voss, Arthur, 1973.B5
"Voyage of Life," 1962.B40
"Voyage to Everywhere," 1962.B14

Waldhorn, Arthur, 1961.B13
Waldrip, Louise, 1969.A2
Walsh, Chad, 1963.B21
Walsh, Thomas F., 1968.B8
Walters, Dorothy Jeanne, 1960.B8
Walton, Eda Lou, 1935.B15
Walton, Edith H., 1935.B16, B17;
    1937.B6; 1939.B18; 1942.B11
Walton, Gerald, 1966.B23
Wanning, Andrews, 1947.B3
Warren, Robert Penn, 1942.B12;
    1953.B12; 1960.B2; 1966.B24
Washburn, Beatrice, 1965.B30
Watkins, Sue, 1962.B74
"Way of Dissent: Katherine Anne
    Porter's Critical Position,
    The," 1954.B3
Weber, Brom, 1962.B75
Weeks, Edward, 1944.B19
"We Get Along Together Just
    Fine," 1963.B16
Welty, Eudora, 1966.B25
"We're All on the Passenger
    List," 1962.B67
Wescott, Glenway, 1936.B2;
    1939.B19; 1944.B20; 1962.B76;
    1966.B5
West, Anthony, 1939.B20
West, Ray B., Jr., 1947.B4;
    1952.B19, B21; 1963.B23
"When Film Gets Good...,"
    1962.B70

INDEX

Whicher, George F., 1944.B21;
    1951.B4
Wiesenfarth, Joseph, 1962.B77;
    1969.B11; 1970.B14; 1971.B5;
    1973.B6
"Wiles and Words," 1953.B11
Wilson, Angus, 1962.B78
Wilson, Edmund, 1944.B22
"Winners' Press Conference,"
    1966.B6
Winsten, Archer, 1937.B7
Winters, Yvor, 1931.B2
"Witness, The," 1964.A1; 1965.A1;
    1971.A1
Wolfe, Bertram D., 1935.B18;
    1942.B13
Wolfe, Peter, 1967.B4
Wolff, Geoffrey, 1970.B15
"World of Katherine Anne Porter,
    The," 1961.B14
"Wreath for Lawrence, A,"
    1960.B1
"Writers as Readers," 1953.B10

"Writers in the Wilderness:
    Katherine Anne Porter,"
    1940.B5
"Writer's Reflections, A,"
    1953.B2
"Writing a Short Story," 1942.B2
Wykes, Alan, 1955.B2

Yanella, Philip R., 1969.B12
Yanitelli, Victor R., 1962.B79
"Yes, But Are They Really
    Novels?", 1962.B17
"Yesterdays of Katherine Anne
    Porter," 1952.B6
Ylvisaker, Miriam, 1962.B80
Yoder, Ed., 1970.B16
Yosha, Lee Williams, 1961.B14
Young, Marguerite, 1945.B7
Young, Vernon A., 1945.B8
"Young Bess" (screenplay),
    1952.B12
Youngblood, Sarah, 1959.B4

Carson McCullers Index

"Break-Through and the Pattern,
    The," 1961.B15
Breit, Harvey, 1950.B9
Brooks, Cleanth, 1959.B3
Brown, John, 1954.B1
Brown, John Mason, 1950.B10
Brustein, Robert, 1965.B5
Buchen, Irving H., 1973.B2
Buckmaster, Henrietta, 1961.B15
Butcher, Fannie, 1961.B16

Callaway, Joe A., 1950.B11
"Call on the Author," 1961.B5
Capote, Truman, 1958.B5
Cargill, Oscar, 1941.B4
Carlton, Ann Ruth, 1972.B4
Carney, Christina F., 1970.B1
Carpenter, Frederick I., 1957.B4
Carr, Virginia Spencer, 1969.B1;
    1975.A1
"Carson McCullers," 1940.B3;
    1941.B1; 1942.B2; 1951.B5,
    B13; 1955.B4; 1958.B3;
    1961.B3; 1963.B5; 1967.B1;
    1969.B3, B4; 1973.B8
"Carson McCullers: A Case of
    Convergence," 1973.B2
"Carson McCullers: A Critical
    Introduction," 1964.B14
"Carson McCullers: A Map of
    Love," 1960.B4
"Carson McCullers and the Failure
    of Dialogue," 1963.B4
"Carson McCullers and the Search
    for Meaning," 1969.B1
"Carson McCullers Completes New
    Novel Despite Adversity,"
    1961.B10
"Carson McCullers Cuts Her Own
    Hair," 1950.B20
"Carson McCullers' Descent to
    Earth," 1972.B11
Carson McCullers: Her Life and
    Work, 1965.A1
"Carson McCullers, La Novelista
    del Fatalismo," 1968.B7
"Carson McCullers' Literary
    Ballad," 1973.B7
"Carson McCullers: Lonely
    Huntress," 1959.B6

"Carson McCullers' Myth of the
    Sad Café," 1967.B8
"Carson McCullers: 1956-1964, A
    Selected Checklist," 1964.B11
"Carson McCullers: 1940-1956: A
    Selected Checklist," 1959.B7
"Carson McCullers: 1917-1947: The
    Conversion of Experience,"
    1966.B6
"Carson McCullers (1917-1967),"
    1969.B9
"Carson McCullers: 1917-1967,"
    1967.B10
"Carson McCullers: 1965-69, A
    Selected Checklist,"
    1970.B8
"Carson McCullers og Hjertenes
    Fangenskap," 1955.B1
"Carson McCullers Omnibus, A,"
    1951.B18
"Carson MacCullers [sic] ou la ca-
    bane de l'enfance," 1962.B13
"Carson McCullers, Pilgrim of
    Loneliness," 1957.B11
"Carson McCullers: Still the
    Lonely Hunter," 1961.B52
"Carson McCullers: The Alchemy
    of Love and Aesthetics of
    Pain," 1959.B4
"Carson McCullers--The Case of
    the Curious Magician,"
    1963.B1
"Carson McCullers' The Heart Is
    a Lonely Hunter," 1961.B39
"Carson McCullers: The Heart Is
    a Timeless Hunter," 1965.B10
"Carson McCullers: Variations on
    a Theme," 1951.B15
"Case of Carson McCullers, The,"
    1964.B4
"Case of the Silent Singer, A
    Revaluation of The Heart Is
    a Lonely Hunter, The,"
    1965.B6
Chapin, Ruth, 1951.B7
Chapman, John, 1950.B12; 1957.B5
"Character of Post-War Fiction in
    America," 1962.B9
Christie, Erling, 1955.B1
"Circling the Squares," 1959.B1

Falk, Signi Lenea, 1961.B19
Feld, Rose, 1940.B5; 1941.B8
Felheim, Marvin, 1964.B6
Ferguson, Otis, 1941.B9
"Fiction Chronicle," 1961.B17
"Fiction in Review," 1946.B14
"Fiction: Odd and Ordinary,"
    1941.B9
Fiedler, Leslie A., 1955.B2;
    1960.B2
Finger, Larry Livingston,
    1972.B6
"First Person Singular,"
    1941.B12
Fleischmann, Wolfgang Bernard,
    1967.B6
Folk, Barbara Nauer, 1962.B6
Ford, Nick Aaron, 1962.B7
"14 Win Admission to Arts
    Institute," 1952.B1
Frank, Joseph, 1946.B6
"Frankie Addams at 50," 1967.B13
"Frankie Addams de Carson
    McCullers," 1949.B1
Freedley, George, 1958.B6
"Free from the Fetters of
    Dogma," 1961.B9
Fremont-Smith, Eliot, 1967.B7
"From a Member," 1950.B13
"From Life into Death," 1961.B8
Fuller, John, 1961.B20
"Full of the Deep South,"
    1972.B15

Gaillard, Dawson F., 1972.B7
Garland, Robert, 1950.B15
Gassner, John, 1952.B3; 1954.B3;
    1956.B2
"Georgia Scene by Carson
    McCullers, The," 1961.B30
"Georgia Ways, Caricatured from
    Life," 1961.B16
Gibbs, Walcott, 1950.B16;
    1957.B10
Gibson, Walker, 1964.B7
"God and No God in The Heart Is
    a Lonely Hunter," 1957.B9
Godden, Rumer, 1961.B21
Gold, Herbert, 1961.B22
Gossett, Louise Young, 1961.B23;
    1965.B8

"Gothic Architecture of The Mem-
    ber of the Wedding, The,"
    1964.B13
Gozzi, Francesco, 1968.B3
Graver, Laurence, 1969.B4
Gray, James, 1946.B7
Griffin, Lloyd W., 1961.B24
Griffith, Albert J., 1967.B8
Grinnell, James W., 1972.B8
Gross, John, 1961.B25
"Growing Up," 1957.B19
Grumbach, Doris, 1961.B26
Gullason, Thomas A., 1971.B3

Haines, Helen E., 1950.B17
Hamilton, Alice, 1970.B3
Hardy, John Edward, 1962.B8
Hart, Jane, 1957.B11
Harte, Barbara, 1963.B5; 1969.B5
Hartt, J. N., 1961.B27
Hassan, Ihab, 1959.B4, B5;
    1962.B9
Hawkins, William, 1950.B18
Haycraft, Howard, 1942.B2
Hayes, Richard, 1957.B12
Heart Is a Lonely Hunter, The
--Reviews
    1940.B1-B2, B4-B7, B9-B14;
    1943.B2
--Major Essays
    1957.B9; 1958.B2; 1960.B2-
    B4; 1961.B39; 1963.B10;
    1964.B1; 1965.A1, B4, B7,
    B10; 1967.B9, B11; 1968.B3
    B10; 1969.B3, B4; 1970.B5;
    1971.B6; 1972.B3; 1975.A2

"Heart Is a Lonely Hunter: A
    Southern Waste Land, The,"
    1960.B3
"Heart Stands Out, The," 1967.B7
Hendrick, George, 1968.B4
Herzberg, Max J., 1962.B10
Hicks, Granville, 1961.B29
Hoffman, Frederick J., 1967.B9
Hogan, William, 1961.B30
"Horror in the Mansion: Gothic
    Fiction in the Works of Tru-
    man Capote and Carson McCul-
    lers, The," 1973.B3

P3